The In-House Counsel's Essential Toolkit

Committee on Corporate Counsel

Corporate Compliance and Ethics

ABA Section of
BUSINESS LAW

Defending Liberty
Pursuing Justice

The In-House Counsel's Essential Toolkit

Committee on Corporate Counsel

Volumes Included:

Corporate Compliance and Ethics

Corporate Governance

Employment Law

General Business Contracts

Intellectual Property

Litigation

Training Outside Counsel

Library of Congress Cataloging-in-Publication Data

The In-house counsel's essential toolkit / ABA Committee on Corporate Counsel.
   p. cm.
  Includes bibliographical references and index.
  ISBN 978-1-59031-662-7 (alk. paper)
   1. Corporate legal departments—United States. 2. Business enterprises—Law and legislation—United States. 3. Contracts—United States.
4. Corporation law—United States—Forms. 5. Corporate lawyers—United States—Handbooks, manuals, etc. I. American Bar Association. Section of Business Law. Committee on Corporate Counsel.

KF1425.164   2007
346.73'065—dc22   2007019680

Table of Contents

Introduction

On behalf of the Committee on Corporate Counsel, welcome to the Corporate Compliance and Ethics volume of *The In-House Counsel's Essential Toolkit: Annotated Forms, Policies, and Advice for Everyday Practice*!

During the 2005 Business Law Section Spring Meeting in Nashville, Tennessee, the Committee leadership was inspired by discussions with colleagues and came up with the idea for this publication. We recognized that in-house counsel often get the most useful information from talking to and comparing notes with colleagues and counsel in other law departments. We also recognized that in-house practice is different from law firm practice in several ways. For instance, unlike outside counsel, most in-house counsel do not have access to a vast collection of form or sample agreements and policies covering a broad range of transactions, industries, and practice areas. Further, most in-house counsel cannot just walk down the hall to a partner's office and get a quick tutorial on a lot of different issues. In addition to lacking these resources, most in-house departments simply do not have the budget or resources to hire outside counsel on everyday matters, which is particularly true for small to medium-sized legal departments. We also recognized that many in the in-house world have specific expertise gleaned from private practice or other experience, but often are expected to become generalists with the ability to competently practice in several different subject matter areas.

In light of this, we decided that the best way to serve the in-house counsel members of our Committee was to collaborate with our colleagues nationwide—both in-house and outside—to create a guidebook filled with annotated forms, general advice, and practical tips. Our desire was to create a publication that in-house counsel could use to quickly understand the key issues in matters that arise often, but that are outside their particular area of expertise. It is our hope that this publication will fill a much-needed gap in corporate counsel libraries.

The In-House Counsel's Essential Toolkit was initially titled *The Pocket Outside Counsel*. As the name suggests, we originally envisioned a pocket-sized guidebook for in-house counsel in small to medium-sized departments. However, once the project gained momentum, the contents of the guidebook expanded by leaps and bounds. Before long we realized we could not call it **The Pocket Outside Counsel** with a straight face! Hence, **The In-House Counsel's Essential Toolkit** was born.

However, we still intend for the **Toolkit** to serve as a practical guide for in-house counsel in small to medium-sized law departments covering matters that frequently arise. Often in such law departments, we join the team to wear one hat, but are soon expected to wear a closet full of chapeaux. Suddenly, the lawyer who spent a few years in private practice counseling clients on labor and employment matters is expected to draft the company's first compliance program; the litigator brought in to manage the increasing volume of product liability cases must negotiate an inbound software licensing deal; and the fifth-year associate who represented a company during its initial public offering finds herself in the position of general counsel and now needs to know a little bit of everything! In those cases, where do you start? The **Toolkit**, of course.

We do, however, offer an important caveat, and it's not exactly a pitch for outside counsel. While the authors have offered practical tips and tried to highlight many of the traps in each area, venturing into an area of law where you do not have deep experience can create bigger problems. We would strongly suggest that if you are dealing with a material issue, a call to your outside counsel can confirm that you are on the right track or save you from yourself.

HOW TO USE THE TOOLKIT

The **Toolkit** is divided into individual volumes that address the following major areas: General Business Contracts, Corporate Governance, Compliance, Employment, Intellectual Property, Anatomy of a Litigation, and Training Your Outside Counsel. Each volume contains introductory remarks, annotated form agreements and policies with explanatory comments, alternative provisions, and practice tips. In order to give you a wide and diverse view, and to avoid geographic and other viewpoint myopia, we collected the materials from a diverse pool of in-house counsel with different-sized legal departments, as well as outside counsel from different types of firms. The lawyers practice in states from New York to California, Arizona to Illinois, and many states in between, plus one or two non-U.S. countries. The lawyers are diverse not only in terms of ethnicity, race, and gender, but also in terms of geography, area of practice, and years of experience. Many of the leaders and contributors are luminaries in their field of practice.

Each form has been reviewed, revised, and annotated by several groups that volunteered to work on this project. In order to ensure that different viewpoints were captured, each form was reviewed by at least one in-house counsel and one outside counsel, although in most cases many sets of eyes reviewed the material. You will see various lawyers identified throughout the publication, and their designations as chapter leaders, working group members, contributors, and editors denote their varying degrees of participation.

This publication is not intended to be so extensive as to serve as a treatise on any particular subject. Instead, think of the **Toolkit** as the first place to go when an issue arises regarding outside counsel about which you know very little, or even nothing. Our hope is that we have given you sufficient information to get a strong head start in the game.

A few things to note: Each agreement has its own set of "boiler-plate" provisions, and we did not attempt to unify these sections across the board. Instead, we offer comments throughout the publication giving different opinions on some of the boilerplate provisions, and leave you with a smorgasbord of possibilities from which to choose.

In addition, each form and policy is intended to be as generic as possible, unless otherwise noted as favorable to one side or the other. Therefore, the forms and policies generally are not state-specific, although we sometimes included references to particularly interesting aspects of state law where appropriate. We thus encourage you to consult with local counsel if you are dealing in an area of the country (or the world) with which you are unfamiliar.

THE STEAM ENGINE

This project involved the teamwork of many experienced lawyers, who devoted countless hours to finding, annotating, and polishing these forms. We were lucky to have an extensive network of extremely fine lawyers, and we are incredibly thankful for the generosity of the lawyers, law firms, and companies involved. As we stated, each form was donated by someone or some firm or company, then reviewed and annotated by more lawyers, then further edited by even more lawyers, making the end result a staggering feat of collaboration. If you have questions about a particular form or subject matter area, or are in need of counsel, we encourage you to contact the lawyers noted. Each volume lists the chapter leaders, who were in charge of gathering the forms, recruiting worker bees, and reviewing and commenting on the substance of each word submitted (the all-around whip-crackers); the working group members, who reviewed and commented on the forms; and the contributors, who submitted forms for our use that often were already annotated after years of contemplation and negotiation.

Finally, we want to give a special thanks to Janet Jacobs, an associate at Stoel Rives LLP in Seattle, Washington, for pinch hitting by request throughout the process, and also to the word processing department at Stoel Rives, particularly Sherry Sherod and Marisue Thomas. From start to finish, they made all of our countless revisions, edits, and tweaks, and endured us doing it over again and again. They were indispensable, and always had a great attitude—even when they had revised the same paragraph several times before.

On behalf of the editors, we wish you luck, and hope you find this volume of the *Toolkit* to be a useful resource for your everyday practice.

Sincerely, Your Editors

Jolene A. Yee, Co-chair, Committee on Corporate Counsel

Mari Valenzuela, Ambassador to the Committee on Corporate Counsel

David Benson, Chair, Subcommittee on Privately Held Companies

Editors' Information

For further information about this publication or the Committee on Corporate Counsel, feel free to contact any one of the editors, and they will be happy to answer your questions (or direct you to someone who can).

Jolene A. Yee
Assistant General Counsel
E. & J. Gallo Winery Legal Department
600 Yosemite Blvd.
Modesto, CA 95354–2760
jolene.yee@ejgallo.com

Mari I. Valenzuela
Corporate Counsel
Microchip Technology Inc.
2355 W. Chandler Blvd.
Chandler, AZ 85224
mari.valenzuela@microchip.com

David Benson
Principle
Stoel Rives LLP
3600 One Union Square
600 University Street
Seattle, WA 98101
dlbenson@stoel.com

Corporate Compliance and Ethics

Chapter Leaders:

**Michael R. Clarke, Vice President,
Chief Ethics and Compliance Officer**
University of Medicine & Dentistry of New Jersey
Newark, New Jersey
clarkemi@umdnj.edu

**David L. Dick, Compliance Consultant
and Attorney at Law**
Larchmont, New York
davidleonarddick@aol.com

Steve A. Lauer, Corporate Counsel
Global Compliance Services
Charlotte, North Carolina
steven.lauer@globalcompliance.com

Contributors:

Jacqueline C. Bares, Special Counsel
Kennedy Covington
Charlotte, North Carolina
jbares@kennedycovington.com

Adam Biegel, Partner
Alston & Bird, LLP
Atlanta, Georgia
Adam.biegel@alston.com

Jamie Boucher, Counsel
Skadden, Arps, Slate, Meagher & Flom LLP
Washington, D.C.
jboucher@skadden.com

Debra M. Brown
Brown & Associates, LLC
Beverly, Massachusetts
www.selfauditor.com

Judy K. Carter, Senior General Attorney
BNSF Railway Company
Fort Worth, Texas
judy.carter@bnsf.com

Michael Clark, Partner
Hamel, Bowers & Clark
Houston, Texas
Clark@hal-pc.org

Jesse A. Davis, III, Associate
Alston & Bird, LLP
Atlanta, Georgia
jess.davis@alston.com

Andrew Demetriou, Partner
Fulbright & Jaworski
Los Angeles, California
ademetriou@fulbright.com

Wesley Fastiff, Chairman Emeritus
Littler Mendelson
San Francisco, California
Wjfastiff@littler.com

David Fein, Partner
Wiggin and Dana
Stamford, Connecticut
dfein@wiggin.com

**William Groves, Assistant General
Counsel and Assistant Secretary**
Exide Technologies
Alpharetta, Georgia
bill.groves@exide.com

**Deborah House, Vice President
and Deputy General Counsel for
Legal Resources and Strategic Initiatives**
Association of Corporate Counsel
Washington, D.C.
house@acc.com

Mary Jones, Associate General Counsel
Deere & Company
Moline, Illinois
JonesMary@JohnDeere.com

Jenny Kim, Senior Associate
Miller & Chevalier Chartered
Washington, D.C.
jkim@milchev.com

Andrew Lauer, Partner, Labor and Employment Group
Thelen Reid Brown, Raysman & Steiner LLP
New York, New York
alauer@thelen.com

Darryl Marsch, Senior Counsel
R.J. Reynolds Tobacco Co.
Winston Salem, North Carolina
marschd@rjrt.com

**Marci Narine, Vice President, Global Compliance,
and Deputy General Counsel**
Ryder System, Inc.
Miami, Florida
Mnarine@ryder.com

Mona Shulman, Assistant General Counsel
Mother Lode Holding Company
Auburn, California
mshulman@mlhc.com

Sajai Singh, Partner
J. Sagar Associates
Bangalore, India
Sajai@jsalaw.com

Thomas J. Smedinghoff, Partner
Wildman Harrold LLP
Chicago, Illinois
smedinghoff@wildmanharrold.com

Michael L. Sommer, President and Counsel
General Counsel on Demand
Cornelius, North Carolina
msommer@gcondemand.com

Radhi Thayu, Associate
Skadden, Arps, Slate, Meagher & Flom LLP
Washington, D.C.
rthayu@skadden.com

**Hilary Wandall, Attorney
and Corporate Privacy Officer**
Merck & Co., Inc.
Whitehouse Station, New Jersey
Hilary_wandall@merck.com

**Jonathan Wilson, Senior Vice President,
Legal and Corporate Development**
Web.com, Inc.
Atlanta, Georgia
Jwilson@web.com

William M. Wood, Partner
Opus Law Group
Seattle, Washington
Bwood@opuslawgroup.com

A. INTRODUCTION: STATEMENT OF PURPOSE

Every business must operate within the law. Such a simple statement belies the difficulties that one might encounter in attempting to ensure that your company does so. The actions of numerous individuals—employees, agents, contractors, and others—can affect the degree to which your company complies with applicable mandates.

Accordingly, many companies have developed "compliance programs." Though people may differ on the details of a compliance program, generally speaking, an effective compliance program consists of a comprehensive system of policies and procedures designed to prevent—or, if they occur, to detect and correct—violations of law or company policy.

This volume of the *Toolkit* will provide tools with which to approach the task of designing and implementing a corporate compliance and ethics program. The contextual background for such a program—the legal basis for that program and some of the primary standards by which the program might be measured—appears at the beginning of this volume. Following that introduction, we include a number of sample policies that address some of the more common substantive areas of focus for corporate compliance programs. Those sample policies contain annotations and notations that highlight some of the considerations to consider when customizing or adapting the sample policies to your own situation.

B. THE LEGAL CONTEXT FOR COMPLIANCE AND ETHICS PROGRAMS

Business organizations always have been expected to operate within the confines of the law, and the companies that did not do so were prosecuted by the government. In earlier days, those confines presented simpler and more familiar constraints. The rules on business behavior were few. Several decades ago, however, that began to change and the "rules of the game" became much more numerous and complex.

In the early 1960s, several companies in the electrical equipment industry were convicted of having committed antitrust violations. Subsequently, some members of that industry established compliance programs—a set of policies and related procedures and practices that, in combination, were intended to prevent and detect wrongdoing—in order to prevent recurrence of that illegal behavior. Failures by many businesses to adhere to the requirements of environmental laws in the 1970s, involving discharges to water and air, and contamination of land with hazardous chemicals, led to the need for environmental compliance programs. Scandals in the 1970s involving the payment by United States-based companies of bribes to foreign government officials in order to secure sales and other business opportunities led to passage of the Foreign Corrupt Practices Act. That statute soon led members of the defense and aerospace industries to begin to develop internal compliance programs. In 1986, 32 major defense contractors established the Defense Industry Initiative to implement principles of business ethics and conduct expressing that industry's federal-procurement-related responsibilities to the government and the public.

Congress enacted the Sentencing Reform Act of 1984, which included business crimes, to introduce greater uniformity and certainty into sentencing decisions by individual federal judges. While the likelihood of a company appearing before a federal judge for sentencing after conviction may seem remote, that statute also created the United States Sentencing Commission ("Sentencing Commission"). The statute also gave the sentencing commission authority to establish rules under which federal judges would achieve that greater uniformity. Under that authority, the commission in 1991 enacted the Sentencing Guidelines for Organizational Defendants. In the Sentencing Guidelines, the Sentencing Commission adopted a "carrot and stick" approach to encourage greater compliance with federal criminal statutes and regulations, rather than relying solely on the traditional approach to criminal sentencing of imposing retroactive punishment for violations of the law. In the sentencing guidelines, the Sentencing Commission introduced the notion that an organizational defendant that had created and maintained, before the criminal violation in question occurred, a compliance program that could be viewed as "effective" would earn credits that would lower its criminal penalty. Simultaneously, the fines that a federal judge could impose on an organization that had failed to demonstrate such a proactive approach to compliance increased. The guidelines provided a form of blueprint for an effective compliance program, and companies began to design their programs to meet the standards set out in the guidelines. In 2004, the Sentencing Commission made significant changes to the guidelines, providing greater detail as to what, in its view, would constitute an "effective corporate compliance and ethics program." The guidelines, as changed by the Sentencing Commission in 2004, appear as Exhibit A at the end of this volume.

The structure and operation of corporate compliance and ethics programs reflect the legal context in which they exist. That context has evolved over time. To fully and properly design, implement, manage, and evaluate such a program, in-house counsel need to understand that context and its evolution. For instance, the Guidelines now reflect an expectation that a company's program will "promote an organizational culture that encourages ethical conduct and a commitment to compliance with the law," rather than simply meeting the minimum requirements set by law.

In order to design and implement a corporate ethics and compliance program that will meet the standards set in the sentencing guidelines, as well as those in prosecutors' guidance and court decisions, in-house counsel must understand what such a program is intended to accomplish and the legal context in which it must operate. This volume contains suggestions on how to create such a program. In addition, we included samples of substantive policies on a variety of legal topics that often appear in companies' ethics and compliance programs. While the specific topics covered in a particular business's program will depend on that business's needs, this material should provide the reader some basis for designing his or her company's program.

The sentencing guidelines had considerable impact on companies, just as the commission had hoped. The year following enactment of the guidelines witnessed formation of the Ethics Officer Association, which its creators intended "to promot[e] ethical business practices and serv[e] as a global forum for the exchange of information and strategies among organizations and individuals responsible for ethics, compliance, and business conduct programs." The association, recently renamed the Ethics and Compliance Officer Association, as well as the Society of Corporate Compliance & Ethics, another national organization, represent reliable resources for counsel, as does the Committee on Corporate Compliance of the American Bar Association's Section of Business Law.

In 1996, the Chancery Court of Delaware focused corporate attention on the guidelines in a noncriminal context by favorably citing them in its landmark *Caremark* ruling regarding liability of corporate directors for failure to prevent criminal conduct by their company. In that decision, Chancellor Allen stated that the "Guidelines offer powerful incentives for corporations today to have in place compliance programs to detect violations of law, promptly to report violations to public officials when discovered, and to take prompt, voluntary remedial efforts." *In re Caremark International Inc. Derivative Litigation*, 698 A. 2d 959 (Del. Chan. 1996).

Compliance programs continued to develop, generally along the lines outlined in the sentencing guidelines. Because the guidelines focus on the sentencing of an organization after conviction of a crime, and a company itself has a remote likelihood of facing a federal judge in that context, whether that company had an effective compliance program and thereby qualifies for a reduced sentence under the guidelines may seem of limited practical value. Other developments, some related to the guidelines, however, have provided considerable additional justification for the effort that such a program requires.

The United States Department of Justice, for example, prosecutes those accused of committing federal crimes. United States Attorneys around the country make the initial determinations as to whom to prosecute (for example, whether to indict officers and/or directors), and the basis on which to do so. Those officials have incorporated the guidelines into the process by which they make those determinations, as outlined in guidance prepared at headquarters of the department of justice in Washington, D.C.

You can find the most recent version of that guidance in the McNulty memorandum, included as Exhibit B in this publication, which replaced earlier, similar instructions by the justice department to the U.S. Attorneys in the field. Section VIII of the McNulty memo advises U.S. Attorneys that "[p]rosecutors should therefore attempt to determine whether a corporation's compliance program is merely a 'paper program' or whether it was designed and implemented in an effective manner. In addition, prosecutors should determine whether the corporation has provided for a staff sufficient to audit, document, analyze, and utilize the results of the corporation's compliance efforts. In addition, prosecutors should determine whether the corporation's employees are adequately informed about the compliance program and are convinced of the corporation's commitment to it. This will enable the prosecutor to make an informed decision as to whether the corporation has adopted and implemented a truly effective compliance program that, when consistent with other federal law enforcement policies, may result in a decision to charge only the corporation's employees and agents."

Other federal agencies have issued rules and guidance documents that also have helped shape the development of corporate compliance and ethics programs. The Department of Health and Human Services, which enforces the Health Insurance Portability and Accountability Act, Medicare, and Medicaid, among other statutes and programs, has issued guidance to various sectors of the healthcare industry regarding the structure and operation of compliance programs. That guidance tracks rather closely the elements set out in the Sentencing Guidelines for an effective corporate compliance and ethics program.

1. Elements of an Effective Compliance Program Under the Guidelines

According to the Sentencing Commission, seven broad elements comprise an effective compliance and ethics program as follows:

1. Standards and procedures: The organization must adopt standards and procedures to detect and deter criminal conduct. These standards typically appear in one or more company codes of conduct and policies. The topics covered depend on the nature of the company's business operations, jurisdictions in which it operates, and other factors.

2. Governing authority (such as the board of directors): The governing authority of the organization must be knowledgeable about the content and operation of the ethics and compliance program, assign overall responsibility for that program to an identified individual within the organization's high-level personnel, specify which employee has operational responsibility for that program (that employee must report periodically to high-level personnel), and provide adequate resources, appropriate authority, and direct access to the organization's governing authority.

3. Delegation of authority: The organization must attempt to prevent the appointment to significant positions in the company of individuals who have engaged in illegal activities or other conduct that is inconsistent with an effective compliance and ethics program.

4. Communication and training: The organization must take steps to communicate to its employees and, as appropriate, its agents, the substance of its standards and procedures. Training constitutes a required method by which to communicate this information,

which must be appropriate to individuals' roles and responsibilities. Prior to the 2004 changes to the sentencing guidelines, training was only an example of appropriate communication of policies and procedures; it is now expected.

5. Reporting mechanisms (for example, hotlines): The organization must take steps: to ensure that its compliance and ethics program is followed, using appropriate monitoring and auditing methods; to evaluate the effectiveness of that program; and to enable individuals to report or seek guidance regarding potential or actual criminal conduct, without fear of retaliation and, if desired, anonymously.

6. Promotion and enforcement: The organization must promote and enforce the compliance and ethics program consistently, using appropriate incentives and disciplinary measures.

7. Response to discovered criminality: If it detects criminal conduct, the organization must take reasonable steps to respond to that criminality and to prevent future similar conduct.

2. The Law Department and a Compliance and Ethics Program

The roles of a law department and of a corporate ethics and compliance program within a company are closely related. The most basic mission of a law department is to safeguard and promote the company's legal interests. In establishing a compliance and ethics program, a company aims to create standards and processes that will enable it to prevent and, if they occur, timely detect violations of the law and other applicable standards. Clearly, the avoidance of violations of the law is a core part of the mission of a corporate law department. Further, many compliance issues revolve around legal issues or the application of legal issues to business problems.

This close relationship between compliance and a law department's more "traditional" role suggests that a company's in-house lawyers should play a leading role in the compliance and ethics program. Where do they fit? The American Bar Association's Task Force on Corporate Responsibility opined that "a prudent corporate governance program should call upon lawyers—notably the corporation's general counsel—to assist in the design and maintenance of the corporation's procedures for promoting legal compliance."

The role of a corporate law department with respect to compliance and ethics also emanates from other sources, such as the Sarbanes-Oxley Act of 2002. That statute, enacted following the corporate scandals at WorldCom, Enron, Adelphia, and other companies, created compliance-related responsibilities—and associated accountability—for several categories of corporate personnel. Directors must establish hotline-like mechanisms for "the receipt, retention, and treatment of complaints received by the [company] regarding accounting, internal accounting controls, or auditing matters." The chief executive and chief compliance officers must sign their company's financial statements, attesting to the accuracy of the information that they contain. In-house lawyers were charged in the statute with functioning, in some respects, as the "conscience" if not the "whistleblower," of the organization because an in-house attorney who identifies a possible violation of relevant statutes is obliged to raise the issue internally to successively higher corporate authority if an adequate response is not forthcoming—even to the board of directors in certain circumstances. Additional requirements for corporate compliance programs are found in the rules of certain stock trading organizations, such as the New York Stock Exchange and NASDAQ.

In-house counsel should review the compliance and ethics program for legal sufficiency. Will that program achieve the legal goals that corporate management sets for it? For example, to ensure that the program will be viewed as an effective one so that the company would qualify for the sentencing credits (upon conviction of a federal crime) available under the Sentencing Guidelines, counsel likely will need to review the company's program in light of those standards. Beyond that, of course, counsel would want to ensure that the program satisfies the various substantive legal requirements that apply to the company's operations. In essence, the law department must advise corporate management on the establishment and structure of the company's compliance and ethics program in light of the objectives set for it by management.

In-house counsel can assume an additional function beyond the design and creation of the program and ensuring its effectiveness. One of the core purposes of a compliance and ethics program is to disseminate among the firm's employees and agents the information necessary for them properly to discharge their responsibilities. In short, and as the Sentencing Commission recognized when it changed the guidelines in 2004, a company's compliance with law and other standards depends on how well its representatives understand what is expected of them and what they must do to meet those expectations.

Very often in the course of their jobs, employees encounter issues or situations where the "right" course of action is not clear. Questions with legal components will arise. In order to navigate through such issues, employees will need timely advice regarding those issues. Accordingly, the attorneys (in-house and, possibly, outside counsel) can and should serve as resources available to employees who encounter such issues, so that those employees can better understand what is expected of them and the risks and duties facing the company.

Other important issues also demand the attention of in-house lawyers. As stated, training is a required component of an effective compliance and ethics program. Further, it must be provided to all employees, including corporate directors. In-house counsel must be involved in determining what training they should receive, and ensuring and documenting that it occurs.

3. The Law Department and the Board of Directors

The law department typically assists the corporation's board of directors with questions regarding corporate governance and procedure. The general counsel usually interacts with directors regularly, presenting information regarding the company's legal matters and providing legal guidance as needed or requested. Much of that interaction derives from the nature of a corporation, the basic mission of a law department and in-house attorneys, and the common law of corporate existence.

In light of the expression by Congress in Sarbanes-Oxley that in-house lawyers serve as gatekeepers and the corporate "conscience" (exemplified by its instruction that the Securities and Exchange Commission "issue rules . . . setting forth minimum standards of professional conduct for attorneys appearing and practicing before the Commission in any way"), in-house lawyers cannot escape playing a prominent role in efforts such as director training, with resulting professional accountability, because that role fits clearly among in-house lawyers' counseling responsibilities.

On one level, the training of board members covers many of the issues about which they regularly interact with the general counsel or chief legal officer. On another level, the training that they require on account of Sarbanes-Oxley, court decisions regarding director liability, the Sentencing Guidelines, and other issues relates closely to the on-going, established role of a corporate law department.

Training should include several elements and cover a number of areas. First, the duties of a corporate board have increased, some-times in ways that represent entirely new responsibilities for di-rectors. The Sentencing Guidelines, for example, require that the "governing authority" of a corporation (the board of directors) be knowledgeable about the organization and operation of the compa-ny's compliance program in order that it is able to exercise an ap-propriate degree of oversight of that program. This seems to exceed the standard described by the Delaware court in the *Caremark* case discussed above. Further, the requirement in Sarbanes-Oxley that the board's audit committee establish procedures that allow for the direct submission of issues regarding accounting and auditing mat-ters places that committee directly within a hotline-like mechanism. Directors may require education regarding the scope of their roles in those contexts.

Second, the Sentencing Guidelines also require that a company educate its employees and, as appropriate, its agents about the compli-ance- and ethics-related responsibilities of their respective roles. The directors' roles call for training with respect to issues that are unique to their roles, in addition to certain subjects that have broader impact. Such "at-risk" training should endeavor to protect the directors from missteps that are unique to their roles in the company.

Third, the directors should undergo training similar to that taken by employees of the company. Issues such as antiharassment, protec-tion of the company's intellectual property, and the company's records management policies constitute what one might call "foundational" training that affects everyone, including the directors.

In the context of the more traditional function of a corporate law department, of course, in-house counsel bears responsibility to ensure that the company properly responds to complaints, particularly in terms of ensuring that adequate investigations follow the receipt of credible complaints. This flows from the responsibility of a corporate law department to protect the company's legal interests. In this age of globalization, of course, the difficulties associated with fulfilling those responsibilities multiply as a business expands into foreign markets that have different legal and social systems.

When a business operates in foreign countries as well as in the United States, its compliance-related concerns multiply. In addition to assuring that the business operations comport with the myriad and differing requirements of the various jurisdictions in which its operations exist, a company's lawyers must take steps to ensure that the compliance atmosphere remains consistent throughout the organization despite those legal distinctions. A United States-based company must comply with the mandates of United States law even when there appears to be some inconsistency between those mandates and the requirements or expectations of other countries' legal systems. Examples of these inconsistencies include incident report hotlines, privacy legislation, and the transmission of personally identifiable information.

4. Creating and Implementing a Compliance and Ethics Program

As discussed, the substantive areas of law and business that might concern a particular business, and therefore warrant coverage by the company's compliance and ethics program will depend on the nature and extent of the business. A variety of factors will affect the design and implementation of an effective program, including the following:

- whether the industry in which the business operates is directly regulated by government;
- whether the business deals with individual consumers directly or with other businesses;
- whether the industry in which the business operates includes many or few competitors; and
- whether the company operates globally or only domestically.

To determine which areas of law represent the greatest concerns, a corporate law department should lead or participate in a risk assessment, a process now required by the Sentencing Guidelines since the 2004 changes became effective, and by Sarbanes-Oxley. This process will require a thorough review of the business of the company and the identification of the various legal standards, requirements, and imperatives that relate to the company's operations. Such an analysis, often labeled "risk assessment," should precede the design of a program. The risk assessment also identifies the substantive areas of law that a company should address in its compliance policies and procedures, and the areas of activity that are most likely to lead to violations of law.

The following sample compliance policies are included in this volume:

- Code of Conduct for NASDAQ-listed companies
- Code of Conduct for NYSE-listed companies
- Antitrust Policy
- Conflicts of Interest Policy
- Employment Law
- Gifts and Entertainment Policy
- Insider Trading Policy
- International Business Practices Policy
- Office of Foreign Asset Control
- Political Activities Policy
- Privacy and Data Protection Policy
- Records Management Policy
- Supplier and Vendor Relations Policy

This volume also provides guidance on developing a legally-compliant corporate information Security Policy.

While the needs of businesses differ significantly from industry to industry, and even within an industry, these policies should serve as starting points for the creation of policies appropriate for your company's needs. Annotations to each policy identify issues or factors you should consider when determining how to apply the sample policy to your situation. The results of a risk assessment should provide guidance as to which of the model policies would be pertinent to a particular business, and whether other substantive areas of law and regulation might be appropriate for additional policies.

The design of the corporate compliance and ethics program will also vary from company to company. Larger companies typically create programs with greater formality and procedures than do smaller companies. The considerations expressed by the Sentencing Commission in the guidelines should animate the process of designing a specific program, and those guidelines are included in this volume for your ease of reference.

C. CODE OF CONDUCT

1. Introduction

Section 406 of the Sarbanes-Oxley Act of 2002 required that a publicly traded company disclose in its annual report whether it has adopted a code of ethics for its principal executive officer and its senior financial officers. If a company has not adopted a code of ethics for those officials, it must explain why not. Any waivers of the provisions of the code of ethics granted to individual corporate officers must be disclosed by the company in a filing with the SEC or on the company's website.

The two primary stock exchanges—NASDAQ exchange (NASDAQ) and the New York Stock Exchange (NYSE)—both incorporated into their listing standards a requirement that a company adopt a code of ethics that applies to all of its employees. NASDAQ and NYSE also provided guidance as to what subjects such a code should cover. The requirements of the two exchanges vary, however, so we have included two different codes of ethics: one is designed to comply with the SEC and NASDAQ rules, while the other satisfies the requirements of the SEC and NYSE rules. Choose the one that fits your company's status.

A code of ethics covers a range of topics that relate to its business. As a rule, however, a code of ethics (or code of conduct, as it is sometimes called) does not include an in-depth treatment of those subjects. To the degree that a company requires that its employees and agents receive guidance on one or more subjects to a greater degree, it probably should adopt a policy that addresses each of those subjects in greater depth, rather than trying to expand the discussion in the code of ethics to include that greater degree of detail. Each general subject touched on in the code of ethics might expand into a distinct, more complete policy. The code of ethics, then, provides an overview of the various topics treated in greater depth in separate policies.

Although private companies are not required by law to establish a code of conduct, depending on the size of the company, it might be a good idea to adopt a code of conduct similar to the public company models, or to include certain provisions in the company's employee handbook or comparable document.

2. Form: Code of Conduct (NASDAQ-traded Companies)

NOTE: *The following sample Code of Business Conduct and Ethics is designed to comply with SEC and NASD regulations.*
Why should a company have a code of conduct?

- *It allows the company to state clearly its values and corporate culture, including principles of honesty, ethical conduct, and integrity.*
- *It ensures that the company's values are recognized by management, employees, and other groups.*
- *It is an essential piece of a corporate compliance program under the Sarbanes-Oxley Act of 2002.*
- *It is taken into account under U.S. sentencing guidelines when a company is under investigation or indicted for criminal acts.*

[COMPANY NAME]
CODE OF BUSINESS CONDUCT AND ETHICS

Adopted ___[date]_____

This Code of Business Conduct and Ethics (this "Code") is designed to:

- provide you with guidance in addressing potentially troublesome situations involving [company name] and our subsidiaries (in the aggregate, the "Company");
- promote honest and ethical conduct, including the ethical handling of actual or apparent conflicts of interest between personal and professional relationships; and
- promote full, fair, accurate, timely, and understandable disclosure in reports and documents that we file with, or submit to, the Securities and Exchange Commission (the "SEC") and in other public communications made by the Company.

NOTE: *The bullet points above address the definition of "code of ethics" as set forth in section 406 of the Sarbanes-Oxley Act of 2002, which requires public companies to disclose: (i) in their annual reports, whether they have adopted a code of ethics for their principal executive officer and senior financial officers or, if not, why not; and (ii) in a Form 8-K or on their public website, any amendment to or waiver of the code of ethics for the specified officers. See SEC Release No. 33-8177 (January 23, 2003).*

In any business, the possibility exists that an employee's, officer's, or director's personal interests or those of such persons' family may conflict with the interests of the employer. You should do your utmost to avoid situations where conflicting loyalties may cause you to compromise your principles and responsibilities for personal gain. Also, you should avoid situations where a conflict of interest may arise due to the involvement of your spouse, immediate family, or members of your household.

This Code covers a wide range of business practices and procedures. It does not cover every issue that may arise, but it sets out basic principles to guide all of our employees, officers, and directors. The absence of a guideline covering a particular situation does not relieve you from the responsibility to operate with the highest ethical standards of business conduct. All of our employees, officers, and members of our board of directors (the "Board") must conduct themselves accordingly and seek to avoid even the appearance of improper behavior. The Code also should be provided to and followed by our agents and representatives, including consultants.

Obeying the law, both in letter and in spirit, is the foundation on which this Company's ethical standards are built. All employees, officers, and directors must respect and obey the applicable governmental laws, rules, and regulations of the cities, states, and countries in which we operate. Although not everyone is expected to know the details of all such laws, it is important to know enough to determine when to seek advice from supervisors, managers, or other appropriate personnel. If a law conflicts with a policy in this Code, you must comply with the law. If you have any questions about these conflicts, you should ask your supervisor, our ethics officer, or our chief financial officer how to handle the situation.

NOTE: *In the absence of in-house legal and ethics departments, questions should be directed to the chief financial officer or director of internal audit, if there is one. Otherwise, companies may consider having questions directed to the general counsel.*

Those who violate the standards in this Code will be subject to disciplinary action, up to and including termination of employment. If you are in a situation that you believe may violate or lead to a violation of this Code, follow the guidelines described in "Violations of this Code."

NOTE: *What topics should be covered in a code of conduct?*

Codes of conduct generally are designed based on specific factors such as the size of the company, the countries in which the company operates, and the company's compliance history and risk tolerance. Appendix A includes a list of issues, topics, and risk areas that could be addressed in a company's code of conduct. While the topics listed in Appendix A are most prevalent in companies' codes of conduct, a company's specific code should be tailored to that company's business, industry, and culture.

General

To whom does this Code apply?

This Code is applicable to the members of the Board and all of our officers and employees, including, but not limited to, the chief executive officer, the chief financial officer, the corporate controller, and any person performing similar functions. Where appropriate to the context, the term "employee," "officer," "director," or "you" shall include your immediate family, your spouse's immediate family, and members of your household.

NOTE: *This code of conduct applies to directors, executive officers, finan-cial officers, and all employees. Some companies elect to have several dif-ferent codes of conduct, which apply to different groups, such as a separate code of conduct for the board of directors, financial officers, and employees. This code of conduct may also supplement an employee handbook.*

What are my responsibilities under this Code?

You are responsible for:

- becoming thoroughly familiar with this Code;
- maintaining an understanding of the standards presented in this Code, and complying with the standards presented in this Code; and
- upon request of your supervisor or an executive officer, correcting any variance with these standards to bring the situation or activi-ties into full compliance.

What are our responsibilities under this Code?

We will distribute copies of this Code and provide training with respect to its terms to all current employees, officers, and directors, and to future employees, officers, and directors when they are hired or become a member of the Board, as the case may be. We will, as part of our regular audit process, test compliance with this Code. The Company also will periodically review these standards and make appropriate additions or changes, and will promptly inform employees, officers, and directors of all changes to this Code.

NOTE: *Dissemination is not enough to have an effective code of conduct. Implementation is necessary. After the code of conduct is drafted with the input of the human resources department, senior management, and the legal department (or outside counsel in the absence of a legal department), senior management and employees should receive training on the substance of the code of conduct, and then the code of conduct should be widely dis-tributed throughout the company and enforced consistently. An unenforced code of conduct will not serve a company well, and may, in some circum-stances, lead to greater difficulty than having no code of conduct at all.*

Conflicts of Interest

When does a conflict of interest exist?

A conflict of interest exists when a person's private interests interfere in any way with the interests of the Company. A conflict situation can arise when an employee, officer, or director takes actions or has interests that may make it difficult to perform his or her duties objectively and effectively. Conflicts of interest also may arise when an employee, officer, or director, or members of his or her family, receives improper personal benefits as a result of his or her position in the Company.

It is almost always a conflict of interest for an employee to work simultaneously for a competitor, customer, or supplier. The best policy is to avoid any direct or indirect business connection with our customers, suppliers, or competitors, except on the Company's behalf. Conflicts of interest are prohibited as a matter of Company policy. Conflicts of interest may not always be clear-cut, so if you have a question, you should consult with your supervisor or the Company's chief financial officer. Any employee, officer, or director who becomes aware of an actual or potential conflict of interest should bring it to the attention of a supervisor or the Company's chief financial officer, or consult the procedures described in "Violations of this Code."

Trading in Company Securities

Can I buy and sell our securities?

If you know any material information about the Company that has not been disclosed to the public (otherwise known as "insider information"), you are prohibited by law and Company policy from engaging in transactions in the Company's stock until such information is disclosed to the public. If you do conduct transactions in the Company's stock while in possession of material nonpublic information, it is more than just a violation of our ethical standards. The Securities Exchange Act of 1934 prohibits insider trading and deceptive practices in stocks and securities. If you violate these provisions, you could be subject to both civil and criminal penalties. If you have any questions regarding buying or selling our stock, please consult with [the responsible corporate officer] prior to engaging in any such transaction.

> **NOTE:** *The title of the corporate official to whom the company delegates the responsibility for enforcement of the company's policy on insider trading varies from company to company. Accordingly, this policy refers to "the responsible corporate officer."*

Use of Company Information

What is considered "material information"?

In general, material information is information that a prudent investor would consider important in reaching a decision to buy or sell stock. Although the following list is not exclusive or exhaustive, it provides several examples of what generally is considered material information:

- Projections of future earnings or losses or other earnings guidance;
- Earnings that are inconsistent with the consensus expectations of the investment community;
- A pending or proposed merger, acquisition, or tender offer, or an acquisition or disposition of significant assets;
- A change in management;
- Major events regarding the Company's securities, including the declaration of a dividend or stock split or the offering of additional securities;
- Financial liquidity problems;
- Actual or threatened major litigation, or the resolution of such litigation;
- New major contracts, orders, suppliers, customers, or finance sources, or the loss thereof;
- A significant increase or reduction in purchases of merchandise by a significant customer;
- A significant change in the amount or timing of replenishment orders, or in the amount or timing of returned merchandise;
- A significant change in inventory, including increases or decreases in obsolete items or the accounting reserves established therefore; and

- The results of operations during any period of any division, subsidiary, or segment, or any significant changes in the components thereof, including its sales, costs of goods sold, or items of expense.

These same criteria also apply to material nonpublic information relating to our customers and suppliers.

What happens if I disclose material nonpublic information to others?

If you possess material nonpublic information, you may not disclose such information to any other person (including family members). If you do disclose such information and others trade in Company securities based on that information, you could be subject to criminal and civil penalties.

Information is a key corporate asset and is considered the property of the Company. Even inadvertent release of business or technical information to third parties may help our competitors by providing them with solutions to an important problem or by allowing them to avoid costly research and development activities. If competitors gain even a very general sense of what we intend to bring to market, it may give them a head start in countering whatever advantages we might have had with our customers. If you have access to proprietary and confidential information, you must take every precaution to keep it confidential. Unauthorized disclosure of confidential information could be extremely harmful and could be the basis of legal action against both the Company and the person disclosing the information.

Financial Reporting

What are my obligations with respect to financial reporting?

As a public company, the integrity of our recordkeeping and reporting systems is of utmost importance. We are required to keep books and records that accurately and fairly reflect our transactions and the dispositions of our assets. All of our books, records, accounts, and financial statements must be maintained in reasonable detail, must appropriately reflect our transactions, and must conform to applicable legal requirements and to our system of internal controls. You are forbidden to use, authorize, or condone the use of "off-the-books" bookkeeping, secret accounts, unrecorded bank accounts, slush funds, falsified books, or any other devices that could be utilized to distort our records or reports or our true operating results and financial condition.

Outside Employment and Activities

What is "moonlighting" and is it permitted?

Generally speaking, "moonlighting" is defined as working at some activity for personal gain outside of your job with the Company. We expect you to devote your full time and attention to your commitment to the Company. As an employee of the Company, you should avoid outside employment or activities that might impair effective performance of your responsibilities to the Company, either because of excessive demands on your time or because of the nature of the employment or activity. If you are an employee and you wish to engage in a trade or profession similar to the services you provide to the Company, you must obtain the prior written approval of your Company supervisor. If you are a member of the Board and you wish to serve on the board of directors of an entity engaged in a business similar to ours, you must obtain the prior written approval of the Board.

Can I have an ownership interest in our customers or suppliers?

You should avoid any direct or indirect financial interests that might influence your decisions or actions as a Company employee. These interests could include, among other things, a personal or family interest in a customer or a supplier if that interest represents a material part of your net worth or income. You also should avoid investments or other financial interests in businesses that compete with the Company. These prohibitions do not include passive investments of not more than 1% of the total outstanding shares of any public company or investments in a single company that do not constitute a significant portion of your net worth.

Unfair Competition

What is unfair competition?

Trade laws and regulations inside and outside of the United States are designed to foster a competitive marketplace and prohibit activities in restraint of trade. Generally, any actions taken either individually, or in combination with others, that are predatory toward a competitor or by their nature restrain competition, are most likely violations of one or more antitrust laws. In order to avoid violations of such laws, as an employee of the Company you may not enter into or discuss any arrangement or understanding with any third party restricting the Company's or anyone else's pricing policies, the terms upon which our products and services may be sold to others, the number and type of products manufactured or sold, or that might in any way be construed as dividing customers or sales territories with a competitor.

Gifts, Bribes, and Kickbacks

A supplier wants to give me a gift. Is this acceptable?

You may not solicit gifts, gratuities, or any other personal benefit or favor of any kind from any supplier or potential supplier. Gifts include not only merchandise and products, but also personal services, theatre tickets, and tickets to sporting events. You may not under any circumstances accept gifts of money.

You may accept unsolicited nonmonetary gifts provided (a) they are items of nominal intrinsic value, or (b) they are advertising or promotional materials, clearly marked with company or brand names. If a proposed gift is of greater than nominal value, you should consult with the Company's chief financial officer prior to accepting any gift.

A supplier wants to take me to a professional sporting event. May I go?

You should not encourage or solicit entertainment from any individual or company with which we do business. Entertainment includes, but is not limited to, activities such as dinner parties, theater parties, or sporting events. From time to time, employees may accept unsolicited entertainment, but only under the following conditions:

- the entertainment occurs infrequently;
- the entertainment involves reasonable, not lavish, expenditures; and
- the entertainment takes place in settings that are appropriate and fitting to employees and their hosts.

Are there restrictions on gifts or entertainment we can offer our customers and suppliers?

You should deal with all of our customers and potential customers honestly and fairly. You may not offer any customer, supplier, or potential customer or supplier any bribes, kickbacks, under-the-table payments, or other similar improper favors. Improper favors include any payment for the benefit of any representative of any supplier or customer and may include the following:

- gifts of other than nominal value;
- cash payments by employees or agents of the Company;
- the uncompensated use of Company services, facilities, or property, unless otherwise authorized by the Company; and
- loans, loan guarantees, or other extensions of credit.

This Code does not prohibit expenditures of reasonable amounts for meals and entertainment of suppliers and customers that are an ordinary and customary business expense, if they are otherwise lawful. Expenditures of this type should be included on expense reports and approved under standard Company procedures.

> **NOTE:** *Your company might wish to prohibit any gifts, even ones of "nominal" value, so as to eliminate any discretion in the application of the code and to avoid any temptation to "game the system."*

What are "kickbacks" and are they permitted?

A kickback is an undisclosed payment or favor that an employee receives from a third party. It is Company policy that corporate purchases of goods or services must not lead to Company employees or their families receiving personal kickbacks or rebates. Acceptance of a kickback or similar favor could lead to termination of your employment.

Interaction With and Payments to Governmental Officials

How should I deal with government officials?

From time to time, you may come into contact with government officials on a wide variety of matters. Employees who make these contacts have a special responsibility to uphold our reputation. If you are in contact with government officials, you should have a thorough understanding of lobbying laws and public disclosure requirements. This information may be obtained by contacting our chief financial officer. You may not make any form of payment, direct or indirect, to any public official as an inducement to having a law or regulation enacted or defeated.

What is the Foreign Corrupt Practices Act?

The Foreign Corrupt Practices Act was enacted in 1977 to penalize U.S. companies and their employees for bribing foreign officials, governments, and political parties in order to secure business. Among other things, it made foreign bribery a crime and mandated accounting control requirements to prevent off-the-book slush fund payments, kickbacks, and other forms of unlawful or improper remuneration. While certain facilitating payments, where necessary to expedite or secure performance of routine governmental actions outside of the United States, are not illegal, you must obtain prior approval from the Company's chief financial officer before a facilitating payment may be offered.

If you violate the Foreign Corrupt Practices Act, the Company could be subject to a criminal fine of up to $2 million and you could be subject to a criminal fine of $100,000 plus up to five years' imprisonment. You also could be subject to a civil penalty of $10,000. The Company expects strict compliance with this law, as well as the other laws of the United States and of any foreign country in which the Company operates or conducts business. Any uncertainties regarding the application of a law, whether domestic or foreign, should be clarified by contacting the Company's chief financial officer.

Political Contributions

Can the Company make political contributions?

Federal law and most state laws prohibit a corporation from contributing to a political campaign or to a political party. Improper corporate contributions could take the form of use of corporate facilities (for example, use of a photocopy machine to reproduce campaign literature), as well as cash contributions. If you participate in partisan political activities, you must never imply that you speak or act for the Company.

Can I participate in political activities?

Our system of government is built on individual participation in the political process. Accordingly, we will not condone any corporate action, direct or indirect, which would infringe on the right of each of our employees to decide individually whether, to whom, and in what amount, he or she will make personal political contributions of money or personal services.

Senior Financial Officers

Are our senior financial officers subject to any additional standards of conduct?

Like all the Company's employees, our chief executive officer, chief financial officer, corporate controller, and any person performing similar functions must engage in honest and ethical conduct, including the ethical handling of actual or apparent conflicts of interest between personal and professional relationships. These officers must provide, or cause to be provided, full, fair, accurate, timely, and understandable disclosure in reports and documents that we file with, or submit to, the SEC and in other public communications made by the Company. These officers also must comply with applicable governmental laws, rules, and regulations, as well as the rules and regulations of the NASDAQ Stock Market, Inc. (NASDAQ).

All violations of this Code by the chief executive officer, chief financial officer, corporate controller, or any person performing similar functions must be reported to the audit committee immediately. These officers' adherence to the foregoing standards is a condition of employment with the Company. Violations are serious matters and will result in disciplinary action, up to and including termination of employment.

Waivers of this Code

Can provisions of this Code be waived?

A waiver of any part of this Code with respect to any employee who is not an officer or director of the Company can be granted only by our chief executive officer, who may condition any such waiver upon receiving approval of the Board. A waiver of any part of this Code with respect to any officer or director of the Company can be granted only by the Board or a committee designated by the Board. Any waivers of this Code will be disclosed promptly, as required by law or NASDAQ.

NOTE: *You must disclose any waiver, defined as a material departure from a provision of the code, and the name of the officer to whom the waiver was granted, on Form 8-K or the company's public website (but only if the company previously disclosed in its most recent Form 10-K that it intended to disclose waivers on its website and listed its website address).*

Violations of this Code

NOTE: *Once a code of conduct is in place, it must be actively supported. The Sentencing Guidelines for Organizational Defendants and the Sarbanes-Oxley Act both place great importance on the degree to which a company's senior management visibly supports the company's compliance program. This is usually done through an audit function, as well as internal and external resources for enforcement. Employees must have a means to report violations, such as the means discussed in this sample policy.*

To whom should I report violations?

You should immediately report any suspected violation of this Code to your supervisor or the chief financial officer. Supervisors receiving such reports should promptly and thoroughly investigate such reports and consult with our chief financial officer, who will consult with our legal counsel. If you are still concerned after speaking with your supervisor or the chief financial officer (for whatever reason), you should call our anonymous hotline at [_____] to report any suspected violations.

Will I get in trouble for reporting violations?

It is the Company's policy not to allow retaliation for reports of misconduct by others made in good faith by employees, officers, and directors, so an employee will not get into trouble simply for reporting what that employee believes is a violation of this Code. You are expected to cooperate in internal or external investigations of misconduct.

What are the consequences of violating this Code?

You will be held accountable for your compliance with this Code. If a violation of this Code is discovered, appropriate corrective action will be taken immediately. Violations may require restitution by the offending employee, officer, and/or director, and could lead to civil or criminal action. Violations may be grounds for discipline, up to and including termination.

How should I approach a particular situation that might give rise to violation of this Code?

We must all work to ensure prompt and consistent action against violations of this Code. However, in some situations, it is difficult to know if a violation has occurred. Since we cannot anticipate every situation that may arise, it is important to have a way to approach a new question or problem. These are the steps to keep in mind:

- **Make sure you have all the facts.** In order to reach the right solutions, we must be as fully informed as possible.
- **Ask yourself, "What specifically am I being asked to do?"** Does it seem unethical or improper? This will enable you to focus on the specific question with which you are faced, and the alternatives you have. Use your judgment and common sense; if something seems unethical or improper, it probably is.
- **Clarify your responsibility and role.** In most situations, there is shared responsibility. Are your colleagues informed? It may help to get others involved and discuss the problem.

- **Discuss the problem with your supervisor.** This is the basic guidance for all situations. In many cases, your supervisor will be more knowledgeable about the question, and will appreciate being brought into the decision making process. Remember that it is your supervisor's responsibility to help solve problems.
- **Seek help from Company resources.** In case it may not be appropriate to discuss an issue with your supervisor, or where you do not feel comfortable approaching your supervisor with your question, discuss it with a manager, the human resources department, the ethics office, or the chief financial officer.
- **You may report ethical violations in confidence and without fear of retaliation.** If your situation requires that your identity be kept secret, your anonymity will be protected to the degree legally possible. The Company does not permit retaliation of any kind against employees, officers, or directors for good faith reports of ethical violations. You also may call our anonymous hotline at [_____].
- **Always ask first, act later.** If you are unsure of what to do in any situation, seek guidance before you act.

APPENDIX A

- Accurate Records, Reporting, & Financial Recordkeeping/Management
- Antitrust/Competitive Information/Fair Competition
- Bribery
- Client Service/Relations/Unethical or Questionable Behavior
  - ➢ Respecting client practices and property
  - ➢ Respecting intellectual property rights of others
- Client/Supplier/Vendor/Contractor-Related Risk
  - ➢ Acceptance and continuance
  - ➢ Risks identified during engagement; third-party illegalities, errors, and irregularities
- Client/Supplier/Vendor/Contractor Confidentiality
- Communications on Behalf of Company (PR, media, speeches, articles)
- Community Activities—Civic Activity
- Compliance With Professional Standards and Related Rules
  - ➢ Independence
  - ➢ Conflicts of interest
  - ➢ Licensure
- Conflicts of Interest
- Contracting (Approvals)
- Copyrightable Material
- Corporate Governance
- Discrimination
- Diversity
- Document Retention
- Drugs and Alcohol
- Electronic Professional Conduct
- Employment Practices (EEO) & Affirmative Action
- Environment
- Expenses Reimbursement & Time Reports
- External Inquiries/Public Disclosure and Reporting
- Family and Personal Relationships
- Family Medical Leave Act
- Fraud
- Gifts, Entertainment, Gratuities, Favors, and Other Items of Value (to/from Clients, Suppliers, Vendors, Contractors, Government Employees)
- Government Contracting
- Government Reporting, Investigations, Subpoenas, and Litigation
- Harassment (Sexual and Otherwise)
- Health and Safety
- International Business & Global Business Practices
  - ➢ Anti-boycott laws
  - ➢ Embargoes
  - ➢ Export/import laws
  - ➢ Foreign Corrupt Practices Act
  - ➢ Foreign economic boycotts
- Marketing, Sales, Advertising, & Promotions
- Money Laundering
- Obligations Relating to Outside Employment
- Outside Employment & Other Activities
  - ➢ Outside Businesses
  - ➢ Professional Organizations
  - ➢ Charities & Community Service
  - ➢ Fundraising
- Personal Conduct
- Political Contributions and Activity: Lobbying, Holding Office, Campaign Finance
- Privacy
- Procurement/Purchasing
- Protecting Company Assets (Use of Company Resources)
  - ➢ Intellectual property and proprietary and confidential information
  - ➢ Property
  - ➢ Computer and network security (information security)
  - ➢ Computer software and hardware
  - ➢ E-mail and voicemail (communications systems)
  - ➢ Internet & Intranet
  - ➢ Industrial espionage & sabotage
- Quality
- Securities Trading & Insider Information
- Security
- Social Responsibility
- Supplier, Vendor, and Contractor Relationships
- Work/Life Balance
- Workplace Violence—Firearms & Weapons

3. Form: Code of Conduct
(New York Stock Exchange-Listed Companies)

> **NOTE:** *The following sample code of business conduct and ethics is designed to comply with SEC and NYSE regulations.*

_____ CORPORATION

Code of Business Conduct and Ethics

Adopted [date_____]

This code of business conduct and ethics is established pursuant to section 406 of the Sarbanes-Oxley Act of 2002, which requires that the Company establish a code of ethics to apply to the Company's principal executive officer and certain of the Company's senior financial officers, including but not limited to the Company's principal financial officer, controller, principal accounting officer, or persons performing similar functions. This code also is intended to satisfy the requirements for listing on the New York Stock Exchange. As such, the code is applicable to all directors, officers, and employees.

Maintaining the highest standard of ethics in the conduct of the Company's business is Company policy, and has always been an integral part of the Company's culture. The Company's reputation for ethical business practices is one of the Company's most valued assets.

Complying With Law

All employees, officers, and directors of the Company and its subsidiaries (in the aggregate the "Company") should respect and comply with the laws, rules, and regulations of all jurisdictions that apply to the Company. For example, legal compliance includes compliance with "insider trading," financial reporting, antitrust, privacy, sexual harassment, nondiscrimination, and other laws.

Conflicts of Interest

All conflicts between the interests of employees, officers, and directors of the Company and the Company's interests are prohibited.

A "conflict of interest" exists whenever an individual's private interests directly or indirectly interfere or conflict in any way with the interests of the Company. Acceptance of gifts, entertainment, or other personal benefits of any significance from customers of or suppliers to the Company always raises the potential for a conflict of interest. A conflict situation can arise when an employee, officer, or director takes actions or has interests that may make it difficult to perform his or her Company work objectively and effectively.

Any employee who becomes aware of a conflict or potential conflict should bring it to the attention of the Company's senior vice president and general counsel or his or her designee. Any director who becomes aware of a conflict or potential conflict should bring it to the attention of the corporate governance and nominating committee and the Company's senior vice president and general counsel or his or her designee. Conflicts of interest involving the Company's senior vice president and general counsel should be brought to the attention of the chief executive officer and the audit committee.

Corporate Opportunity

Except under guidelines approved by the board of directors, employees, officers, and directors are prohibited from (a) taking for themselves personally opportunities that properly belong to the Company or are discovered through the use of Company property, information, or position; (b) using Company property, information, or position for personal gain; and (c) competing with the Company.

Confidentiality

Employees, officers, and directors of the Company must maintain the confidentiality of confidential information entrusted to them by the Company or its suppliers or customers, except when disclosure is authorized by the senior vice president and general counsel or his or her designee, or is required by laws, regulations, or legal proceedings.

Fair Dealing

Each employee, officer, and director should endeavor to deal fairly with the Company's customers, suppliers, competitors, and each other. None should take advantage of anyone through manipulation, concealment, abuse of privileged information, misrepresentation of material facts, or any other unfair dealing practice.

Protection and Proper Use of Company Assets

All employees, officers, and directors should protect the Company's assets and ensure their efficient use for legitimate business purposes. Theft, carelessness, and waste have a direct negative impact on the Company's profitability and reputation.

Reporting Any Illegal or Unethical Behavior

You are encouraged to talk to supervisors, managers, or other appropriate personnel about observed behavior that may be illegal or unethical and, when in doubt, about the best course of action in a particular situation. Employees and officers who are concerned that violations of this code or that other illegal or unethical conduct by employees, officers, or directors of the Company has occurred or may occur should contact their supervisor or superiors. If they do not believe it appropriate or are not comfortable approaching their supervisors or superiors about their concerns or complaints, then they should contact the senior vice president and general counsel of the Company or his or her designee or the audit committee. Directors should contact the Company's senior vice president and general counsel or the corporate governance and nominating committee. If an employee's concerns or complaints require confidentiality, including keeping his or her identity anonymous, then this confidentiality will be protected, subject to applicable law, regulation, or legal proceedings.

No Retaliation

The Company will not permit retaliation of any kind by or on behalf of the Company and its employees, officers, and directors in response to good faith reports or complaints of violations of this code or other illegal or unethical conduct.

Public Company Reporting

As a public company, it is of critical importance that the Company's filings with the Securities and Exchange Commission be accurate and timely. Depending on your position with the Company, you may be called upon to provide necessary information to ensure that the Company's public reports are complete, fair, and understandable. The Company expects you to take this responsibility very seriously and to provide prompt and accurate answers to inquiries related to the Company's public disclosure requirements.

Amendment, Modification, and Waiver

This code may be amended by the board of directors. Any waiver of this code for executive officers or senior financial officers may be authorized only by the board or the audit committee. Waivers of this code for directors may be authorized only by the board or the corporate governance and nominating committee. Any waiver of this code for other employees may be authorized only by the Company's senior vice president and general counsel or his or her designee.

RESEARCH REFERENCES:

17 CFR Parts 228 and 229, § 228.406 (Item 406) Code of Ethics.

U.S. Securities and Exchange Commission Release No. 33-8177, dated January 23, 2003, available at www.sec.gov.

New York Stock Exchange listing requirements, available at www. nyse.com.

D. ANTITRUST POLICY

1. Introduction

Antitrust laws include several different laws enacted by the federal government and the state governments. Nonetheless, they are based on the concept of open competition, and try to prevent businesses from undermining that concept by various types of behavior by one or several firms.

Penalties that may be applied to companies and individuals who violate antitrust laws are severe. Moreover, violations might easily result from misunderstandings of the applicable legal requirements. Accordingly, companies are well advised to consider whether their employees and agents could violate antitrust laws in the course of their day-to-day dealings, and whether the risk is sufficiently great to warrant memorializing policies and procedures to address the issue in that regard in policies and procedures. The following policy can serve as a starting point when your company has determined to adopt a policy addressing antitrust issues.

Those involved in pricing decisions, or who engage in direct contact with competitors are especially at risk for potential antitrust concerns and should therefore become thoroughly familiar with this policy.

2. Form: Corporate Antitrust Guidelines

I. INTRODUCTION

While the U.S. antitrust laws are a complex and difficult subject, all employees must become sufficiently familiar with them to be able to recognize potential antitrust problems when they arise. These guidelines have a limited objective: To help employees recognize situations in which the advice of the law department should be sought. The guidelines *do not* attempt to delineate the outer boundaries of conduct that may be permissible. Employees who have questions concerning the company's policy on compliance with the antitrust laws are encouraged to contact the law department.

NOTE: *More than 100 countries have implemented some form of competition law. Thus, companies conducting business outside the United States should be aware that other countries' competition laws may be implicated in global commerce, and that the law of other countries often differs from U.S. antitrust law.*

II. SUMMARY OF ANTITRUST LAWS

The Sherman Act of 1890 reflects in general terms the fundamental rules that govern all business activity. This statute outlaws agreements that *unreasonably* restrain interstate and foreign trade, and prohibits monopolization, conspiracies, and attempts to monopolize.

The Sherman Act was supplemented by the Clayton Act of 1914, which regulates mergers and acquisitions. The Clayton Act also prohibits specific types of conduct that may be anticompetitive and restrain trade under certain circumstances, such as exclusive dealing arrangements. The Clayton Act was amended and supplemented in 1936 by the Robinson-Patman Act, which deals with discrimination in prices, services (such as advertising), or facilities.

Business conduct also is governed by the Federal Trade Commission Act of 1914, which declares that unfair methods of competition and unfair or deceptive acts or practices are unlawful. It incorporates the principles of the antitrust laws so far as anticompetitive conduct is concerned. It also deals with false, misleading, or unethical business practices, such as unfair or deceptive advertising.

In addition to these federal laws, most states have antitrust or unfair competition laws, which often mirror the federal statutes.

III. ENFORCEMENT OF THE ANTITRUST LAWS

Primarily, the federal antitrust laws are enforced by the Department of Justice, the Federal Trade Commission, and private plaintiffs. State antitrust laws are enforced by state enforcement agencies and private plaintiffs.

The Antitrust Division of the Department of Justice enforces the Sherman Act through both criminal prosecutions and civil suits in the federal courts. It also has jurisdiction to enforce the Clayton and

Robinson-Patman Acts, though it has generally left responsibility for Robinson-Patman Act enforcement to the Federal Trade Commission (FTC), an administrative agency with concurrent jurisdiction. In investigating serious antitrust violations, the Antitrust Division works closely with the Federal Bureau of Investigation (FBI).

The FTC has concurrent jurisdiction with the Department of Justice over enforcement of the Clayton and Robinson-Patman Acts, and also enforces the Federal Trade Commission Act that, among other things, incorporates the rules of the Sherman Act. Generally, FTC proceedings—which are civil rather than criminal—take place within the agency, and the final determinations of the FTC are appealable to the federal courts.

Finally, subject to certain limitations, any person injured in his business or property by reason of a federal antitrust law violation can sue in a federal court. Indeed, the total number of private antitrust suits far exceeds the number of suits brought by the Department of Justice and the FTC.

IV. CONSEQUENCES OF ANTITRUST VIOLATIONS

The consequences of violating the antitrust laws are severe for both corporations and individuals. An individual who authorizes, orders, or participates in conduct found to violate the Sherman Act may be punished by heavy fines and imprisonment, even if the individual is working on behalf of a corporation. A corporation found guilty of violating the Sherman Act may be fined heavily for each offense, up to $100 million, or twice the gain or loss caused by the violation. Additionally, damages in these suits are automatically tripled, emphasizing the seriousness with which anticompetitive conduct is viewed by U.S. policymakers.

NOTE: *In addition to criminal fines and jail sentences, antitrust laws provide for injunctive relief that can impose long-term and often very severe restrictions on the conduct of corporations and individuals. For example, a corporation may be required to divest some of its assets, license patents, or technology, or change its established ways of doing business. Individuals may be enjoined from engaging in certain types of employment or business activity.*

V. TYPES OF CONDUCT COVERED

The antitrust laws prohibit the restraint of free competition by means of collusion, coercion, or abuse of economic power. Generally, the laws are written in broad terms that do not identify all types of unlawful conduct, which gives courts and enforcement agencies flexibility in applying the laws to prohibit only conduct that is "unreasonable." Conduct generally is judged under the "rule of reason," under which a restraint of trade is determined to be "reasonable" if, overall, it enhances competition to the ultimate benefit of consumers. However, courts have declared certain conduct to be unlawful *per se*, meaning that it is prohibited absolutely regardless of any claimed justification, and without proof of any actual effect on competition.

> **NOTE:** *Such "agreements" need not be written or even expressed, but may be inferred from a course of conduct by the parties. Generally speaking, the best way to avoid unlawful agreements is to make all business decisions on the basis of the company's completely independent judgment and self-interest, without any communication with competitors or coercion of customers or suppliers.*

The following guidelines should be followed in order to achieve the company's business goals in compliance with the letter and spirit of the antitrust laws:

A.   Relations with Competitors: Prohibited Conduct
    1.   Pricing Agreements
Any agreement with competitors concerning prices, terms of sale, price changes, discounts, credit terms, rebates or special financing, pricing methods, warranties, transportation charges, or any other matter relating to or affecting prices or any element of price is absolutely prohibited.

> **NOTE:** *To avoid any circumstances in which any improper agreement might be inferred, there should be no communication of any kind between the company and its competitors regarding pricing or other selling terms.*

2.   Agreements Limiting Production or Markets

Agreements with competitors to: (1) control or limit production; (2) restrict or allocate exports or imports; (3) control or limit product quality or research; or (4) divide or otherwise allocate sales according to customers, territories, or products, are absolutely prohibited.

> **NOTE:** *There should be no communication of any kind directly or indirectly between the company and its competitors regarding such matters.*

3.   Joint Refusals to Deal (Boycotts)

The company is generally free to choose its own customers and suppliers, provided that such choices are not taken in an effort to monopolize any part of commerce. However, agreements among competitors not to do business or to limit business with a particular buyer or seller could be seen as prohibited conduct, and is therefore banned as a matter of company policy.

4.   Bid Rigging

All forms of bid rigging, including agreements to submit certain bids, to rotate bids, to refrain from bidding, and to compare bids prior to submission, are absolutely prohibited.

B.   Relations With Competitors: Conduct Requiring Advance Approval

It is important to avoid conduct that might give the appearance of collusion. Any contact or communication with competitors holds this potential, but there are limited situations in which communication with competitors is permissible and serves legitimate purposes and needs. In any of the situations discussed below, employees who have occasion to have contact with competitors should work closely with the law department to ensure not only that such contacts are limited to proper subjects, but also that appropriate procedures are followed to record the nature and scope of these activities.

1.   Trade Associations and Professional Societies

Trade associations and professional societies perform many necessary and legitimate functions. However, they must not be used for contacts or communications with competitors that are prohibited by company policy, such as discussions of prices.

NOTE: *Because any contact or joint activity with competitors could potentially be construed as anticompetitive, you should not participate in trade association activities without the consent of appropriate management and advance approval and monitoring by the law department. The law department may require the participation of an antitrust lawyer or the reading of a reminder concerning conduct at trade association meetings to ensure compliance with the antitrust laws.*

---

2. Safety

Any contact with competitors with respect to any product safety issue or standard must be cleared in advance and monitored by the law department.

3. Standardization Activities

Appropriate activities involving the standardization of products or materials may be lawful, but care must be taken to avoid any potential anticompetitive consequences that could be caused by such activities. There can be no agreement among competitors requiring adherence to standards; adherence to standards always must be voluntary. Performance standards are generally preferable to design standards, provided performance standards are not established at levels so high that they constitute unreasonable restraints. Again, contacts with competitors concerning standards must be approved in advance and monitored by the law department.

4. Benchmarking Activities, Plant Visits, and Requests for Information

Legitimate reasons exist for competitors to provide technical information to one another or to visit one another's facilities. However, you should secure clearance from the law department before providing information to, or obtaining information from, a competitor, or before an employee or a competitor visits a facility of the other.

5. Group Buying

In many instances, participation in a buying group or purchasing cooperative can produce cost savings and other efficiencies. Because such activities also may be challenged as unlawful agreements with competitors, you must not participate in buying groups unless the law department has approved that participation in advance.

    6.   Mergers, Acquisitions, and Joint Ventures

Mergers, acquisitions, and joint ventures between competing firms often involve antitrust law issues. The law department must be consulted in advance of any discussion outside the company concerning any possible merger or acquisition.

C.   Relations with Customers: Prohibited Conduct

    1.   Pricing Agreements – Minimum Prices

Restrictions or agreements with customers (direct accounts, distributors, wholesalers, or retailers) regarding minimum resale prices are prohibited absolutely. No threats should be communicated or other coercion applied with respect to minimum resale prices. The establishment of minimum resale prices by the company's customers must remain in their sole discretion.

NOTE: *For example, threatening to withdraw certain benefits or programs from a distributor or customer in order to persuade that customer or distributor to sell the company's products at a specified minimum price is prohibited.*

---

    2.   Joint Refusals to Deal

Decisions by the company to restrict or allocate production, or to accept orders for, or limit sales to, particular products, territories, or customers must be made unilaterally, and not by any agreement or understanding with other customers.

D.   Relations With Customers: Conduct Requiring Advance Approval

    1.   Pricing Agreements—Maximum Prices

Restrictions or agreements with customers regarding maximum resale prices must be evaluated and approved in advance by the law department.

2. Tying

Without advance approval by the law department, the company must not require that customers purchase one product in order to obtain a separate product.

3. Restrictions on Resale

Without advance approval by the law department, the company should not implement restrictions or agreements with customers to limit their resale to particular customers, territories, or products.

4. Company Pricing

Pricing should always be done independently with a view toward maintaining a competitive position in the marketplace, and not for the purpose of driving a competitor from the market. Consultation with, and advance approval by, the law department are required with respect to:

a. Sales Below Cost or at Unusually Low Prices

Sales at unprofitable, marginally profitable, or discriminatory prices may be construed as evidence of predatory conduct. In addition to federal laws, many states have specific laws prohibiting sales below cost absent special circumstances.

b. Potentially Discriminatory Prices or Merchandising Assistance

Generally, the same prices must be available to all customers at the same level of distribution, and merchandising services or promotional payments must be proportionally equal, unless lower prices to particular customers can be justified by actual cost savings, or because the prices, services, or payments are offered in good faith to meet, but not beat, terms offered by a competitor. Without prior approval by the law department, the company must not offer disparate prices, terms, or programs to customers.

NOTE: *See Appendix A for detailed guidance regarding compliance with the law on pricing and merchandising assistance.*

---

5. Exclusive Dealing and Requirements Contracts

You must obtain advance approval from the law department prior to entering into any agreement that requires a purchaser to buy all or a specified portion of its requirements from the company, or not to purchase from another company.

    6.   Licensing Restrictions

Any restrictive terms or conditions in the licensing of patents, trademarks, copyrights, trade secrets, or know-how require prior law department review for antitrust considerations.

        a.   Complaining Customers

Customer complaints about other discounting customers are a frequent source of potential antitrust liability. You should avoid becoming involved in mediating or attempting to settle disputes between customers or distributors. Such involvement may limit the company's ability to terminate the customer or distributor for legitimate business reasons.

NOTE: *If the company is contacted by a customer complaining about another customer's pricing, the best response is, "Thank you for the information, but I cannot tell you if or when I may act on it. All of the company's decisions in that regard are unilateral and not for discussion with other customers."*

E.   Relations with Suppliers

    1.   Independent Selection of Suppliers

The company must select suppliers independently. Employees should not discuss supplier selection with other actual or potential buyers of the same supplies, and under no circumstances can the company enter into agreements or understandings with other buyers concerning supplier selection.

NOTE: *To avoid problems, employees should not disclose outside the company or its affiliates the prices, terms, or conditions of the company's purchases, and should not solicit or accept any comparable information from any other buyer.*

---

2. Inducing or Receiving Discriminatory Prices or Promotional Benefits

Section 2(f) of the Robinson-Patman Act prohibits what in some companies may be a common negotiating tool for its procurement department. While the company should negotiate vigorously with its suppliers in order to obtain the best possible prices for the goods and services that it requires, a buyer cannot, however, knowingly induce or receive discriminatory prices, promotional services, and allowances. A buyer could be liable if the buyer knew or reasonably should have known that the seller violated the law in granting the discriminatory price, service, or allowance. Consult with the law department if there is reason to believe the price or promotional service or allowance is not available to the company's competitors.

3. Exclusive Dealing and Requirements Contracts

You must not enter into any agreement requiring the company to purchase all or a significant portion of its overall requirements from certain suppliers, or requiring suppliers to sell all or a portion of their output only to the company unless the law department has approved such an agreement in advance.

4. Reciprocity

Agreements to purchase goods or services from a supplier on condition that the supplier will make purchases from the company, or to sell goods or services to a customer with the understanding that the company will make purchases from the customer can create antitrust problems. Accordingly, obtain prior approval from the law department before considering such arrangements.

F. Other Conduct

1. Exclusionary Conduct

The antitrust laws encourage vigorous competition. Accordingly, having a monopoly position as a consequence of a superior product, business acumen, or historic accident is not unlawful. However, predatory or exclusionary conduct intended to obtain or preserve a monopoly is prohibited. The company should compete on the basis of superior products and services, and competitive prices, and not by actions (either joint or independent) intended to injure another company or to force it out of or prevent it from entering the market.

2. <u>Unfair Methods of Competition and Deceptive Practices</u>

The Federal Trade Commission Act prohibits unfair methods of competition and unfair or deceptive acts or practices. Although the statute does not define these terms, they have been construed to include acts or practices that have the capacity or tendency to deceive an ordinary person, acting reasonably, to the person's detriment. Many states have similar statutes. The company's public statements not only must be true, but should not be misleading or readily susceptible to misinterpretation.

The company also must avoid unethical and unfair methods of competition. Practices such as shipping unordered merchandise, use of "push money" without knowledge of the recipient's employer, commercial bribery, and coercion, intimidation, or harassment of customers, competitors, or suppliers are prohibited.

VI. GOVERNMENT INQUIRIES

The company sometimes receives inquiries from government agencies and departments. These inquiries may take the form of letters, subpoenas, telephone calls, or personal visits. It is the policy of the company to comply with all applicable laws, and to cooperate with any reasonable requests for information from the federal, state, and local governments. However, in doing so, it is imperative that the legal rights of the company and its employees be preserved and protected.

Whenever a request for information is received from any government branch, agency, or department, the law department should be notified promptly, before making any response or acknowledgment. No employee should answer any question, submit to any interview, produce any company information, or hold any discussion or conversation with any government representative without prior consultation with the law department.

The same considerations apply to communications from attorneys representing parties other than the company.

NOTE: *Remember, the company is the holder of the attorney-client privilege, not the employee. Thus, employees should consult with the law department before discussing confidential or potentially privileged information with any third party.*

APPENDIX A

The Robinson-Patman Act is a technically complex statute that tends to restrain the very price competition the Sherman Act encourages. Despite years of criticism from both buyers and sellers, the price discrimination statute is still the law of the land. Stated very simply, the law prohibits charging competing buyers (for resale) different prices for the same type of goods.

NOTE: *The Robinson-Patman Act applies only to goods, not services or intangibles. Note also that the prohibition on discrimination applies only to goods of "like grade and quality." That language refers to physical similarity, regardless of brand names or packaging. Superficial differences between products are not sufficient to justify different prices.*

The prohibitions on price differences are not absolute. Only price differences that cause competitive injury to disfavored customers or (in unusual circumstances) to competing suppliers are prohibited. However, even slight differences in price have been found to be unlawful in highly competitive, price-sensitive markets. Although the Robinson-Patman Act has a tendency to require uniform sales prices, the law does recognize some situations where different prices are permissible. Specifically:

A. Functional Prices

Since the act prohibits only price differences that have an adverse effect on competition, a supplier may charge different prices to customers who perform different distribution functions and who, therefore, do not compete against each other.

NOTE: *For example, the company may provide a functional discount to wholesalers as a reasonable reimbursement for the value to the company of their warehousing, marketing, and distribution services. Retailers, since they perform a different function in the distribution chain, and do not provide these services, may lawfully be excluded from receiving the discount.*

B.   Practical Availability

If a price, term, or discount is available to all competing customers as a practical matter, the act is not violated if some customers choose not to avail themselves of the favorable price, term, or discount. The type of outlet is not relevant to this inquiry. The right question to ask often is, "Do these two customers compete with each other?"

C.   Cost Justification

The act does not prevent price differentials that reflect differences in the cost of manufacture, sale, or delivery. The cost justification defense is highly technical and must be supported by detailed cost studies based on sound accounting principles. The company should undertake cost studies before it charges different prices based on an assumed cost justification. Rough approximations, estimates, and after-the-fact studies are usually insufficient. Price differences based on differences in cost may not be instituted without advance approval by the law department.

> **NOTE:** *As a practical matter, the cost justification defense is so difficult to prove that it is almost never used. If such a defense is used, a contemporaneously prepared cost study should also be used.*

D.   Geographic Price Differences

It may sometimes be desirable to sell at different prices in different geographic market areas. Not surprisingly, problems arise under such programs at the "borders" of designated areas where resellers who may have purchased at different prices compete against each other. Geographic price variations cannot be instituted without advance approval by the law department.

E.   Meeting Competition

The statute allows a supplier to justify a lower price to one or more competing customers by showing that the lower price was made in good faith to meet an equally lower price of a competitor. The meeting competition defense has been rejected where the seller either knew or should have known that: (1) the lower price went beyond meeting competition and beat the competing price; (2) the lower price granted by the competitor was unlawful; (3) the lower price was not limited to only those customers to whom a lower price was available from a competitor; and (4) the competitor's lower price was no longer available.

Even though the meeting competition defense has been relied on heavily in some markets over the years, it has some important limitations. Any questions regarding use of the meeting competition defense to justify a price difference should be referred to the law department for review and approval.

NOTE: *Many companies require that "meet comp" forms be used routinely and thoroughly completed when a lower price is made to one or more customers in order to meet competition. Regardless, companies may choose to observe third-party pricing in the marketplace so that observations can be incorporated into strategic business documents. Employees should never contact a competitor to verify or learn of pricing, but employees are encouraged to request written proof of pricing already provided by competitors to customers.*

F. Changes in Market Conditions

The act permits changes in response to changing conditions affecting the marketability of the products involved, such as obsolescence, deterioration of perishable goods, and sales in good faith in discontinuing a line of products.

G. Sales to Nonprofit Institutions and Government Entities

The Robinson-Patman Act exempts sales to charitable institutions not operated for profit, unless those buyers are purchasing for resale. Sales to the federal government also are exempt, and sales to state and local governments for their own use are also generally exempt.

H. Sale for Use, Consumption, or Resale Abroad

Sales for use, consumption, or resale outside the United States and its territories are not covered by the price discrimination prohibition of the Robinson-Patman Act. There may however, be foreign laws that prohibit price discrimination; the Law Department, therefore, should be consulted.

I. Discrimination in Merchandising Assistance

The Robinson-Patman Act prohibits payments to a customer as compensation for any services or facilities furnished by the customer (*e.g.*, payment for the placement of the company's merchandising fixtures, advertising, or promotions at retail) unless the payments are available on proportionally equal terms to all other competing customers. The act contains a similar prohibition against the furnishing of services or facilities in connection with the resale of the product. The prohibitions are absolute, and proof of a violation does not depend on a showing that there has been an adverse effect on competition.

NOTE: *Nonproportional merchandising assistance to competing customers may in some cases be defended on the basis of a good-faith meeting of competition, but this defense is subject to the same limitations discussed above.*

E. CONFLICTS OF INTEREST POLICY

1. Introduction

An employer expects its employees will act with only the employer's interests at heart. Sometimes, however, an employee's self-interest can undermine that loyalty or create the appearance of divided loyalties.

Such divergent interests might be acceptable so long as the employee notifies the employer. For example, if an employee has a preexisting ownership interest in a competing company, but does not work in the relevant corporate department. The employer might wish to ban other types of personal interests of employees that conflict with its interests.

The following policy will guide employees and other agents as to the types of interests that conflict with those of the employer.

You may incorporate this policy into a larger document that also includes codes of conduct and corporate ethics, as well as specific guidelines for such matters as gifts (*see infra*). If this policy is incorporated into a code of ethics required by section 406 of Sarbanes-Oxley, you must post it on your company's website, and file any waivers or changes on a Form 8-K with the SEC. Your company may have different policies that apply to officers and employees at various levels within the organization, since the code of ethics required by section 406 need only cover "senior financial officers" and may be reserved to a separate document.

2. Form: Conflicts of Interest Policy

Overview

The company expects that all employees, officers, and directors will conduct the company's business with honesty and integrity, and adhere to the highest ethical standards. The company's employees owe to the company their undivided loyalty in respect of their job-related responsibilities.

Although the company respects the rights of individuals to manage their personal affairs and investments, employees should avoid situations that create an actual or a potential conflict between their personal, social, financial, political, or other interests and the interests of company. This policy seeks to address any direct or indirect participation in activities that could impair, or be perceived to impair, an individual's business judgment on behalf of the company.

Scope

This policy applies to any and all transactions and conduct undertaken on behalf of the company, and is directed to all officers, directors, and employees of company.

Policy Details

Company officers, directors, and employees are expected to avoid or to disclose any activities, financial interests, or relationships that may present a potential conflict of interest or the appearance of a conflict. While some particular conflicts are set forth within this policy, the list is not exhaustive and may not include all conflicts that should be avoided and disclosed.

  1. Ownership or Financial Interest in Other Businesses

Each employee should avoid, at a minimum, the following: (a) holding an undisclosed, substantial financial interest in a supplier, competitor, or customer, by either the employee, officer, director, or a family member; (b) having an undisclosed interest in a transaction in which the company is known to be involved or interested; and (c) receiving undisclosed fees, commissions, other compensation, or other benefits from a supplier, competitor, or customer of the company.

NOTE: *Consider providing a definition of "substantial financial interest," which may vary depending upon the entity in which the interest is held. For example, the policy might exempt a de minimis holding in a public company, while a similar interest in a privately-held supplier or customer may not be acceptable.*

For directors, the applicable standard may mirror the company's requirement for a director to be "independent," which in turn may *depend on the listing requirements of the stock exchange on which the company's securities are traded. The New York Stock Exchange standard for independence is that the director not have a "material relationship" with another firm with which the listed company has a relationship. NYSE Listed Company Manual § 303A.02(a). The NASDAQ Stock Market Rules imposes a similar requirement, applicable to partners, controlling shareholders, or executive officers of organizations that have a financial relationship with the listed company involving payments to or from the listed company exceeding the greater of 5% of the recipient's gross revenues or $200,000. NASDAQ Corporate Governance Rule 4200(a)(15).*

The policy might also include limitations on service as an executive officer or controlling person, without regard to ownership. The NYSE rules on independence impose a special standard for executive officers (or directors whose immediate family members are executive officers) of companies whose employer makes or receives payments exceeding the greater of 2% of consolidated gross revenues or $1 million. Such individuals are not considered independent until three years after the financial relationship has fallen below the threshold. NYSE Listed Company Manual § 303A.02(b)(v).

2. <u>Acceptance of Gifts, Entertainment, Loans, or Other Favors</u>

Although business courtesies are to be encouraged, the company generally discourages the acceptance of gifts, gratuities, entertainment, loans, and guarantees of any obligations or other items of more than token or nominal monetary value, on a regular basis, from actual or potential suppliers, vendors, or customers. Moreover, such gifts may be permitted only if they are not made or received on a regular or frequent basis. Employees, officers, or directors should never accept any gifts that could affect the judgment or actions of the recipient in the performance of his or her duties. The specific criteria for accepting gifts are governed by the company's policy relating to gifts and entertainment.

> **NOTE:** *Some organizations have a policy that contemplates tiers of reporting or advance approval depending upon the fair market value of a gift. For example, gifts of under $50 may be accepted without reporting, while those with a greater value must be reported, and, above a certain higher threshold, returned to the donor or turned over to the company. In addition, use of certain types of gifts, such as tickets to sporting or cultural events, must be approved by the relevant ethics authority or compliance officer in advance of use.*
>
> *Alternatively, rather than prohibiting gifts that "could" affect an employee's judgment, your company might choose to prohibit gifts that "might reasonably be deemed to" affect such judgment. This is a subjective test, which implies a judgment by a compliance authority rather than the individual receiving the gift. In such a case, the policy should reference the individual or body that can make such a finding.*
>
> *This test imposes an obligation on the recipient to make a judgment as to whether the gift will influence his or her actions.*
>
> *Consider attaching the policy or having a cross-reference or link to it here.*

3. Outside Employment

Any outside employment that affects motivation, performance, or the amount of time and attention dedicated to company job responsibilities is to be avoided. In the case of directors of the company, this policy does not apply to their principal occupation, so long as such occupation is consistent with the standards for service as a director.

> **NOTE:** *Alternatively this could be stated as "employment inconsistent with the performance of the individual's job duties or contractual obligations to the company," which is a more concrete test.*
>
> *There should be a caveat of this type, since most outside directors are employed in some capacity. It may not be necessary if a director is not considered to have "job responsibilities" as used in the policy, but this should be clarified.*

4. Relatives and Personal Relationships

No officer, director, or employee is permitted to direct company business or corporate opportunities to a vendor managed by, or in which an ownership interest is held by, a relative, spouse, or domestic partner. In addition, any employment of a family member, spouse, or domestic partner with a supplier, competitor, or customer may result in a conflict of interest and should be disclosed to management, as described in paragraph 6, below.

NOTE: *Consider whether this should be subject to the standards described above with respect to financial interests or positions of service held by employees, officers, directors, or family members of such individuals.*

Direct involvement in the hiring of, the direct supervision of, or any direct responsibility for promotional and compensation determinations about spouses, relatives, domestic partners, or close personal friends employed by the company is not permitted. In addition, any personal relationships that may create conflicts with any employee's company responsibilities or that may compromise the company's interests should be avoided.

5. Personal Use of Company Assets

Employees, officers, and directors are prohibited from taking personal or financial advantage of corporate opportunities for themselves while employed with the company. Further, no one is permitted to use the company's property, information, resources, facilities, or position for personal gain.

6. Disclosure

Management, in consultation with the Office of Ethics (OE) and the Office of General Counsel (OGC), is responsible for determining whether or not an actual or potential conflict of interest exists, for establishing any guidelines or controls, and for resolving any conflicts in writing. Each individual is responsible for disclosing any activity that may give rise to an actual or potential conflict, in the following manner:

NOTE: *There are many possible variations for the assignment of the responsibility for resolving such conflicts. In this example, "management" is defined by the context of the reporting person, and thus varies depending upon his or her rank. The institution of an ethics office, independent of the general counsel's office, implies a relatively sophisticated management hierarchy that may not be present in smaller companies or those in which, due to limited regulation of their business activities, compliance issues arise only rarely. In some organizations, the function of receiving reports is delegated to a corporate compliance officer or department, which in turn may report and make recommendations to a special committee appointed by the board of directors or the board's audit committee. Some firms assign the role of analyzing conflict issues to a member of the general counsel's office, with a reporting relationship to a senior manager or an organ of the board. Dual review by a compliance officer and a legal officer will bring their differing perspectives to bear on the issues, which may be helpful to senior management or a committee charged with making the ultimate determination.*

    a. employees of the company should disclose any potential conflicts to the next level of management, who will then consult with the OE and the OGC to resolve any conflicts;

    b. any vice president or senior vice president below the management committee level should disclose any potential conflicts to the management committee member responsible for his or her business area and to the chief executive officer (CEO), who will consult with the OE and the OGC to resolve any conflicts; or

    c. the CEO, any executive vice president, or senior vice president at the management committee level, and any director shall disclose any actual or potential conflicts to the board of directors.

E.   Annual Certifications

Certifications concerning outside activities that may involve actual or potential conflicts of interest shall be completed and filed annually by all directors, officers, and key employees.

NOTE: *The use of the term "outside" limits the certification obligation. In some instances, your company may wish to have a broader certification as to compliance with all provisions of the conflict of interest policy.*

Consider a definition tied to actual job titles in use at the company to make clear who has a certification obligation.

F. EMPLOYMENT LAW
1. Introduction

When it comes to employment compliance, many employers are apprehensive and uncertain. So, what exactly is "employment compliance"? Broadly speaking, employers must comply with all applicable federal, state, and local laws (and to the extent that the company has non-US operations, all applicable foreign laws) pertaining to their employees. Certain laws have size thresholds. For example, some laws apply only to employers with 15 or more employees (such as Title VII and the Americans with Disabilities Act) and some laws apply to only employers with 50 or more employees (such as the Family and Medical Leave Act). Additionally, depending upon the location, an employer may be required to comply with local regulations like posting regulations that notify employees of their rights under the appropriate federal, state, and local laws.

The most prevalent employment laws are antidiscrimination laws. Accordingly, policies against discrimination, and training on such policies, are very important. Compliance, however, is not limited to antidiscrimination laws. Employers also have to navigate a wide-ranging field of laws and regulations, ranging from employees on military leave (Uniformed Services Employment and Reemployment Rights Act) to laws that protect an employee who takes medical leave (Family and Medical Leave Act).

Why is compliance such an important issue for employers? For one, the result of noncompliance or the inadvertent mishandling of a personnel matter can leave an employer, among other things, in the midst of a lawsuit or government investigation. Additionally, employee morale may suffer if laws and regulations are not adhered to.

Staying current with the ever-changing employment law landscape is critical for all employers. From Title VII (federal antidiscrimination law) to sex harassment to the Family and Medical Leave Act, and wage and hour laws, employers must stay on top of the most recent changes in order to remain compliant.

Compliance also is about preventing lawsuits and other complications in the workplace. The savviest employers recognize the need for preventive maintenance in order to minimize the risk of a lawsuit or audit. One of the best ways to mitigate such risks is to avail yourself of the latest forms and policies, and to educate your employees regarding the relevant employment laws.

The area of employment law compliance is vast. This section, while not exhaustive, should provide employers with the basic policies, forms, and guidance necessary to comply with most major federal laws. Nevertheless, you should consult with employment counsel to ensure that your employment policies, forms, and/or practices are legal and appropriate.

For additional guidance on employment policies and agreements, you should also refer to the employment volume of this publication.

2. Title VII

a. Introduction

Title VII of the Civil Rights Act of 1964 is the primary federal antidiscrimination law. Title VII applies to employers that have 15 or more employees. It prohibits workplace discrimination on the basis of race, color, sex, national origin, and religion. It is also unlawful under Title VII for an employer to take retaliatory action against an individual for opposing employment practices made unlawful by Title VII, such as for filing a charge of discrimination or for testifying, assisting, or participating in an investigation, proceeding, or hearing concerning an alleged violation of Title VII.

At one time or another, many employers likely will face a Title VII discrimination charge or complaint. To prepare for such a complaint, there are various steps an employer should take. First, an employer should implement a strongly worded policy that explains the zero-tolerance attitude the employer has toward discrimination and harassment. The employer should require employees to sign such a policy (it could be part of a handbook) and return it to the employer. The employer must maintain and inform employees of the existence of a complaint procedure. Having a clearly defined procedure can act as a preventative measure and can help an employer determine problem areas within the workplace. An antidiscrimination policy may be as simple as the sample policy below.

There is no magical way for employers to comply with Title VII. But, employers should keep three things in mind at all times: Regularly monitor employee behavior; educate employees, especially supervisors; and enforce policies in a consistent manner. Employers should also ensure that all employment decisions are based upon legitimate, nondiscriminatory business reasons, and supported by accessible documentation.

Employment discrimination claims can present themselves in different forms, such as discrimination in the hiring process, failure to promote, or wrongful termination. For example, in order for an employee to establish a *prima facie* case that he or she was discriminated against in the hiring process, under *McDonnell Douglas v. Green*, 411 U.S. 792, 802 (1973), the employee must successfully allege that:

- he or she belongs to a protected class;
- he or she applied and was qualified for a job for which the employer was seeking applicants;
- he or she was rejected for the position despite his or her qualifications; and
- the position remained open after his or her rejection, and the employer continued to seek applications from other people with similar qualifications to the plaintiff.

If the employee is successful in establishing the *prima facie* case, the burden of production shifts to the employer to articulate a legitimate, nondiscriminatory reason for the plaintiff's rejection. If the employer sustains the burden, the plaintiff then has the opportunity to present evidence showing that the employer's stated reason for the rejection was merely pretextual.

For each protected category (race, religion, gender, etc.) and the discrimination claim that can result, an employee must set forth a *prima facie* case (slightly varied from above, depending upon the protected characteristic and the nature of the claim). Employers should be cognizant of the most powerful defense to such an action—the legitimate business reason. Documenting an employee's lack of qualification or poor performance will go a long way toward establishing this defense.

In *Kolstad v. American Dental Association*, 527 U.S. 526 (1999), the Supreme Court held that employers can be vicariously liable for punitive damages when employees who serve in a managerial capacity intentionally discriminate while acting within the scope of their employment. The Supreme Court created an affirmative defense to such an action, promoting the statute's goal of motivating employers to deter discrimination. Employers who make "good-faith efforts to prevent discrimination in the workplace" are not liable for punitive damages under Title VII when their employees, contrary to these efforts, engage in discriminatory behavior. A written antiharassment policy can be an extremely important part of asserting this defense.

b. Form: Antidiscrimination Policy

[Company] strives to maintain an atmosphere that is free from illegal discrimination or harassment of any kind, including discrimination or harassment on the basis of an individual's race, color, religion, sex (including pregnancy), age, disability, marital status, sexual orientation, national origin, or any other characteristic protected by federal, state, or local law.

[Company] has a complaint procedure that employees should follow in the event any employee feels that he or she has been the subject of unlawful harassment, including sexual harassment or discrimination. Any employee found to have violated this policy will be subject to disciplinary action, up to and including immediate termination.

NOTE: *cf the introduction to Title VII. Some of these listed here are in addition to what is required under Federal Law.*

3. Equal Employment Opportunity (EEO)

Every employer covered by the nondiscrimination and EEO laws is required to post an "Equal Employment Opportunity is the Law" poster on the premises. The notice must be displayed prominently, where employees and applicants for employment can readily see it. The notice provides information concerning the laws and procedures for filing complaints of violations of the EEO laws. The form poster is shown below.

A. SAMPLE EEO POSTER

Equal Employment Opportunity is

THE LAW

Employers Holding Federal Contracts or Subcontracts

Applicants to and employees of companies with a Federal government contract or subcontract are protected under the following Federal authorities:

RACE, COLOR, RELIGION, SEX, NATIONAL ORIGIN

Executive Order 11246, as amended, prohibits job discrimination on the basis of race, color, religion, sex or national origin, and requires affirmative action to ensure equality of opportunity in all aspects of employment.

INDIVIDUALS WITH DISABILITIES

Section 503 of the Rehabilitation Act of 1973, as amended, prohibits job discrimination because of disability and requires affirmative action to employ and advance in employment qualified individuals with disabilities who, with reasonable accommodation, can perform the essential functions of a job.

VIETNAM ERA, SPECIAL DISABLED, RECENTLY SEPARATED, AND OTHER PROTECTED VETERANS

38 U.S.C. 4212 of the Vietnam Era Veterans' Readjustment Assistance Act of 1974, as amended, prohibits job discrimination and requires affirmative action to employ and advance in employment qualified Vietnam era veterans, qualified special disabled veterans, recently separated veterans, and other protected veterans.

Any person who believes a contractor has violated its nondiscrimination or affirmative action obligations under the authorities above should contact immediately:

The Office of Federal Contract Compliance Programs (OFCCP), Employment Standards Administration, U.S. Department of Labor, 200 Constitution Avenue, N.W., Washington, D.C. 20210 or call (202) 693-0101, or an OFCCP regional or district office, listed in most telephone directories under U.S. Government, Department of Labor.

Private Employment, State and Local Governments, Educational Institutions

Applicants to and employees of most private employers, state and local governments, educational institutions, employment agencies and labor organizations are protected under the following Federal laws:

RACE, COLOR, RELIGION, SEX, NATIONAL ORIGIN

Title VII of the Civil Rights Act of 1964, as amended, prohibits discrimination in hiring, promotion, discharge, pay, fringe benefits, job training, classification, referral, and other aspects of employment, on the basis of race, color, religion, sex or national origin.

DISABILITY

The Americans with Disabilities Act of 1990, as amended, protects qualified applicants and employees with disabilities from discrimination in hiring, promotion, discharge, pay, job training, fringe benefits, classification, referral, and other aspects of employment on the basis of disability. The law also requires that covered entities provide qualified applicants and employees with disabilities with reasonable accommodations that do not impose undue hardship.

AGE

The Age Discrimination in Employment Act of 1967, as amended, protects applicants and employees 40 years of age or older from discrimination on the basis of age in hiring, promotion, discharge, compensation, terms, conditions or privileges of employment.

SEX (WAGES)

In addition to sex discrimination prohibited by Title VII of the Civil Rights Act of 1964, as amended (see above), the Equal Pay Act of 1963, as amended, prohibits sex discrimination in payment of wages to women and men performing substantially equal work in the same establishment.

Retaliation against a person who files a charge of discrimination, participates in an investigation, or opposes an unlawful employment practice is prohibited by all of these Federal laws.

If you believe that you have been discriminated against under any of the above laws, you should contact immediately:

The U.S. Equal Employment Opportunity Commission (EEOC), 1801 L Street, N.W., Washington, D.C. 20507 or an EEOC field office by calling toll free (800) 669-4000. For individuals with hearing impairments, EEOC's toll free TDD number is (800) 669-6820.

Programs or Activities Receiving Federal Financial Assistance

RACE, COLOR, RELIGION, NATIONAL ORIGIN, SEX

In addition to the protection of Title VII of the Civil Rights Act of 1964, as amended, Title VI of the Civil Rights Act prohibits discrimination on the basis of race, color or national origin in programs or activities receiving Federal financial assistance. Employment discrimination is covered by Title VI if the primary objective of the financial assistance is provision of employment, or where employment discrimination causes or may cause discrimination in providing services under such programs. Title IX of the Education Amendments of 1972 prohibits employment discrimination on the basis of sex in educational programs or activities which receive Federal assistance.

INDIVIDUALS WITH DISABILITIES

Sections 501, 504 and 505 of the Rehabilitation Act of 1973, as amended, prohibits employment discrimination on the basis of disability in any program or activity which receives Federal financial assistance in the federal government. Discrimination is prohibited in all aspects of employment against persons with disabilities who, with reasonable accommodation, can perform the essential functions of a job.

If you believe you have been discriminated against in a program of any institution which receives Federal assistance, you should contact immediately the Federal agency providing such assistance.

4. Sex Harassment

a. Introduction

The concept of sex harassment emanates from Title VII. Similarly, harassment based on other protected classifications, such as race or religion, which is becoming increasingly more prevalent, originates from the same source. Generally speaking, an employer is subject to Title VII if it has 15 or more employees. Under Title VII, employees are protected from sex harassment by coworkers in the workplace. There are two general types of sex harassment. The first is *quid pro quo* harassment, where a person is required to submit to some sexual act as a condition of hiring, keeping one's job, or receiving some other benefit in the workplace. The other general form of sex harassment is "hostile work environment harassment." Hostile work environment sex harassment involves a sexually unwelcome or offensive work environment.

The most common form of sex harassment is the hostile work environment and an allegation of an offensive work environment. In addition, while the harassment may be sexual in nature, it may also include nonsexual conduct that singles out a person for harassment because of some other protected category such as race or religion.

In *Burlington Industries, Inc. v. Ellerth*, 118 S. Ct. 2257, 2261 (1998) and *Faragher v. City of Boca Raton*, 118 S. Ct. 2275, 2279 (1998), the U.S. Supreme Court held that an employer can be found liable for actionable hostile environment sexual harassment by a supervisor with higher authority over the employee who claimed harassment. If the supervisor's harassment resulted in termination or some other "tangible employment action," the employer will be held to a strict liability standard. However, if no tangible employment action was taken, the employer may have a defense available if the employer can show that "(a) the employer exercised reasonable care to prevent and correct promptly any sexually harassing behavior, and (b) the plaintiff employee unreasonably failed to take advantage of any preventive or corrective opportunities provided by the employer or to avoid harm otherwise."

In establishing such a defense, an antiharassment policy is important because it lets employees know that harassment will not be tolerated in the workplace and that the employer is exercising reasonable care to prevent such behavior. Furthermore, a well-drafted policy identifies specific behaviors that are prohibited and the repercussions for violating the policy. Additionally, if the employer has a complaint procedure in place, the employer should be able to satisfy the second prong of the defense. Thus, with an antiharassment policy/complaint mechanism in place, employers will be less likely to have to defend a harassment claim.

A key step to successfully preventing and/or defending against a claim of sex harassment is to educate supervisors and employees. Systematic instruction in what is and what is not sex harassment is an important part of the process. In some states, employers are required by law to give sex harassment training to their employees. In addition, employers may also be required to record employees' attendance at these training sessions. To that end, employers should also know whether training is required in their state. For instance, in California, employers with 50 or more employees are required to give supervisors located in California two hours of sex harassment training, and repeat it once every two years thereafter.

Many, if not all, employers choose to include a sex harassment policy in their employee handbooks. Such a practice is wise and can help stop sex harassment before it starts. Sex harassment policies typically prohibit unwanted sexual advances, but a good policy will be very detailed and explain exactly what is and is not permissible.

Employers often prohibit:

- supervisors or managers explicitly or implicitly suggesting sex in return for a hiring, compensation, promotion, or retention decision;
- verbal or written sexually suggestive or obscene comments, jokes, or propositions;
- unwanted physical contact, such as touching, grabbing, or pinching;
- displaying sexually suggestive objects, pictures, or magazines;
- continual expression of sexual or social interest after an indication that such interest is not desired;
- conduct with sexual implications when such conduct interferes with the employee's work performance or creates an intimidating work environment; and/or

- suggesting or implying that failure to accept a request for a date or sex would adversely affect the employee with respect to a performance evaluation or promotion.

A sample antiharassment policy may look like this:

b. Form: ANTIHARASSMENT POLICY

It is the policy of the company to maintain a work environment free from sexual harassment or conduct that might reasonably be perceived as constituting sexual harassment or creating/contributing to a sexually hostile work environment.

Sexual harassment means any unwelcome sexual advances or requests for sexual favors or any conduct of a sexual nature when:

- Submission to such conduct is made either explicitly or implicitly a term or condition of an individual's employment;
- Submission to or rejection of such conduct by an individual is used as the basis for an employment decision affecting such individual; or
- Such conduct has the purpose or effect of substantially interfering with an individual's work performance or creating an intimidating, hostile, or offensive working environment.

The following are examples of conduct that the company absolutely prohibits. This list is not all-inclusive.

- Offensive comments, jokes, or other sexually oriented statements or depictions.
- Unwelcome sexual advances or flirtations.
- Suggestive or lewd remarks.
- Unwanted hugs, touches, kisses, or other touching.
- Requests for sexual favors.
- Derogatory, offensive, or pornographic posters, signs, cartoons, or drawings.
- Transmitting or forwarding e-mails containing offensive, suggestive, or lewd attachments, statements, or jokes.
- Uploading, downloading, or viewing inappropriate pictures or material onto company computer systems.

The above list is only illustrative of types of conduct that would violate this policy and, as such, by no means represents an exclusive list of conduct or types of conduct that could lead to disciplinary action, up to and including termination of employment. Offensive and inappropriate behavior need not rise to the level of sexual harassment within the meaning of applicable state and federal law to be deemed a violation of this policy.

All employees must comply with this nonharassment policy and take appropriate measures to ensure that such conduct does not occur.

In addition to discipline by the company, individuals who engage in acts of sexual harassment may also be subject to civil and criminal penalties.

c. Complaint Procedure

Employers also should establish a complaint procedure for employees in the event an employee believes he/she has been subjected to harassment. The complaint procedure generally cannot guarantee confidentiality to an employee who utilizes the complaint procedure. Furthermore, the employer should take steps to ensure that the procedure is distributed to all employees; a complaint procedure that remains unknown to employees is ineffective and simply not useful. The final component of a successful complaint procedure is a means by which an employer can resolve a dispute before it evolves into protracted litigation.

c. Form: Complaint Procedure

Employees who believe they have been subject to conduct that violates this policy, including sexual harassment or any other form of unlawful harassment or discrimination on account of their membership in a protected class, should immediately report the matter to [the director of human resources and administration], [to his or her supervisor], or to any officer at the company. Under no circumstances does the employee need to report the harassment to an individual with whom the employee does not feel comfortable (for example, if his or her supervisor is the one engaging in improper conduct).

Employees who in good faith come forward with complaints or concerns about any type of harassment or discrimination, or those who cooperate in investigations of same, will not be subject to any type of retaliation or retribution by the company or any of its employees. Employees engaging in retaliatory conduct of any kind will be subject to discipline up to and including immediate termination.

Supervisors who receive complaints of harassment or discrimination from an employee are to forward them immediately to [designated person at company, who could include the director of human resources and/or a representative from the legal department].

Any and all complaints of harassment or discrimination will be investigated. Although the company cannot guarantee complete confidentiality in matters of harassment and discrimination, it will conduct its investigation in as confidential a manner as possible under the circumstances.

If the investigation confirms that harassment, discrimination, or other conduct in violation of this policy has occurred, the company will take prompt and effective action designed to ensure that the offending conduct or act(s) does not continue.

Any employee found to have engaged in conduct prohibited by this policy will be subject to discipline, up to and including termination. The company does not consider conduct in violation of this policy to be within the course and scope of employment or the direct consequence of the discharge of one's duties. Accordingly, to the extent permitted by law, the company reserves the right not to provide a defense or pay damages assessed against employees for conduct in violation of this policy.

5. Americans with Disabilities Act (ADA)

a. Introduction

The Americans with Disabilities Act (ADA) presents many compliance requirements for employers. The ADA prohibits employers with at least 15 employees from discriminating against qualified individuals with disabilities. Employers may believe that their obligation to disabled employees starts and ends with accommodations on the job. However, employers should be aware that the ADA permeates all areas of an employer's business, including recruitment, hiring, firing, promotion, job assignments, training, leave, lay-off, and benefits.

From the moment a disabled applicant contacts an employer, the employer must ensure compliance with the ADA. An employer should clearly identify to all supervisors which questions are acceptable during the interview process.

It is important for an employer to effectively communicate its disability policy. Supervisors and managers should carefully document the "interactive process" when an accommodation is requested by an employee. During the interactive process, the employer should try to identify the precise physical or mental limitations resulting from the disability and potential reasonable accommodations needed to overcome these limitations.

The ADA generally requires an employer to "reasonably accommodate" an applicant's or employee's disability if such applicant or employee can perform the "essential functions" of the position with such reasonable accommodation. A reasonable accommodation includes, but is not limited to: making facilities readily accessible; modifying work schedules or job restructuring; and/or acquiring or modifying equipment or devices to assist persons with disabilities.

Furthermore, employers should take note of the different standards for the qualification of a "disability" under federal and state law. While the federal definition of a "disability" is fairly well-established, state laws can be dramatically different and may encompass more injuries/conditions (*see, for example,* New York's disability law). For instance, in New York, a very temporary disability often can be considered a "disability" for purposes of the state's Human Rights Law, while under federal law, temporary disabilities often are not considered disabilities under the Americans with Disabilities Act. Employers also should make sure they post the proper state and federal posters related to the disability laws and disability discrimination.

When an employer is challenged with a disability claim, job descriptions can be very useful in demonstrating that the employee could not perform the "essential functions" of the position, even with the requested "reasonable accommodation." One preventative measure that employers have used to aid in litigation (should such a situation arise) is defined job descriptions. Therefore, updating job descriptions on a yearly regular basis to reflect the changing work environment is essential.

b. Form: ADA Policy

The Americans with Disabilities Act (ADA) requires employers to reasonably accommodate qualified individuals with disabilities. It is the policy of the company to comply with all federal and state laws concerning the employment of persons with disabilities.

It is company policy not to discriminate against qualified individuals with disabilities with respect to application procedures, hiring, advancement, discharge, compensation, training, or other terms, conditions, and privileges of employment.

Company will reasonably accommodate qualified individuals with a temporary or long-term disability so that they can perform the essential functions of a job.

An individual who can be reasonably accommodated for a job, without undue hardship, will be given the same consideration for that position as any other applicant.

All employees are required to comply with safety standards. Applicants who pose a direct threat to the health or safety of other individuals in the workplace, which threat cannot be eliminated by reasonable accommodation, will not be hired. Current employees who pose a direct threat to the health or safety of the other individuals in the workplace will be placed on appropriate leave until an organizational decision has been made with respect to the employee's immediate employment situation.

The human resources department is responsible for implementing this policy, including resolution of reasonable accommodation, safety, and undue hardship issues.

Definitions

As used in this policy, the following terms have the indicated meaning, and will be adhered to in relation to the ADA policy.

- "Disability" refers to a physical or mental impairment that substantially limits one or more of the major life activities of an individual. An individual who has such impairment, has a record of such an impairment, or is regarded as having such impairment is a "disabled individual."
- "Direct threat to safety" means a significant risk to the health or safety of others that cannot be eliminated by reasonable accommodation.
- A "qualified individual with a disability" means an individual with a disability who, with or without reasonable accommodation, can perform the essential functions of the employment position that the individual holds or has applied for.
- "Reasonable accommodation" means making existing facilities readily accessible to and usable by individuals with disabilities; job restructuring, part-time or modified work schedules; reassignment to a vacant position; acquisition or modification of equipment or devices; adjustment or modification of examinations; adjustment or modification of training materials; adjustment or modification of policies; and similar activities.
- "Undue hardship" means an action requiring significant difficulty or expense by the employer. The factors to be considered in determining an undue hardship include: (1) the nature and cost of the accommodation; (2) the overall financial resources of the facility at which the reasonable accommodation is to be made; (3) the number of persons employed at that facility; (4) the effect on expenses and resources or other impact upon that facility; (5) the overall financial resources of the company; (6) the overall number of employees and facilities; (7) the operations of the particular facility, as well as the entire company; and (8) the relationship of the particular facility to the company. These are not all of the factors but merely examples.
- "Essential job functions" refers to those activities of a job that are the core to performing said job for which the job exists that cannot be modified.

6. Age Discrimination in Employment Act (ADEA)

a. Introduction

Employers with 50 or more employees are subject to the requirements of the Age Discrimination in Employment Act. The ADEA aims to prevent discrimination against employees over the age of 40. In passing this legislation, Congress noted that "older workers find themselves disadvantaged in their efforts to retain employment, and [find it hard] to regain employment when displaced from jobs." Congress sought to promote employment based on an employee's ability rather than the employee's age. Finally, Congress aimed to "help employers and workers find ways of meeting problems arising from the impact of age on employment."

Aside from general restrictions on discrimination against employees over the age of 40, the ADEA also imposes restrictions on employers when it comes to executing release agreements with employees upon separation or termination of employment. Any time an employer terminates an employee who is over the age of 40, and the employee is asked to sign a release, the employer must give the employee 21 days to consider the release and seven days to revoke the release.

In the event that multiple employees are terminated, pursuant to the Older Workers' Benefit Protection Act (OWBPA), the obligations become more difficult. To remain compliant under the OWBPA when terminating multiple employees, employers must give the employees 45 days in which to consider the release and seven days to revoke the release. More importantly, however, employers must detail the "eligibility factors" for the terminated employees, as well as a list of the "decisional unit" considered for termination. In this context, the "decisional unit" is the group of employees that were considered for termination.

Without a proper OWBPA release, employers may subject themselves to future ADEA liability, in spite of the signed release.

b. Form: Sample ADEA/OWBPA-related Component of Release Agreement

Employee acknowledges that s/he was given at least twenty-one (21) days (45 days if multiple employees are terminated at the same time) in which to consider this Agreement. Employee further acknowledges that

(a) s/he took advantage of the time s/he was given to fully consider this Agreement before signing it; (b) s/he carefully read the Agreement; (c) s/he fully understands it; (d) s/he is entering the Agreement voluntarily; (e) s/he is receiving valuable consideration in exchange for her/his execution of the Agreement that s/he would not otherwise be entitled to receive; and (f) Company, by this writing, advised Employee to consult with an attorney before signing it, and that s/he did so to the extent s/he deemed appropriate.

This Agreement shall not become effective until the eighth day following Employee's signing of this Agreement, provided that Employee does not revoke same within the seven days after Employee executes the Agreement. Employee may revoke this Agreement by giving notice in writing of such revocation, which must be received within seven days after Employee's execution of the Agreement, such notice of revocation to be provided to Company. If Employee revokes this Agreement prior to the eighth day after Employee's execution, this Agreement, and the promises contained therein, shall automatically be deemed void.

7. Fair Labor Standards Act (FLSA)

a. Introduction

The Fair Labor Standards Act (FLSA) regulates four areas of law related to payment of wages:

- Establishes minimum wage and overtime standards;
- Distinguishes between covered (nonexempt) and excluded (exempt) employees;
- Establishes overtime threshold (40 hours); and
- Specifies record-keeping requirements

There is no minimum employee count for an employer to be obligated to comply with the FLSA. Whether an employer must comply is determined by the nature of the employee's work or the nature of the employer's work (for example, is the employee/employer engaged in interstate commerce?). For more information on the Fair Labor Standards Act and whether it applies to your business, visit www.dol.gov/esa/whd/flsa/index.htm.

Complying with the Fair Labor Standards Act can be one of the most complex and difficult areas of law for employers and human resources personnel. Failure to follow the relevant statutes can result in severe penalties and costly class-action lawsuits. The FLSA class action has gained popularity amongst the plaintiff's bar in recent years. For example, if employers are not careful about their classification of employees or payment of overtime, they may pay for it down the road, as has been seen in class-action suits brought against Wal-Mart, Intel, IBM, and other corporations.

The first step for an employer is the proper classification of employees: Who is an employee? Who is an independent contractor? What tasks does the employee perform? Is he/she eligible for overtime? Is the employee exempt? Does he/she fit the administrative exemption? Professional exemption? Another category? Determining the answers to these basic questions can go a long way in avoiding lawsuits for an employer.

There are six main exemptions under the FLSA. A brief overview of each exemption follows below:

(1) Executive Exemption
- The employee must be paid on a salary basis and earn more than $455 per week;
- The primary duty of the employee is the management of the enterprise or a recognized department or subdivision of the enterprise;
- The employee customarily and regularly directs the work of two or more other full-time employees; and
- The employee has the authority to hire or fire other employees.

(2) Administrative Exemption
- Compensated on a salary or fee basis of at least $455 per week;
- Primary duty is the performance of office or nonmanual work directly related to the management or general business operations of the employer or the employer's customers; and
- Primary duty includes the exercise of discretion and independent judgment with respect to matters of significance.

(3) Learned Professional Exemption
- Paid on a salary basis and earns at least $455 per week;
- Primary duty involves the performance of work requiring knowledge of an advanced type;
- The advanced knowledge is in a field of science or learning; and
- The advanced knowledge is customarily acquired by a prolonged course of specialized intellectual instruction.

(4) Creative Professional Exemption
- Paid on a salary basis and earns at least $455 per week; and
- Primary duty is to perform work requiring invention, imagination, originality, or talent in a recognized field of artistic or creative endeavor, as opposed to routine mental, manual, mechanical, or physical work.

(5) Computer Professional Exemption
- Paid on a salary basis and earns at least $455 per week or not less than $27.63 an hour;
- Employee is a computer systems analyst, computer programmer, software engineer, or other similarly skilled worker in the computer field; and
- Computer professional's primary duty consists of the application of systems analysis techniques and procedures, including

consulting with users, to determine hardware, software, or system functional specifications; the design, development, documentation, analysis, creation, testing, or modification of computer systems or programs, including prototypes, based on and related to user or system design specifications; the design, documentation, testing, creation, or modification of computer programs related to machine operating systems; or a combination of the aforementioned duties, the performance of which requires the same level of skills.

(6) Outside Sales Exemption
   • Primary duty is to make sales or to obtain orders or contracts for services or for the use of facilities for which consideration will be paid by the client or customer;
   • Customarily and regularly engaged away from the employer's place or places of business; and
   • Unlike the exemptions listed above, there is no minimum salary requirement for outside salespersons.

The FLSA is not the only statute an employer must consider when addressing wage and overtime issues. Very often, there are various state laws to consider as well. For example, the state minimum wage may be different from the federal minimum wage. The overtime rate may be different as well. Therefore, it is wise to consult local and state laws to ensure compliance when determining employee pay rates.

Another important component of the FLSA is recordkeeping. Employers are required to keep fairly detailed records of hours worked and compensation payments made to employees. Every covered employer must keep certain records for each nonexempt worker. The act requires no particular form for the records, but does require that the records include certain identifying information about the employee and data about the hours worked and the wages earned. The law requires this information to be accurate. The following is a listing of the basic records that an employer must maintain:

   • Employee's full name and social security number;
   • Home address, including zip code;
   • Birth date, if younger than 19;
   • Gender and occupation;

- Time and day of week when employee's work week begins;
- Hours worked each day;
- Total hours worked each work week;
- Basis on which employee's wages are paid (for example, "$6 an hour," "$220 a week," "piecework");
- Regular hourly pay rate;
- Total daily or weekly straight-time earnings;
- Total overtime earnings for the work week;
- All additions to or deductions from the employee's wages;
- Total wages paid each pay period; and
- Date of payment and the pay period covered by the payment.

Keeping accurate records of wages can help an employer defend an FLSA claim down the road. Without accurate records, it will be difficult to dispute an employee's or a class of employees' claim(s) regarding unpaid wages.

Finally, employers must display a poster explaining the Fair Labor Standards Act. There is likely to be a required state poster as well. Posters must be displayed in a public place somewhere at the employer's headquarters or main place of business.

b. SAMPLE FLSA POSTER

Your Rights Under the Fair Labor Standards Act

Federal Minimum Wage

$4.75 *per hour*
beginning October 1, 1996

$5.15 *per hour*
beginning September 1, 1997

Employees under 20 years of age may be paid $4.25 per hour during their first 90 consecutive calendar days of employment with an employer.

Certain full-time students, student learners, apprentices, and workers with disabilities may be paid less than the minimum wage under special certificates issued by the Department of Labor.

<u>Tip Credit</u> – Employers of "tipped employees" must pay a cash wage of at least $2.13 per hour if they claim a tip credit against their minimum wage obligation. If an employee's tips combined with the employer's cash wage of at least $2.13 per hour do not equal the minimum hourly wage, the employer must make up the difference. Certain other conditions must also be met.

Overtime Pay

At least $1^1/_2$ times your regular rate of pay for all hours worked over 40 in a workweek.

Child Labor

An employee must be at least **16** years old to work in most non-farm jobs and at least **18** to work in non-farm jobs declared hazardous by the Secretary of Labor. Youths **14** and **15** years old may work outside school hours in various non-manufacturing, non-mining, non-hazardous jobs under the following conditions:

No more than –

- 3 hours on a school day or **18** hours in a school week;
- 8 hours on a non-school day or **40** hours in a non-school week.

Also, work may not begin before **7 a.m.** or end after **7 p.m.**, except from **June 1** through **Labor Day**, when evening hours are extended to **9 p.m.** Different rules apply in agricultural employment.

Enforcement

The Department of Labor may recover back wages either administratively or through court action, for the employees that have been underpaid in violation of the law. Violations may result in civil or criminal action.

Fines of up to $10,000 per violation may be assessed against employers who violate the child labor provisions of the law and up to $1,000 per violation against employers who willfully or repeatedly violate the minimum wage or overtime pay provisions. This law <u>prohibits</u> discriminating against or discharging workers who file a complaint or participate in any proceedings under the Act.

Note: • Certain occupations and establishments are exempt from the minimum wage and/or overtime pay provisions.
• Special provisions apply to workers in American Samoa.
• Where state law requires a higher minimum wage, the higher standard applies.

For Additional Information, Contact the Wage and Hour Division office nearest you – listed in your telephone directory under United States Government, Labor Department.

This poster may be viewed on the Internet at this address: http://www.dol.gov/esa/regs/compliance/posters/flsa.htm

The law requires employers to display this poster where employees can readily see it.

U.S. Department of Labor
Employment Standards Administration
Wage and Hour Division
Washington, D.C. 20210

WH Publication 1088
Revised October 1996

NOTE: *Employers also should post the applicable state minimum wage poster. In most cases, the applicable state minimum wage is higher than the federal minimum wage, and employers are required to pay the higher of the two.*

8. Family and Medical Leave Act (FMLA)

a. Introduction

The Family and Medical Leave Act is a federal law that requires certain employers to provide qualifying employees up to a total of 12 weeks of unpaid leave during a 12-month period for:

- For the birth and care of the newborn child of the employee;
- For placement with the employee of a son or daughter for adoption or foster care;
- To care for an immediate family member (spouse, child, or parent) with a serious health condition; or
- To take medical leave when the employee is unable to work because of a serious health condition.

The FMLA requires employers with 50 or more employees to restore employees who have taken FMLA leave to the same position (or an equivalent position) they had prior to taking the leave. An employer may request a medical certification from an employee who has requested leave for a serious health condition.

While many states have enacted laws similar to the federal FMLA, some states' laws provide greater rights to employees who take leave. In some instances, employees have the right to take leave for additional reasons beyond the reasons granted by the federal law, or they may have the opportunity to take leave for a longer period of time. As a general rule, the employer must follow the state or federal law that is more beneficial to the employee.

The FMLA presents many challenges for employers. The task of addressing an employee's leave is a difficult one. First, an employer must determine if the employee meets the FMLA eligibility requirements: Has the employee worked long enough in the previous calendar year to qualify for FMLA leave? If he/she has qualified, is the basis for the leave request sufficient? Has the employee already taken leave during the calendar year?

Below is a sample FMLA policy, as well as a number of forms an employer should have on hand for when an employee requests leave and a standard poster that must be displayed onsite.

b. Form: FMLA Policy

The Family and Medical Leave Act (FMLA) gives employees the right to take time off in order to recover from a serious health condition, to care for a family member with a serious health condition, in the event of the birth of the employee's child, or in the event a child is placed with the employee either by adoption or for foster care. [Company] (the "Company") fully complies with state and federal laws related to family and medical leaves. [Moreover, although employees in the [location] and [location] offices are not presently eligible for leave under the FMLA due to the size of their respective offices, [Company] has decided as a matter of policy to provide the same level of benefits to otherwise eligible employees in each of its offices.]

Employees considering applying for an FMLA leave should review this policy and their specific circumstances with the benefits manager.

Leave Entitlement

Eligible employees may request up to 12 weeks of unpaid leave in a 12-month period for any of the following reasons:

- Birth of the employee's child or placement of a child into the employee's family by adoption or by foster care arrangement;
- In order to care for the employee's spouse, child, or parent who has a serious health condition; or
- The employee's own serious health condition.

Eligible Employees
An employee is eligible for FMLA leave if employed for at least 12 months, and for at least 1,250 hours of service in the 12-month period immediately preceding the commencement of leave.

12-Month Period
The 12-month period referred to in the previous paragraph is a "rolling" period measured backward from the time that leave is commenced. Thus, as of the day that leave is commenced, an eligible employee is entitled to 12 weeks leave less any family and medical leave taken in the preceding 12 months.

Pay During Leave

Family and medical leave shall be unpaid. However, employees may elect to use all accrued vacation and personal days during the leave. In addition, employees requesting leave for their own serious health condition or that of a spouse, child, or parent also may elect to use all accrued sick leave during the FMLA leave. Employees must use accrued time during the FMLA leave or, for any unpaid FMLA leave, subject to the discussion below, add it to the end of the FMLA leave period. Accrued time will be paid in accordance with Company policy.

Health Benefits

Health benefits are continued for the duration of the FMLA leave, or any period of paid leave thereafter, under the same conditions as if the employee had continued to work during this period, and therefore, the employee is required to pay his/her portion of the premium costs (for FMLA leave without pay, employees must pay via personal check). If an employee does not return to work after the expiration of the FMLA leave, the employee will be required to reimburse the Company for the full cost (employee and employer portions) of health insurance premiums that were paid on employee's behalf during the period of unpaid leave, unless the reasons for not returning were the continuation, recurrence, or onset of a serious health condition of the employee or for other circumstances beyond the employee's control.

Benefit Leave Accrual

No employment benefits, including, without limitation, vacation, sick days, personal days, and any other length-of-service related benefits, will accrue during any unpaid portion of FMLA leave.

Conditions Applicable to Certain Leave Requests

a. Birth of the employee's child or placement of a child into the employee's family by adoption or by a foster care arrangement.
   (i) Intermittent leave or working a reduced number of hours is not permitted unless approved in writing by the benefits manager and office administrator. If approved, Company may temporarily transfer the employee to another job with equivalent pay and benefits that better accommodates that type of leave.
b. In order to care for the employee's spouse, child, or parent who has a serious health condition or for the employee's own serious health condition.

(i) Definition of "child" as it pertains to family leave is a biological, adopted, step, or foster child or legal ward, under the age of 18, or 18 years of age or older and "incapable of self-care because of mental or physical disability."

(ii) If leave is for the illness of a child and both parents are employed by Company, each parent is entitled to 12 weeks of leave.

(iii) If leave is to care for a parent with a serious medical condition, and both husband and wife are employed by Company, the combined leave shall not exceed 12 weeks.

(iv) Leave taken to care for a child, spouse, or parent with a serious medical condition, or for the employee's own serious health condition, may be taken intermittently or on a reduced-hours basis only if such leave is medically necessary. Requests for intermittent leave under these circumstances should be made to the benefits manager or the office administrator. If intermittent or reduced hours leave is required, Company may temporarily transfer the employee to another job with equivalent pay and benefits that better accommodates that type of leave.

(v) Leave taken for the employee's own serious health condition that is covered by workers' compensation or disability benefits will be considered part of the 12 weeks allowed under the FMLA.

Application for Leave

Requests for leave must be submitted on a Leave of Absence Application Form to the benefits manager or the office administrator. They can provide you with copies of this form. When the necessity for leave is foreseeable, the employee must provide at least 30 days' notice before the leave commences. If the date of birth or placement of a child, or the date of treatment for a serious health condition, requires leave to begin in less than 30 days, employees shall give notice as soon as is practicable, generally within two business days of learning of the need for leave.

Failure of the employee to provide timely notice may result in the denial of FMLA leave until at least 30 days after the employee provides such notice.

Medical Certification

A "certification of health condition" must be submitted for leave requests in connection with the employee's serious health condition or the serious health condition of a child, spouse, or parent. This certification must be submitted no later than 15 days from the date that leave is requested.

Failure to submit the requested certification within 15 days may result in the denial of FMLA leave until certification is provided.

Employees who have taken leave for their own serious health condition will be required to provide certification from their health care provider that they are eligible to return to work.

Return from Leave

At the conclusion of a family and medical leave, to the extent required by law, employees will be entitled to return to the position held when leave began, or to an equivalent position with equivalent pay and other terms and conditions. Company's obligation to restore an employee, however, ends at the conclusion of the 12-week FMLA period (or such greater period as may be required by state law). If an employee fails to return at that time for any reason, Company cannot guarantee that the employee will be restored to his or her position or an equivalent position upon return, and his/her employment may be terminated.

Status Reports During Leave

Employees taking family and medical leave must report to the benefits manager or the office administrator once a month concerning their status and expected return date. Additionally, updated documentation must be submitted on a monthly basis by your medical provider.

c. Form: Employee Leave Request

_____, Inc.

EMPLOYEE LEAVE REQUEST

(Please complete this form every time you use any paid or unpaid leave.)

EMPLOYEE NAME: _____

TODAY'S DATE: _____

Have you worked for [company] for at least six months? ☐ Yes ☐ No

I request one day or less: _____ _____
                                      date   hours

I request more than one day: _____ _____
                                   beginning date   return date

Total number of hours taken: _____

I request that my leave be charged to:

- ☐ Vacation ☐ Sick
- ☐ Unpaid Leave ☐ Comp Time
- ☐ Personal ☐ Other _____

IF FMLA/[state leave act] LEAVE, PLEASE COMPLETE THIS SECTION [note: check state leave laws to see if applicable].
OTHERWISE, YOU MAY PROCEED TO SIGNATURE LINE AT BOTTOM OF PAGE.

Please check one of the following:

☐ Your serious health condition {DO NOT IDENTIFY THE CONDITION}/Certification may be required
☐ Family members with serious health condition {DO NOT IDENTIFY THE CONDITION}/Certification may be required
☐ Pregnancy (includes prenatal care, childbirth, and recovery)
☐ Care for a newborn child
☐ Placement/adoption of child or adult dependent

If you are requesting an altered or reduced work schedule for medical reasons, either for yourself or family members, please indicate your scheduling needs:

_____

(Attach a separate sheet if necessary.)

EMPLOYEE SIGNATURE: _____

Confidentiality: Any medical information will be kept in a confidential file and will be used only to determine eligibility for FMLA and to track leave.

☐ Leave Approved ☐ Not Approved   Supervisor's Signature: _____

d. Form: Employer Response

Employer Response to Employee
Request for Family or Medical Leave
(Optional Use Form -- See 29 CFR § 825.301)

U.S. Department of Labor
Employment Standards Administration
Wage and Hour Division

(Family and Medical Leave Act of 1993)

Date:

OMB No. : 1215-0181
Expires : 08-31-07

To: _____
(Employee's Name)

From: _____
(Name of Appropriate Employer Representative)

Subject: REQUEST FOR FAMILY/MEDICAL LEAVE

On _____ , you notified us of your need to take family/medical leave due to:
(Date)

☐ The birth of a child, or the placement of a child with you for adoption or foster care; or

☐ A serious health condition that makes you unable to perform the essential functions for your job: or

☐ A serious health condition affecting your ☐ spouse, ☐ child, ☐ parent, for which you are needed to provide care.

You notified us that you need this leave beginning on _____ and that you expect
(Date)
leave to continue until on or about _____ .
(Date)

Except as explained below, you have a right under the FMLA for up to 12 weeks of unpaid leave in a 12-month period for the reasons listed above. Also, your health benefits must be maintained during any period of unpaid leave under the same conditions as if you continued to work, and you must be reinstated to the same or an equivalent job with the same pay, benefits, and terms and conditions of employment on your return from leave. If you do not return to work following FMLA leave for a reason other than: (1) the continuation, recurrence, or onset of a serious health condition which would entitle you to FMLA leave; or (2) other circumstances beyond your control, you may be required to reimburse us for our share of health insurance premiums paid on your behalf during your FMLA leave.

This is to inform you that: *(check appropriate boxes; explain where indicated)*

1. You are ☐ eligible ☐ not eligible for leave under the FMLA.

---

2. The requested leave ☐ will ☐ will not be counted against your annual FMLA leave entitlement.

---

3. You ☐ will ☐ will not be required to furnish medical certification of a serious health condition. If required, you must furnish certification by _____ *(insert date)* (must be at least 15 days after you are notified of this requirement), or we may delay the commencement of your leave until the certification is submitted.

---

4. You may elect to substitute accrued paid leave for unpaid FMLA leave. We ☐ will ☐ will not require that you substitute accrued paid leave for unpaid FMLA leave. If paid leave will be used, the following conditions will apply: *(Explain)*

Form WH-381
Rev. June 1997

5. (a) If you normally pay a portion of the premiums for your health insurance, these payments will continue during the period of FMLA leave. Arrangements for payment have been discussed with you, and it is agreed that you will make premium payments as follows: *(Set forth dates, e.g., the 10th of each month, or pay periods, etc. that specifically cover the agreement with the employee.)*

(b) You have a minimum 30-day *(or, indicate longer period, if applicable)* grace period in which to make premium payments. If payment is not made timely, your group health insurance may be cancelled, *provided* we notify you in writing at least 15 days before the date that your health coverage will lapse, or, at our option, we may pay your share of the premiums during FMLA leave, and recover these payments from you upon your return to work. We ☐ will ☐ will not pay your share of health insurance premiums while you are on leave.

(c) We ☐ will ☐ will not do the same with other benefits (*e.g.*, life insurance, disability insurance, etc.) while you are on FMLA leave. If we do pay your premiums for other benefits, when you return from leave you ☐ will ☐ will not be expected to reimburse us for the payments made on your behalf.

6. You ☐ will ☐ will not be required to present a fitness-for-duty certificate prior to being restored to employment. If such certification is required but not received, your return to work may be delayed until certification is provided.

7. (a) You ☐ are ☐ are not a "key employee" as described in § 825.217 of the FMLA regulations. If you are a "key employee:" restoration to employment may be denied following FMLA leave on the grounds that such restoration will cause substantial and grievous economic injury to us as discussed in § 825.218.

(b) We ☐ have ☐ have not determined that restoring you to employment at the conclusion of FMLA leave will cause substantial and grievous economic harm to *us*. *(Explain (a) and/or (b) below. See §825.219 of the FMLA regulations.)*

8. While on leave, you ☐ will ☐ will not be required to furnish us with periodic reports every _____ _____ *(indicate interval of periodic reports, as appropriate for the particular leave situation)* of your status and intent to return to work *(see § 825.309 of the FMLA regulations)*. If the circumstances of your leave change and you are able to return to work earlier than the date indicated on the reverse side of this form, you ☐ will ☐ will not be required to notify us at least two work days prior to the date you intend to report to work.

9. You ☐ will ☐ will not be required to furnish recertification relating to a serious health condition. *(Explain below. if necessary, including the interval between certifications as prescribed in §825.308 of the FMLA regulations.)*

This optional use form may be used to satisfy mandatory employer requirements to provide employees taking FMLA leave with Written notice detailing spectfic expectations and obligations of the employee and explaining any consequences of a failure to meet these obligations. (29 CFR 825.301(b).)

Note: Persons are not required to respond to this collection of information unless it displays a currently valid OMB control number.

Public Burden Statement

We estimate that it will take an average of 5 minutes to complete this collection of information, including the time for reviewing instructions. searching existing data sources, gathering and maintaining the data needed, and completing and reviewing the collection of information. If you have any comments regarding this burden estimate or any other aspect of this collection of information, including suggestions for reducing this burden. send them to the Administrator, Wage and Hour Division, Department of Labor, Room S-3502. 200 Constitution Avenue, N.W., Washington. DC 20210.

DO NOT SEND THE COMPLETED FORM TO THE OFFICE SHOWN ABOVE.

e. Form: Employee Medical Certification

Certification of Health Care Provider
(Family and Medical Leave Act of 1993)

U.S. Department of Labor
Employment Standards Administration
Wage and Hour Division

(When completed, this form goes to the employee, Not to the Department of Labor.)

OMB No.: 1215-0181
Expires: 07/31/07

---

1. Employee's Name

2. Patient's Name *(If different from employee)*

---

3. Page 4 describes what is meant by a **"serious health condition"** under the Family and Medical Leave Act. Does the patient's condition[1] qualify under any of the categories described? If so, please check the applicable category.

(1) _____ (2) _____ (3) _____ (4) _____ (5) _____ (6) _____ , or None of the above _____

---

4. Describe the **medical facts** which support your certification, including a brief statement as to how the medical facts meet the criteria of one of these categories:

---

5. a. State the approximate **date** the condition commenced, and the probable duration of the condition (and also the probable duration of the patient's present **incapacity**[2] if different):

b. Will it be necessary for the employee to take work only **intermittently or to work on a less than full schedule** as a result of the condition (including for treatment described in Item 6 below)?

If yes, give the probable duration:

c. If the condition is a **chronic condition** (condition #4) or **pregnancy**, state whether the patient is presently incapacitated[2] and the likely duration and frequency of **episodes of incapacity**[2]:

---

[1] Here and elsewhere on this form, the information sought relates **only** to the condition for which the employee is taking FMLA leave.

[2] "Incapacity," for purposes of FMLA, is defined to mean inability to work, attend school or perform other regular daily activities due to the serious health condition, treatment therefor, or recovery therefrom.

Form WH-380
Revised December 1999

6. a. If additional **treatments** will be required for the condition, provide an estimate of the probable number of such treatments.

If the patient will be absent from work or other daily activities because of **treatment** on an **intermittent** or **part-time** basis, also provide an estimate of the probable number of and interval between such treatments, actual or estimated dates of treatment if known, and period required for recovery if any:

b. If any of these treatments will be provided by **another provider of health services** (e.g., physical therapist), please state the nature of the treatments:

c. **If a regimen of continuing treatment** by the patient is required under your supervision, provide a general description of such regimen (*e.g.*, prescription drugs, physical therapy requiring special equipment):

7. a. If medical leave is required for the employee's **absence from work** because of the **employee's own condition** (including absences due to pregnancy or a chronic condition), is the employee **unable to perform work** of any kind?

b. If able to perform some work, is the employee **unable to perform any one or more of the essential functions of the employee's job** (the employee or the employer should supply you with information about the essential job functions)? If yes, please list the essential functions the employee is unable to perform:

c. If neither a. nor b. applies, is it necessary for the employee to be **absent from work for treatment?**

8. a. If leave is required to **care for a family member** of the employee with a serious health condition, **does the patient require assistance** for basic medical or personal needs or safety, or for transportation?

   b. If no, would the employee's presence to provide **psychological comfort** be beneficial to the patient or assist in the patient's recovery?

   c. If the patient will need care only **intermittently** or on a part-time basis, please indicate the probable **duration** of this need:

Signature of Health Care Provider

Type of Practice

Address

Telephone Number

Date

To be completed by the employee needing family leave to care for a family member:

State the care you will provide and an estimate of the period during which care will be provided, including a schedule if leave is to be taken intermittently or if it will be necessary for you to work less than a full schedule:

Employee Signature

Date

A **"Serious Health Condition"** means an illness, injury impairment, or physical or mental condition that involves one of the following:

1. Hospital Care

    Inpatient care (*i.e.*, an overnight stay) in a hospital, hospice, or residential medical care facility, including any period of incapacity[2] or subsequent treatment in connection with or consequent to such inpatient care.

2. Absence Plus Treatment

    (a) A period of incapacity[2] of **more than three consecutive calendar days** (including any subsequent treatment or period of incapacity[2] relating to the same condition), that also involves:

        (1) **Treatment**[3] **two or more times** by a health care provider, by a nurse or physician's assistant under direct supervision of a health care provider, or by a provider of health care services (*e.g.*, physical therapist) under orders of, or on referral by, a health care provider; or

        (2) **Treatment** by a health care provider on **at least one occasion** which results in a **regimen of continuing treatment**[4] under the supervision of the health care provider.

3. Pregnancy

    Any period of incapacity due to **pregnancy**, or for **prenatal care**.

4. Chronic Conditions Requiring Treatments

    A **chronic condition** which:

        (1) Requires **periodic visits** for treatment by a health care provider, or by a nurse or physician's assistant under direct supervision of a health care provider;

        (2) Continues over an **extended period of time** (including recurring episodes of a single underlying condition); and

        (3) May cause **episodic** rather than a continuing period of incapacity[2] (*e.g.*, asthma, diabetes, epilepsy, etc.).

5. Permanent/Long-term Conditions Requiring Supervision

    A period of **Incapacity**[2] which is **permanent or long-term** due to a condition for which treatment may not be effective. The employee or family member must be **under the continuing supervision of, but need not be receiving active treatment by, a health care provider**. Examples include Alzheimer's, a severe stroke, or the terminal stages of a disease.

6. Multiple Treatments (Non-Chronic Conditions)

    Any period of absence to receive **multiple treatments** (including any period of recovery therefrom) by a health care provider or by a provider of health care services under orders of, or on referral by, a health care provider, either for **restorative surgery** after an accident or other injury, **or** for a condition that **would likely result in a period of Incapacity**[2] **of more than three consecutive calendar days in the absence of medical intervention or treatment**, such as cancer (chemotherapy, radiation, etc.), severe arthritis (physical therapy), and kidney disease (dialysis).

This optional form may be used by employees to satisfy a mandatory requirement to furnish a medical certification (when requested) from a health care provider, including second or third opinions and recertification (29 CFR 825.306).

Note: Persons are not required to respond to this collection of information unless it displays a currently valid OMB control number.

---

[3] Treatment includes examinations to determine if a serious health condition exists and evaluations of the condition. Treatment does not include routine physical examinations, eye examinations, or dental examinations.

[4] A regimen of continuing treatment includes, for example, a course of prescription medication (*e.g.*, an antibiotic) or therapy requiring special equipment to resolve or alleviate the health condition. A regimen of treatment does not include the taking of over-the-counter medications such as aspirin, antihistamines, or salves; or bed-rest, drinking fluids, exercise, and other similar activities that can be initiated without a visit to a health care provider.

Public Burden Statement

We estimate that it will take an average of 20 minutes to complete this collection of information, including the time for reviewing instructions, searching existing data sources, gathering and maintaining the data needed, and completing and reviewing the collection of information. If you have any comments regarding this burden estimate or any other aspect of this collection of information, including suggestions for reducing this burden, send them to the Administrator, Wage and Hour Division, Department of Labor, Room S-3502, 200 Constitution Avenue, N.W., Washington, D.C. 20210.

DO NOT SEND THE COMPLETED FORM TO THIS OFFICE; IT GOES TO THE EMPLOYEE.

f. Sample FMLA Poster

(4)

Your Rights
under the
Family and Medical Leave Act of 1993

FMLA requires covered employers to provide up to 12 weeks of unpaid, job-protected leave to "eligible" employees for certain family and medical reasons. Employees are eligible if they have worked for their employer for at least one year, and for 1,250 hours over the previous 12 months, and if there are at least 50 employees within 75 miles. The FMLA permits employees to take leave on an intermittent basis or to work a reduced schedule under certain circumstances.

Reasons for Taking Leave:

Unpaid leave must be granted for *any* of the following reasons:

• to care for the employee's child after birth, or placement for adoption or foster care;
• to care for the employee's spouse, son or daughter, or parent who has a serious health condition; or
• for a serious health condition that makes the employee unable to perform the employee's job.

At the employee's or employer's option, certain kinds of *paid* leave may be substituted for unpaid leave.

Advance Notice and Medical Certification:

The employee may be required to provide advance leave notice and medical certification. Taking of leave may be denied if requirements are not met.

• The employee ordinarily must provide 30 days advance notice when the leave is "foreseeable."
• An employer may require medical certification to support a request for leave because of a serious health condition, and may require second or third opinions (at the employer's expense) and a fitness for duty report to return to work.

Job Benefits and Protection:

• For the duration of FMLA leave, the employer must maintain the employee's health coverage under any "group health plan."

• Upon return from FMLA leave, most employees must be restored to their original or equivalent positions with equivalent pay, benefits, and other employment terms.
• The use of FMLA leave cannot result in the loss of any employment benefit that accrued prior to the start of an employee's leave.

Unlawful Acts by Employers:

FMLA makes it unlawful for any employer to:
• interfere with, restrain, or deny the exercise of any right provided under FMLA:
• discharge or discriminate against any person for opposing any practice made unlawful by FMLA or for involvement in any proceeding under or relating to FMLA.

Enforcement:

• The U.S. Department of Labor is authorized to investigate and resolve complaints of violations.
• An eligible employee may bring a civil action against an employer for violations.

FMLA does not affect any Federal or State law prohibiting discrimination, or supersede any State or local law or collective bargaining agreement which provides greater family or medical leave rights.

For Additional Information:

If you have access to the Internet visit our FMLA website: http://www.dol.gov/esa/whd/fmla. To locate your nearest Wage-Hour Office, telephone our Wage-Hour toll-free information and help line at 1-866-4USWAGE (1-866-487-9243): a customer service representative is available to assist you with referral information from 8am to 5pm **in your time zone**; or log onto our Home Page at http://www.wagehour.dol.gov.

U.S. Department of Labor
Employment Standards Administration
Wage and Hour Division
Washington, D.C. 20210

WH Publication 1420
Revised August 2001

*U.S. GOVERNMENT PRINTING OFFICE 2001-476-344/49051

9. Occupational Safety and Health Act

a. Introduction

All employers engaged in interstate commerce must follow the requirements of the Occupational Safety and Health Act (OSHA). According to the U.S. Department of Labor, OSHA's mission is to ensure the safety and health of America's workers by setting and enforcing standards; providing training, outreach, and education; establishing partnerships; and encouraging continual improvement in workplace safety and health.

In theory, OSHA regulations, if followed, are designed to reduce worker injuries. An injured worker can bring a lawsuit against an employer for failure to follow OSHA guidelines and/or the DOL can seek to investigate and/or enforce OSHA regulations. Therefore, it is imperative that employers follow applicable guidelines.

There are several general requirements for employers under OSHA. Employers should have the following plans/policies in place:

- Hazard Communication Standard;
- Emergency Action Plan Standard;
- Fire Safety;
- Exit Routes;
- Walking/Working Surfaces; and
- Medical and First Aid.

Additionally, employers should keep track of injuries and illnesses that occur onsite. Every employer covered by OSHA who has more than 10 employees, except for employers in certain low-hazard industries in the retail, finance, insurance, real estate, and service sectors, must maintain three types of OSHA-specified records of job-related injuries and illnesses. There is a specific form for injury and illness recordkeeping (Log of Work-Related Injuries and Illnesses). There is also a specific accident report form that should be filled out by employers in the event of an accident at the workplace. Employers with 10 or fewer employees, or in "statistically low-hazard" industries, are exempt from the recordkeeping requirements. Employers should visit www.osha.gov to find out if they are considered to be in a "low hazard" industry.

b. Sample Log of Work-Related Injuries and Illnesses

OSHA's Form 300 (Rev. 01/2004)

Log of Work-Related Injuries and Illnesses

Attention: This form contains information relating to employee health and must be used in a manner that protects the confidentiality of employees to the extent possible while the information is being used for occupational safety and health purposes.

Year 20___

U.S. Department of Labor
Occupational Safety and Health Administration

OSHA's Form 300A (Rev. 01/2004)

Summary of Work-Related Injuries and Illnesses

Year 20___

U.S. Department of Labor
Occupational Safety and Health Administration

Number of Cases

Number of Days

Injury and Illness Types

Establishment Information

Employment Information

Sign here

Post this Summary page from February 1 to April 30 of the year following the year covered by the form.

Optional

Worksheet to Help You Fill Out the Summary

At the end of the year, OSHA requires you to enter the average number of employees and the total hours worked by your employees on the summary. If you don't have these figures, you can use the information on this page to estimate the numbers you will need to enter on the Summary page at the end of the year.

How to figure the average number of employees who worked for your establishment during the year:

❶ **Add** the total number of employees your establishment paid in all pay periods during the year. Include all employees: full-time, part-time, temporary, seasonal, salaried, and hourly.

The number of employees paid in all pay periods = ❶ _____

❷ **Count** the number of pay periods your establishment had during the year. Be sure to include any pay periods when you had no employees.

The number of pay periods during the year = ❷ _____

❸ **Divide** the number of employees by the number of pay periods.

❶ _____ ÷ ❷ = ❸

❹ **Round** the answer to the next highest whole number. Write the rounded number in the blank marked *Annual average number of employees.*

The number rounded = ❹ _____

For example, Acme Construction figured its average employment this way:

For pay period...	Acme paid this many employees...
1	10
2	0
3	15
4	30
▼	40
24	20
25	15
26	+10
	830

- Number of employees paid = 830
- Number of pay periods = 26
- 830 ÷ 26 = 31.92
- 31.92 rounds to 32
- 32 is the annual average number of employees

How to figure the total hours worked by all employees:

Include hours worked by salaried, hourly, part-time and seasonal workers, as well as hours worked by other workers subject to day to day supervision by your establishment (e.g., temporary help services workers).

Do not include vacation, sick leave, holidays, or any other non-work time, even if employees were paid for it. If your establishment keeps records of only the hours paid or if you have employees who are not paid by the hour, please estimate the hours that the employees actually worked.

If this number isn't available, you can use this optional worksheet to estimate it.

Optional Worksheet

_____ **Find** the number of full-time employees in your establishment for the year.

X _____ **Multiply** by the number of work hours for a full-time employee in a year.

This is the number of full-time hours worked.

+ _____ **Add** the number of any overtime hours as well as the hours worked by other employees (part-time, temporary, seasonal).

_____ **Round** the answer to the next highest whole number. Write the rounded number in the blank marked *Total hours worked by all employees last year.*

OSHA's Form 301
Injury and Illness Incident Report

Attention: This form contains information relating to employee health and must be used in a manner that protects the confidentiality of employees to the extent possible while the information is being used for occupational safety and health purposes.

U.S. Department of Labor
Occupational Safety and Health Administration

Form approved OMB no. 1218-0176

This *Injury and Illness Incident Report* is one of the first forms you must fill out when a recordable work-related injury or illness has occurred. Together with the *Log of Work-Related Injuries and Illnesses* and the accompanying *Summary*, these forms help the employer and OSHA develop a picture of the extent and severity of work-related incidents.

Within 7 calendar days after you receive information that a recordable work-related injury or illness has occurred, you must fill out this form or an equivalent. Some state workers' compensation, insurance, or other reports may be acceptable substitutes. To be considered an equivalent form, any substitute must contain all the information asked for on this form.

According to Public Law 91-596 and 29 CFR 1904, OSHA's recordkeeping rule, you must keep this form on file for 5 years following the year to which it pertains.

If you need additional copies of this form, you may photocopy and use as many as you need.

Completed by _____

Title _____

Phone (___) ___ - ___   Date ___ / ___ / ___

Information about the employee

1) Full name _____

2) Street _____
City _____ State _____ ZIP _____

3) Date of birth ___ / ___ / ___
4) Date hired ___ / ___ / ___
5) ☐ Male
   ☐ Female

Information about the physician or other health care professional

6) Name of physician or other health care professional _____

7) If treatment was given away from the worksite, where was it given?
Facility _____
Street _____
City _____ State _____ ZIP _____

8) Was employee treated in an emergency room?
☐ Yes
☐ No

9) Was employee hospitalized overnight as an in-patient?
☐ Yes
☐ No

Information about the case

10) Case number from the Log _____ (Transfer the case number from the Log after you record the case.)
11) Date of injury or illness ___ / ___ / ___
12) Time employee began work _____ AM / PM
13) Time of event _____ AM / PM ☐ Check if time cannot be determined

14) What was the employee doing just before the incident occurred? Describe the activity, as well as the tools, equipment, or material the employee was using. Be specific. Examples: "climbing a ladder while carrying roofing materials"; "spraying chlorine from hand sprayer"; "daily computer key-entry."

15) What happened? Tell us how the injury occurred. Examples: "When ladder slipped on wet floor, worker fell 20 feet"; "Worker was sprayed with chlorine when gasket broke during replacement"; "Worker developed soreness in wrist over time."

16) What was the injury or illness? Tell us the part of the body that was affected and how it was affected; be more specific than "hurt," "pain," or "sore." Examples: "strained back"; "chemical burn, hand"; "carpal tunnel syndrome."

17) What object or substance directly harmed the employee? Examples: "concrete floor"; "chlorine"; "radial arm saw." If this question does not apply to the incident, leave it blank.

18) If the employee died, when did death occur? Date of death ___ / ___ / ___

Public reporting burden for this collection of information is estimated to average 22 minutes per response, including time for reviewing instructions, searching existing data sources, gathering and maintaining the data needed, and completing and reviewing the collection of information. Persons are not required to respond to the collection of information unless it displays a current, valid OMB control number. If you have any comments about this estimate or any other aspects of this data collection, including suggestions for reducing this burden, contact: US Department of Labor, OSHA Office of Statistical Analysis, Room N-3644, 200 Constitution Avenue, NW, Washington, DC 20210. Do not send the completed forms to this office.

c. Sample OSHA Poster

Finally, employers subject to the Occupational Safety and Health Act (OSHA) are required to post the notice below informing employees of the act's protections. This exact notice can be obtained at the OSHA website (www.osha.gov).

Sample OSHA Poster

You Have a Right to a Safe and Healthful Workplace.

IT'S THE LAW!

- ❑ You have the right to notify your employer or OSHA about workplace hazards. You may ask OSHA to keep your name confidential.
- ❑ You have the right to request an OSHA inspection if you believe that there are unsafe and unhealthful conditions in your workplace. You or your representative may participate in the inspection.
- ❑ You can file a complaint with OSHA within 30 days of discrimination by your employer for making safety and health complaints or for exercising your rights under the *OSH Act*.
- ❑ You have a right to see OSHA citations issued to your employer. Your employer must post the citations at or near the place of the alleged violation.
- ❑ Your employer must correct workplace hazards by the date indicated on the citation and must certify that these hazards have been reduced or eliminated.
- ❑ You have the right to copies of your medical records or records of your exposure to toxic and harmful substances or conditions.
- ❑ Your employer must post this notice in your workplace.

The *Occupational Safety and Health Act of 1970 (OSH Act)*, P.L. 91-596, assures safe and healthful working conditions for working men and women throughout the Nation. The Occupational Safety and Health Administration, in the U.S. Department of Labor, has the primary responsibility for administering the *OSH Act*. The rights listed here may vary depending on the particular circumstances. To file a complaint, report an emergency, or seek OSHA advice, assistance, or products, visit our website at www.osha.gov or call 1-800-321-OSHA or your nearest OSHA office:

Atlanta (404) 562-2300
Denver (303) 844-1600
San Francisco (415) 975-4310

Boston (617) 565-9860
Kansas City (816) 426-5861
Seattle (206) 553-5930

Chicago (312) 353-2220
New York (212) 337-2378
Teletypewriter (TTY) 1-877-889-5627

Dallas (214) 767-4731
Philadelphia (215) 861-4900

If you work in a state operating under an OSHA-approved plan, your employer must post the required state equivalent of this poster.

1-800-321-OSHA

OSHA Occupational Safety and Health Administration

www.osha.gov   U.S. Department of Labor

OSHA 3165-09R

10. Workers' Compensation Laws

a. Introduction

Workers' compensation laws vary from state to state, so employers should check local and state statutes to ensure compliance. Issues that may arise include proper classification of employees/independent contractors, and whether workers' compensation coverage is elective. Depending upon the state, there is likely to be a requirement that the employer post a workers' compensation poster notifying employees of their rights under the applicable law.

b. Sample Workers' Compensation Poster (check your state labor department for appropriate poster)

TO THE EMPLOYER: THIS NOTICE MUST BE POSTED IN A CONSPICUOUS PLACE UPON YOUR PREMISES.

NOTICE

REGARDING WORKERS' COMPENSATION INSURANCE

ALL WORKERS EMPLOYED BY THE UNDERSIGNED ARE HEREBY NOTIFIED THAT THE EMPLOYER HAS COMPLIED WITH THE LAW AS TO SECURING THE PAYMENT OF COMPENSATION TO EMPLOYEES AND THEIR DEPENDENTS, IN ACCORDANCE WITH THE PROVISIONS OF THE WORKERS' COMPENSATION LAW.

_____
Employer

_____
Date

By _____
Employer's Authorized Agent

An employee receiving an injury by accident must immediately notify his/her supervisor, superintendent, or the undersigned, who will provide medical attendance.

Claim for compensation must be made in writing and given to the employer. Forms for giving notice of injury and making claim for compensation will be furnished by the employer; by the surety,

or upon application, by the Industrial Commission in Boise, Idaho.

ICREV 11/94 EMP

11. Uniformed Services Employment and Reemployment Rights Act

a. Introduction

The Uniformed Services Employment and Reemployment Rights Act (USERRA) protects service members' reemployment rights when returning from a period of service in the uniformed services, including those called up from the reserves or National Guard, and prohibits employer discrimination based on military service or obligation. USERRA applies to nearly all employers, public or private, regardless of size.

Employers are required to post a USERRA poster entitled, "Your Rights under USERRA" in a visible location in the workplace. The USERRA notice of rights poster is the only required form related to the act, but employers also should be aware that if their health plan is subject to COBRA, the employer must provide a COBRA election notice to the employee because a military call-up generally is a COBRA-qualifying event.

More information on USERRA is available at the Department of Labor's website at www.dol.gov.

b. Sample: USERRA Policy

An employee who is a member of the United States Army, Navy, Air Force, Marines, Coast Guard, National Guard, Reserves, or Public Health Service will be granted a [insert: paid, partially paid, or unpaid] leave of absence for military service, training, or related obligations in accordance with applicable law. [If unpaid leave, insert: Employees on military leave may substitute their accrued paid leave time for unpaid leave.] At the conclusion of the leave, upon the satisfaction of certain conditions, an employee generally has a right to return to the same position he or she held prior to the leave, or to a position with like seniority, status, and pay that the employee is qualified to perform.

Continuation of Health Benefits

During a military leave of less than 31 days, an employee is entitled to continued group health plan coverage under the same conditions as if the employee had continued to work. For military leaves of more than 30 days, an employee may elect to continue his/her health coverage for up to 24 months of uniformed service, but may be required to pay all or part of the premium for the continuation coverage.

NOTE: *Employees and/or dependents who elect to continue their coverage may not be required to pay more than 102% of the full premium for the coverage elected. The premium is to be calculated in the same manner as that required by COBRA.*

Requests for Leave

Leave for active or reserve duty

Upon receipt of orders for active or reserve duty, an employee should notify his/her supervisor, as well as human resources, as soon as possible, and submit a copy of the military orders to his/her supervisor and the human resources department (unless he/she is unable to do so because of military necessity or it is otherwise impossible or unreasonable).

Leave for training and other related obligations (e.g., fitness for service examinations)

Employees also will be granted time off for military training (normally 14 days plus travel time) and other related obligations, such as for an examination to determine fitness to perform service. Employees should advise their supervisor and/or department head of their training schedule and/or other related obligations as far in advance as possible.

Return from Military Leave

Notice Required

Upon return from military service, an employee must provide notice of or submit an application for reemployment in accordance with the following schedule:

1) An employee who served for less than 31 days, or who reported for a fitness examination, must provide notice of reemployment at

the beginning of the first full regular scheduled work period that starts at least eight hours after the employee has returned from the location of service.

2) An employee who served for more than 30 days, but less than 181 days, must submit an application for reemployment no later than 14 days after completing his/her period of service, or, if this deadline is impossible or unreasonable through no fault of the employee, then on the next calendar day when submission becomes possible.

3) An employee who served for more than 180 days must submit an application for reemployment no later than 90 days after the completion of the uniformed service.

4) An employee who has been hospitalized, or is recovering from an injury or illness incurred or aggravated while serving, must report to the human resources department (if the service was less than 31 days), or submit an application for reemployment (if the service was greater than 30 days), at the end of the necessary recovery period (which may not exceed two years).

Required Documentation

An employee whose military service was for more than 30 days must provide documentation within two weeks of his/her return (unless such documentation does not yet exist or is not readily available) showing the following: (i) the application for reemployment is timely (i.e., submitted within the required time period); (ii) the period of military service has not exceeded five years; and (iii) the employee received an honorable or general discharge.

c. Sample USERRA Poster

FOR USE BY PRIVATE SECTOR AND STATE GOVERNMENT EMPLOYERS

YOUR RIGHTS UNDER USERRA
THE UNIFORMED SERVICES EMPLOYMENT
AND REEMPLOYMENT RIGHTS ACT

USERRA protects the job rights of individuals who voluntarily or involuntarily leave employment positions to undertake military service or certain types of service in the National Disaster Medical System. USERRA also prohibits employers from discriminating against past and present members of the uniformed services, and applicants to the uniformed services.

REEMPLOYMENT RIGHTS

You have the right to be reemployed in your civilian job if you leave that job to perform service in the uniformed service and:

☆ you ensure that your employer receives advance written or verbal notice of your service;

☆ you have five years or less of cumulative service in the uniformed services while with that particular employer;

☆ you return to work or apply for reemployment in a timely manner after conclusion of service; and

☆ you have not been separated from service with a disqualifying discharge or under other than honorable conditions.

If you are eligible to be reemployed, you must be restored to the job and benefits you would have attained if you had not been absent due to military service or, in some cases, a comparable job.

RIGHT TO BE FREE FROM DISCRIMINATION AND RETALIATION

If you:

☆ are a past or present member of the uniformed service;
☆ have applied for membership in the uniformed service; or
☆ are obligated to serve in the uniformed service;

then an employer may not deny you:

☆ initial employment;
☆ reemployment;
☆ retention in employment;
☆ promotion; or
☆ any benefit of employment

because of this status.

In addition, an employer may not retaliate against anyone assisting in the enforcement of USERRA rights, including testifying or making a statement in connection with a proceeding under USERRA, even if that person has no service connection.

HEALTH INSURANCE PROTECTION

☆ If you leave your job to perform military service, you have the right to elect to continue your existing employer-based health plan coverage for you and your dependents for up to 24 months while in the military.

☆ Even if you don't elect to continue coverage during your military service, you have the right to be reinstated in your employer's health plan when you are reemployed, generally without any waiting periods or exclusions (e.g., pre-existing condition exclusions) except for service-connected illnesses or injuries.

ENFORCEMENT

☆ The U.S. Department of Labor, Veterans Employment and Training Service (VETS) is authorized to investigate and resolve complaints of USERRA violations.

☆ For assistance in filing a complaint, or for any other information on USERRA, contact VETS at **1-866-4-USA-DOL** or visit its **website at http://www.dol.gov/vets**. An interactive online USERRA Advisor can be viewed at **http://www.dol.gov/elaws/userra.htm**.

☆ If you file a complaint with VETS and VETS is unable to resolve it, you may request that your case be referred to the Department of Justice for representation.

☆ You may also bypass the VETS process and bring a civil action against an employer for violations of USERRA.

The rights listed here may vary depending on the circumstances. This notice was prepared by VETS, and may be viewed on the internet at this address: http://www.dol.gov/vets/programs/userra/poster.htm. Federal law requires employers to notify employees of their rights under USERRA, and employers may meet this requirement by displaying this notice where they customarily place notices for employees.

U.S. Department of Justice

**U.S. Department of Labor
1-866-487-2365**

1-800-336-4590

Publication Date—January 2006

12. COBRA

a. Introduction

The Consolidated Omnibus Budget Reconciliation Act (COBRA) is a statute that requires employers to allow eligible former employees, retirees, spouses, former spouses, and dependent children to continue their health insurance coverage at group rates post-employment. Employers with 20 or more employees on staff for more than 50 percent of their ordinary business days in the prior year generally are subject to the regulations of COBRA.

Employees and other covered individuals generally are entitled to COBRA coverage if a "qualifying event" occurs. Examples of qualifying events for an employee include voluntary or involuntary employment termination for reasons other than gross misconduct, or a reduction in work hours. Employers should be aware of the necessary forms for proper COBRA compliance.

Most importantly, employers should be aware of when and how they should notify employees of their COBRA rights. Currently, COBRA requires employers and plan administrators to notify eligible individuals of their continuation coverage rights on at least two occasions: When their coverage under the plan commences, and on the occurrence of a qualifying event.

There are many forms that an employer should use to comply with COBRA. Complying with COBRA is complex and should be given extra consideration. Some of the required forms include:

- Model General Notice of COBRA Continuation Coverage Rights;
- Model COBRA Continuation Coverage Election Notice;
- Notice of Qualifying Event from Employer to Plan Administrator;
- Qualifying Event Notice Information for Employee to Send to Plan Administrator;
- Acknowledgment of Receipt of COBRA Notice;
- COBRA Continuation Waiver Letter;
- Employer/Plan Administrator Notice to Employee of Unavailability of Continuation Coverage;
- Notice from Employer to Employee Regarding Early Termination of Continuation Coverage;
- Model Certificate: Group Health Plan Coverage; and
- COBRA Notice Timing/Delivery Chart.

It is recommended that employers contact outside counsel in order to ensure COBRA compliance and to obtain the appropriate forms.

Questions that administrators and human resources personnel need to consider include: Who is entitled to COBRA coverage? What are qualifying events? How long is the employee entitled to COBRA coverage? What must be provided? Has the employee been properly notified? Who bears the responsibility for COBRA premiums?

Finally, it is worth noting that COBRA coverage can be an important component of a settlement and/or release agreement, and many of the above issues may present themselves in that context.

What follows below is a sample "notice of right to elect COBRA continuation coverage." The employer gives this form to employees after the occurrence of a COBRA qualifying event. After a COBRA qualifying event, the employer ordinarily gives this form to the employee, notifying the employee of the right to elect COBRA coverage and the terms associated with the coverage.

b. Form: Notice of Right to Elect Cobra Continuation Coverage

Notification Date:

Your termination of employment on _____ will result in loss of coverage under the _____ health plan on _____ [date]. Under provisions of the Consolidated Omnibus Budget Reconciliation Act of 1985, this is a "Qualifying Event" that will entitle you and your covered spouse and dependent children, if any, to elect to continue coverage (known as "COBRA coverage") under the plan for up to 18 months from the date of your Qualifying Event.

Electing COBRA Coverage

You can elect to continue your coverage by completing and returning the enclosed election agreement to the plan administrator at the address on the form no later than the election end date of _____.

COBRA gives each eligible family member the right to elect coverage independently. Any eligible family member may elect any options shown below without including those family members who do not wish continued coverage.

Coverage Options and Cost

You must pay the full cost of coverage, plus a 2% administration fee. The actual premium amounts are shown below. Your first payment will be for the period beginning _____, and ending with the premium period in which your election was made. The initial payment must be received within 45 days of the date that you sign the election agreement. Subsequently, you will receive a monthly statement indicating the premium amount, due date, and where to send payment. If your first payment is not received by the due date, or any subsequent payment is not received within the 30-day grace period, you will lose your option to continue the coverage.

<u>Carrier</u>　　　　<u>Coverage</u>　　　<u>Premium</u>　　　<u>Billing Period</u>

Our records show the following dependents on file:

Length of COBRA Coverage

If you and your spouse or dependent children, if any, elect coverage, it can be continued for up to 18 months from the date of your Qualifying Event. The coverage period may be extended for the following reasons:

Death of employee, divorce, legal separation, or dependent status change

If any of the above events occur during the original 18-month period of coverage, your spouse and dependent children, if any, may extend coverage for an additional 18 months, resulting in a total of 36 months of coverage from your original Qualifying Event date.

To get the extension, you and/or your spouse and/or dependent children must notify the plan administrator within 60 days of the latest of: (1) the date the Qualifying Event occurs; (2) the date on which there is a loss of coverage; or (3) the date on which you are informed, either through the summary plan description or general COBRA notice, of your obligation to provide notice and the procedures for providing such notice.

Medicare entitlement of employee

If you become entitled to Medicare before your Qualifying Event, your spouse and dependent children, if any, can extend COBRA coverage for up to the greater of:

(a) 36 months from the date of your Medicare entitlement; or

(b) 18 months from your Qualifying Event date.

If you become entitled to Medicare after your Qualifying Event date, but within 18 months of your Qualifying Event, your spouse and dependent children, if any, may extend coverage for an additional 18 months.

Medicare entitlement generally means that you have applied for Social Security Income payments or have filed an application for benefits under Part A or Part B of Medicare.

Disability determination

If it is determined that you and your spouse or dependent children, if any, were disabled (for Social Security purposes) during the first 60 days of COBRA coverage, the 18-month period may be extended to 29 months for all individuals covered under COBRA coverage from the date of the Qualifying Event. The SSA disability determination is the **only** disability determination that extends COBRA coverage, and you **must** provide a copy of that determination. To receive this extension, you must notify the plan administrator within 60 days of the latest of: (1) the date of the disability determination by the Social Security Administration (SSA); (2) the date on which the Qualifying Event occurs; (3) the date on which the qualified beneficiary loses (or would lose) coverage under the plan as a result of the Qualifying Event; or (4) the date on which you are informed, either through the summary plan description or general COBRA notice, of your obligation to provide notice and the procedures for providing such notice. Such notice must be provided before the end of the 18-month period of COBRA continuation coverage.

Bankruptcy filing

If an employer files for bankruptcy reorganization and retiree health coverage is lost within one year before or after the bankruptcy filing, COBRA coverage could continue until the death of a retiree (or a surviving spouse of a deceased retiree) or for 36 months from the retiree's death (after the bankruptcy filing) in the case of the spouse and dependent children.

Newborns and Adopters

A child who is born to or placed for adoption with the covered employee during a period of COBRA coverage will be eligible to become a qualified beneficiary. In accordance with the terms described fully in the summary plan description and requirements of federal law, these qualified beneficiaries can be added to COBRA coverage upon proper notification to the plan administrator.

Termination of COBRA coverage

COBRA coverage will terminate if:

(a) The required premium payments are not paid when due.

(b) After the date of your COBRA election, you and your spouse or dependent children, if any, become covered under another group health plan that does not contain any exclusion or limitation for any of your preexisting conditions. The Health Insurance Portability and Accountability Act of 1996 (HIPAA) limits the extent to which health plans may impose preexisting condition limitations. If you become covered by another group health plan with a preexisting condition limitation that affects you, your COBRA coverage can continue. If the other plan's preexisting condition rule does not apply to you by reason of HIPAA's restrictions on preexisting conditions clauses, your COBRA coverage may be terminated.

(c) You, your spouse, or dependent children, if any, become entitled to Medicare benefits.

(d) The company terminates its group health plan(s).

(e) Coverage is extended to 29 months due to disability, and a determination is made by SSA that the individual is no longer disabled. Federal law requires you to inform the plan administrator within 30 days of the latest of: (1) the date of the final determination by the Social Security Administration that the qualified beneficiary is no longer disabled; or (2) the date on which the qualified beneficiary is informed, either through the summary plan description other statutory notice, of their obligation to provide notice and the procedures for providing such notice.

COBRA coverage is provided subject to your eligibility. The plan administrator may terminate your COBRA coverage retroactively if you are determined to be ineligible for coverage. Please advise us of any change in your address promptly.

Your coverage will remain **terminated** until you complete and return the enclosed election form along with your premium payment to _____. Make all payments payable to _____.

IMPORTANT NOTICE:

You may access your account on the web at _____. Your user name is _____. Your password is _____.

For additional information, contact the person below:

c. Form: Election Agreement

Your rights and the cost of COBRA continuation coverage are summarized on the enclosed Notice of Right to Elect Cobra Continuation Coverage. Additional information can be found in your summary plan description or by contacting the plan administrator shown at the end of this form.

ELECTING COVERAGE

Each eligible family member may elect coverage independently by completing a separate copy of this election agreement. The primary qualified beneficiary may elect to continue coverage on behalf of all eligible dependents who were covered the day before the qualifying event, but only a dependent or legal guardian may elect or decline coverage that the primary qualified beneficiary has declined. Your completed election agreement must be returned by _____ _____ or you will lose your right to COBRA continuation coverage.

I elect the coverage(s) that I have checked below for myself and my eligible dependents, if any:

<u>Carrier</u>   <u>Coverage</u>   <u>Premium</u>   <u>Billing Period</u>

You must provide the information below for any dependent not shown who will be covered. Complete any missing information for any dependents listed below.

<u>Name (last, first, MI)</u>   <u>Date of Birth</u>   <u>Sex</u>   <u>Relationship</u>   <u>Soc. Sec.</u>

Please make all checks payable to _____

I have read the Notice of Right to Elect Cobra Continuation Coverage, and understand my election rights. I agree to notify the plan administrator if I or any covered dependents become covered by another group health plan or entitled to Medicare or have a change of address.

<u>Signature</u>   <u>Date</u>   <u>Phone Number</u>

For further information please contact: _____

13. HIPAA

a. Introduction

The Health Insurance Portability and Accountability Act of 1996 (HIPAA) is a federal law that gives patients greater access to their own medical records and more control over how their health information is used. HIPAA seeks to protect personal health information (PHI) that doctors or health insurance companies have in their files. The HIPAA regulations also address the obligations of healthcare providers and health plans to protect health information.

The rules and regulations under HIPAA are very complicated, particularly if an employer is a "covered entity." An employer should take the following to steps to determine what obligations it has under HIPAA:

- Conduct a covered-entity analysis—if the employer is a covered entity, compliance with the HIPAA privacy, transaction, and security requirements will be required.
- Conduct a covered-entity analysis of its employee benefit plans—if the plan is covered, it must comply with applicable HIPAA requirements including privacy, security, and standard transactions.
- Analyze how health information is gathered and disseminated—employers must determine who has access to health information and how it can protect that information from inadvertent disclosure.

HIPAA compliance is much more complex than it may appear, as employer relationships with their employee benefit plans and use of PHI must be carefully scrutinized to ensure compliance.

b. HIPAA Compliance Notice for Employee Handbook

To put employees on notice that an employer abides by HIPAA, and is cognizant of its regulations, we suggest you include the following notice in your employee handbooks:

HIPAA COMPLIANCE

"All Company employees must comply with the privacy regulations within the Health Insurance Portability and Accountability Act of 1996 (HIPAA), and shall report any suspected or actual violations of HIPAA to Human Resources."

c. Privacy Considerations

An employer that sponsors a fully insured plan can avoid most of the compliance obligations of the privacy regulations if it elects to receive from the plan—or the plan's third-party administrator—only enrollment information and summary claims data for purposes of obtaining bids from carriers or to modify or terminate the plan. For such plans, the compliance obligations will primarily reside with the insurer, as a covered entity, and the employer is not required to do anything further. In contrast, sponsors of self-insured plans or fully insured plans that receive PHI beyond summary data and enrollment information are required to undertake additional steps described. While not required, we recommend that an employer retain a privacy officer to help oversee HIPAA compliance, or at least assign the responsibilities of a privacy officer to someone currently employed.

For more information, you can visit www.dol.gov/dol/topic/health-plans/portability.htm.

14. Immigration

a. Introduction

Since the terrorist attacks of September 11, 2001, the government has stepped up enforcement of the Immigration Reform and Control Act of 1986 (IRCA). IRCA requires that *every* employer verify the identity and work authorization of *every* employee. That means checking original documents within three days of hire and completing Form I-9 regardless of whether the new employee is a citizen, refugee, asylee, lawful permanent resident (colloquially known as "green card" holder), or nonimmigrant. In verifying documents, the employer needs to note whether the employment authorization document has an expiration date. If so, documents need to be reverified prior to that date. The employer also needs to know the difference between blanket work authorization allowing an individual to work for *any* employer, and employer-specific work authorization pursuant to particular nonimmigrant status, such as H-1B or L-1.

Also, employers must be able to distinguish between a visa and an I-94 card. A visa is affixed to a foreign citizen's passport by the U.S. State Department, and allows an individual to apply to *enter* the U.S. during the validity of the visa. The I-94 card is stapled into the passport at the port of entry by Customs and Border Protection (CBP) or issued to the individual by the U.S. Citizenship and Immigration Service (USCIS). The prospective employee's work authorization is measured from the I-94, not the visa. An individual can have a valid I-94 authorizing employment and an expired visa.

There are civil penalties and criminal sanctions for IRCA violations. Employers should refer to the websites of the various agencies for more information, and implement procedures under the tutelage of immigration counsel. Useful websites include the USCIS site (www.uscis.gov), the state department site (www.travel.state.gov), and the CBP site (www.cbp.gov).

While employers must meticulously comply with the IRCA, they also must take care not to discriminate on the basis of national origin or alienage. The Office of Special Counsel for Immigration-Related Unfair Employment Practices provides excellent guidance on its website (www.usdoj.gov.crt/osc), and it has a toll-free number for employers to get answers to questions on work authorization issues to help them reduce inadvertent discrimination.

Finally, employers need to understand the interface between immigration law and the Social Security and tax systems. The Social Security Administration (SSA) sends out mismatch letters if the Social Security Number on a W-2 Form doesn't match with the name on SSA records. The Internal Revenue Service (IRS) requires correction of incorrect information returns. And, increasingly, these agencies are coordinating their efforts with USCIS.

The federal I-9 form can be found at www.uscis.gov/graphics/ formsfee/forms/files/i-9.pdf.

b. Sample I-9 Form

Department of Homeland Security
U.S. Citizenship and Immigration Services

OMB No. 1615-0047; Expires 03/31/07
Employment Eligibility Verification

INSTRUCTIONS
PLEASE READ ALL INSTRUCTIONS CAREFULLY BEFORE COMPLETING THIS FORM.

Anti-Discrimination Notice. It is illegal to discriminate against any individual (other than an alien not authorized to work in the U.S.) in hiring, discharging, or recruiting or referring for a fee because of that individual's national origin or citizenship status. It is illegal to discriminate against work eligible individuals. Employers **CANNOT** specify which document(s) they will accept from an employee. The refusal to hire an individual because of a future expiration date may also constitute illegal discrimination.

Section 1- Employee. All employees, citizens and noncitizens, hired after November 6, 1986, must complete Section 1 of this form at the time of hire, which is the actual beginning of employment. **The employer is responsible for ensuring that Section 1 is timely and properly completed.**

Preparer/Translator Certification. The Preparer/Translator Certification must be completed if Section 1 is prepared by a person other than the employee. A preparer/translator may be used only when the employee is unable to complete Section 1 on his/her own. However, the employee must still sign Section 1 personally.

Section 2 - Employer. For the purpose of completing this form, the term "employer" includes those recruiters and referrers for a fee who are agricultural associations, agricultural employers or farm labor contractors.

Employers must complete Section 2 by examining evidence of identity and employment eligibility within three (3) business days of the date employment begins. If employees are authorized to work, but are unable to present the required document(s) within three business days, they must present a receipt for the application of the document(s) within ninety (90) days. However, if employers hire individuals for a duration of less than three business days, Section 2 must be completed at the time employment begins. **Employers must record: 1)** document title; **2)** issuing authority; **3)** document number, **4)** expiration date, if any; and **5)** the date employment begins. Employers must sign and date the certification. Employees must present original documents. Employers may, but are not required to, photocopy the document(s) presented. These photocopies may only be used for the verification process and must be retained with the I-9. **However, employers are still responsible for completing the I-9.**

Section 3 - Updating and Reverification. Employers must complete Section 3 when updating and/or reverifying the I-9. Employers must reverify employment eligibility of their employees on or before the expiration date recorded in Section 1. Employers **CANNOT** specify which document(s) they will accept from an employee.

- If an employee's name has changed at the time this form is being updated/reverified, complete Block A.

- If an employee is rehired within three (3) years of the date this form was originally completed and the employee is still eligible to be employed on the same basis as previously indicated on this form (updating), complete Block B and the signature block.

- If an employee is rehired within three (3) years of the date this form was originally completed and the employee's work authorization has expired **or** if a current employee's work authorization is about to expire (reverification), complete Block B and:

- examine any document that reflects that the employee is authorized to work in the U.S. (see List A or C),

- record the document title, document number and expiration date (if any) in Block C, and

- complete the signature block.

Photocopying and Retaining Form I-9. A blank I-9 may be reproduced, provided both sides are copied. The Instructions must be available to all employees completing this form. Employers must retain completed I-9s for three (3) years after the date of hire or one (1) year after the date employment ends, whichever is later.

For more detailed information, you may refer to the Department of Homeland Security (DHS) Handbook for Employers, (Form M-274). You may obtain the handbook at your local U.S. Citizenship and Immigration Services (USCIS) office.

Privacy Act Notice. The authority for collecting this information is the Immigration Reform and Control Act of 1986, Pub. L. 99-603 (8 USC 1324a).

This information is for employers to verify the eligibility of individuals for employment to preclude the unlawful hiring, or recruiting or referring for a fee, of aliens who are not authorized to work in the United States.

This information will be used by employers as a record of their basis for determining eligibility of an employee to work in the United States. The form will be kept by the employer and made available for inspection by officials of the U.S. Immigration and Customs Enforcement, Department of Labor and Office of Special Counsel for Immigration Related Unfair Employment Practices.

Submission of the information required in this form is voluntary. However, an individual may not begin employment unless this form is completed, since employers are subject to civil or criminal penalties if they do not comply with the Immigration Reform and Control Act of 1986.

Reporting Burden. We try to create forms and instructions that are accurate, can be easily understood and which impose the least possible burden on you to provide us with information. Often this is difficult because some immigration laws are very complex. Accordingly, the reporting burden for this collection of information is computed as follows: 1) learning about this form, 5 minutes; 2) completing the form, 5 minutes; and 3) assembling and filing (recordkeeping) the form, 5 minutes, for an average of 15 minutes per response. If you have comments regarding the accuracy of this burden estimate, or suggestions for making this form simpler, you can write to U.S. Citizenship and Immigration Services, Regulatory Management Division, 111 Massachuetts Avenue, N.W., Washington, DC 20529. OMB No. 1615-0047.

NOTE: This is the 1991 edition of the Form I-9 that has been rebranded with a current printing date to reflect the recent transition from the INS to DHS and its components.

EMPLOYERS MUST RETAIN COMPLETED FORM I-9
PLEASE DO NOT MAIL COMPLETED FORM I-9 TO ICE OR USCIS

Form I-9 (Rev. 05/31/05) Y

Department of Homeland Security
U.S. Citizenship and Immigration Services

OMB No. 1615-0047; Expires 03/31/07
Employment Eligibility Verification

Please read instructions carefully before completing this form. The instructions must be available during completion of this form. ANTI-DISCRIMINATION NOTICE: It is illegal to discriminate against work eligible individuals. Employers CANNOT specify which document(s) they will accept from an employee. The refusal to hire an individual because of a future expiration date may also constitute illegal discrimination.

Section 1. Employee Information and Verification. To be completed and signed by employee at the time employment begins.

Print Name: Last	First	Middle Initial	Maiden Name

Address (Street Name and Number)	Apt. #	Date of Birth (month/day/year)

City	State	Zip Code	Social Security #

I am aware that federal law provides for imprisonment and/or fines for false statements or use of false documents in connection with the completion of this form.

I attest, under penalty of perjury, that I am (check one of the following):
☐ A citizen or national of the United States
☐ A Lawful Permanent Resident (Alien #) A _____
☐ An alien authorized to work until _____
(Alien # or Admission #)

Employee's Signature	Date (month/day/year)

Preparer and/or Translator Certification. (To be completed and signed if Section 1 is prepared by a person other than the employee.) I attest, under penalty of perjury, that I have assisted in the completion of this form and that to the best of my knowledge the information is true and correct.

Preparer's/Translator's Signature	Print Name

Address (Street Name and Number, City, State, Zip Code)	Date (month/day/year)

Section 2. Employer Review and Verification. To be completed and signed by employer. Examine one document from List A OR examine one document from List B and one from List C, as listed on the reverse of this form, and record the title, number and expiration date, if any, of the document(s).

List A	OR	List B	AND	List C
Document title:				
Issuing authority:				
Document #:				
Expiration Date (if any):				
Document #:				
Expiration Date (if any):				

CERTIFICATION - I attest, under penalty of perjury, that I have examined the document(s) presented by the above-named employee, that the above-listed document(s) appear to be genuine and to relate to the employee named, that the employee began employment on (month/day/year) **and that to the best of my knowledge the employee is eligible to work in the United States. (State employment agencies may omit the date the employee began employment.)**

Signature of Employer or Authorized Representative	Print Name	Title

Business or Organization Name	Address (Street Name and Number, City, State, Zip Code)	Date (month/day/year)

Section 3. Updating and Reverification. To be completed and signed by employer.

A. New Name (if applicable)	B. Date of Rehire (month/day/year) (if applicable)

C. If employee's previous grant of work authorization has expired, provide the information below for the document that establishes current employment eligibility.

Document Title:	Document #:	Expiration Date (if any):

I attest, under penalty of perjury, that to the best of my knowledge, this employee is eligible to work in the United States, and if the employee presented document(s), the document(s) I have examined appear to be genuine and to relate to the individual.

Signature of Employer or Authorized Representative	Date (month/day/year)

NOTE: This is the 1991 edition of the Form I-9 that has been rebranded with a current printing date to reflect the recent transition from the INS to DHS and its components.

Form I-9 (Rev. 05/31/05)Y Page 2

c. Sample Immigration Status Provision for Vendor Contracts

In light of the fact that many employers contract with outside vendors for various services, employers should consider a provision in the vendor agreement regarding the immigration status of the vendor's employees. A sample is below.

Consultant Staff.

The term "Personnel" when used in this Agreement in relation to Consultant, shall refer to Consultant's employees as well as any corporate subcontractors of Consultant permitted by [company] to provide Services. Consultant agrees to present to [company] only those Personnel who are authorized to work for Consultant in the United States pursuant to relevant statutes and regulations. Consultant warrants that it fully complies with the employment verification requirements of the Immigration Reform and Control Act of 1986, as amended, and, upon request of [company], will make Forms I-9 available for inspection by [company]. Consultant further warrants that it will advise [company] if it receives a notification from the Department of Homeland Security and/or Social Security Administration with respect to Personnel and the disposition thereof. Consultant represents, warrants, and covenants that it does not and will not discriminate against its personnel on the basis of race, color, religion, handicap status, gender, national origin, age, or any other basis that is prohibited by law with respect to the hiring, training, promotion, extension of benefits, or any other term or condition of employment, and shall comply with all applicable laws, regulations, and rules applicable to it as an employer or contractor of such personnel. Upon request by [company], Consultant shall provide to [company] the resumes and other applicable documentation establishing the qualifications of any Personnel providing or anticipated to provide Services under this Agreement, and [company] shall have the right to reject the assignment of any such Personnel in its sole discretion.

G. GIFTS AND ENTERTAINMENT POLICY

1. Introduction

The purpose of a gifts and entertainment policy is to provide guidance to employees on providing or accepting gifts. Such a policy should set forth clear, but not overly burdensome, rules on whether, and under what circumstances, they may accept or provide gifts and entertainment (sometimes referred to as "business courtesies") from or to persons or entities actually doing business, or seeking to do business, with the company.

2. Form: Gifts and Entertainment Policy

*Effective Date:*_____

I. Statement of Purpose

    This gifts and entertainment policy (the "Policy") articulates specific guidelines governing employees of [company] (the "Company"). The Company believes that providing and accepting reasonable, acceptable, and customary gifts and entertainment is a standard business practice that may be beneficial to the Company's business interests if properly exercised. Employees must be careful, however, not to provide, accept, or approve gifts or entertainment that pose or create an actual or apparent conflict of interest, violate applicable laws or regulations, or violate a policy governing the recipient's conduct. Employees also must use good business judgment in deciding whether to provide or accept gifts or entertainment, ask questions when in doubt, and decline all gifts and entertainment that may create a negative perception or otherwise undermine the Company's reputation for operating with integrity.

> **NOTE:** *Simple monetary limits are the most helpful in defining what gifts and entertainment may be accepted; in some instances they may vary by location. However, because this can be an imprecise science, a general self-defining standard for what constitutes an appropriate gift or entertainment also should be established. Here "reasonable, acceptable, and customary" is used. Another approach might*

> *be to prohibit gifts or entertainment that carry an "appearance of impropriety," defined as "attempting to improperly influence relationships or business outcomes." Still another approach is to set forth any number of criteria to determine whether gifts or entertainment are appropriate, such as whether they: (1) promote successful business relationships; (2) are reasonable and justifiable under the circumstances; (3) cannot be interpreted as an attempt to gain an improper advantage; (4) will not cause embarrassment to the company; (5) conform to the reasonable and ethical practices in the marketplace; (6) have all necessary written pre-approvals; (7) are properly documented; or (8) otherwise comply with company procedures.*
>
> *In any event, interpretation and application of the standards should be centralized and documented so that precedents will be established that will promote consistent application.*

This Policy also specifies some gift and entertainment rules that apply specifically to contractors. For legal reasons, it is important that Company employees understand that, while contractors provide valuable services to the Company, the same opportunities and benefits available to employees are not extended to contractors.

> **NOTE:** *With increasing frequency, companies are using contractors to provide services that previously were provided by employees or to supplement services provided by existing employees. To avoid the potential tax and other legal consequences of the contractors being treated as employees, company policies may want to draw distinctions. See e.g., Vizcaino v. Microsoft Corporation, 173 F.3d 713 (9th Cir. 1999).*

II. Application

This Policy applies to all employees of the Company.

> **NOTE:** *Some companies apply their gifts and entertainment policy to directors and even contractors. Consider whether such applicability would be appropriate.*

III. Definitions

Entertainment. An entertainment event (e.g., holiday, retirement and going away parties, and customer dinners and lunches). An entertainment event that is not attended by the employee or Third Party providing the Entertainment shall be considered a Gift (e.g., tickets to a baseball game). Entertainment must be reasonable, acceptable, and customary.

Fair Market Value. The amount the Gift would cost you if you bought it on a retail basis. The Fair Market Value of a Gift may be greater than its face value (e.g., tickets to an event that is sold out or that are hard to obtain, such as Super Bowl tickets).

> **NOTE:** *In the policies of some companies, the face value of tickets is definitive.*

Gift. Any item of value for which the recipient does not pay Fair Market Value (e.g., tickets to plays or sporting events, promotional or recognition items such as jackets, clocks, watches, etc., travel or lodging, or the use of the Company's property or facilities).

Government Employees. Employees of the legislative, judicial, or executive branch of any foreign, federal, state, or local government or any branch thereof, including independent regulatory agencies, regardless of whether they are elected or not elected.

> **NOTE:** *Some government employees may accept minor gifts and entertainment, and others may not. For example, as a general matter, federal government employees in the executive branch may accept a gift or entertainment with a value of no more than $20 per event, with a ceiling of $50 total from any one source in a calendar year. Some local government employees are constrained from receiving anything, including a cup of coffee. Because the requirements may vary widely, change often, and be difficult to obtain and analyze (particularly with regard to local governments), companies must be cautious in this arena and control such activities. This is why it is advisable to require employees to secure pre-clearances for gifts and entertainment of government employees.*

Foreign government employees also may include employees of government-owned or government-controlled state enterprises or a "public international organization," any person acting in an official capacity for or on behalf of a foreign government, government entity, or public international organization, and any foreign political party or party official or any candidate for foreign political office.

Internal Gifts. Gifts, gratuities, entertainment, financial consideration of any type between and among divisions, departments, or business areas of the Company, and between individual employees of the Company where reimbursement for the Internal Gift is sought from the Company.

NOTE: *An extension of gifts and entertainment policies to include "internal gifts" to employees for which reimbursement is sought may seek to protect the company's budget, avoid possibly questionable gifts to favored employees or employee groups, and avoid possible tax implications (e.g., provision of gifts to employees may constitute reportable income).*

Third Party. A person or organization seeking to do or doing business with the Company, or that has interests that may substantially be affected by the Company's actions (e.g., choosing a particular supplier or declining to choose that supplier). Gifts or Entertainment expensed to a Third Party are considered as being provided by that Third Party.

NOTE: *A common question is whether a gift may be accepted from a personal friend (or relative) who happens to work for a third party. Acceptance of gifts offered in friendship is appropriate. However, where the gift is expensed to a third party, it loses its "friendship" character and takes on a business one.*

Significant Entertainment. Entertainment that costs more than what is considered reasonable, acceptable, and customary business practice.

> **NOTE:** *Whether something is within the applicable standard may have to be determined in context. A golf game is fairly reasonable, customary, and acceptable business entertainment. However, while greens fees at the local course may be $50, at Pebble Beach they could be in excess of $450, and the value of participating in a pro-am golf tournament could exceed that amount. Entertainment also may have to be considered cumulatively. Entertainment at one event might not be limited to the greens fee, but might also include travel, lodging, and gifts. Elaborate entertainment has been the subject of coverage in the press, (see, "SEC Targets Fidelity Traders," The Boston Globe (September 29, 2005)), and a recent focus of regulating entities such as NASD, which proposed new standards to address this issue in early 2006.*

Significant Gift. One or more Gifts from or to a single Third Party in a calendar year with an aggregate Fair Market Value of more than $100, a loan made on any basis other than arm's-length terms, or any substantial favor.

> **NOTE:** *The phrase "substantial favor" is meant to serve as a catchall phrase for gifts not subject to a fair market value assessment (for example, a third party arranging for the admission of a company employee's child at an exclusive school).*

IV. Policy Requirements
  A. General Limitations
     A Company employee **may not** use, or direct the use of, Company resources to make Gifts of cash or securities, or provide or direct the provision of any Gifts or Entertainment that pose or create an actual or apparent conflict of interest, violate any applicable law or regulation, or violate a policy governing the recipient's conduct. Other than as set forth in this Policy, Company employees **may not** use Company resources to provide Gifts or Entertainment. Employee requests for reimbursement for the provision of Gifts or Entertainment must comply with all provisions of the expense report policy. Employees may not use their own funds to provide Gifts or Entertainment for nonemployees, including Government Employees, if such expenditures would otherwise not be permissible under this Policy.

B. Providing Gifts and Entertainment (other than to Government Employees)

<u>Entertainment:</u> An employee may provide Entertainment that serves a Company business purpose if: (1) the expenses related to the Entertainment are reasonable, acceptable, and customary; **and** (2) a Company officer approves the Entertainment. Significant Entertainment must have the written approval of a senior vice president (or higher if the Entertainment is being provided by a senior vice president) and the office of ethics.

NOTE: *The office of ethics should be involved in such a decision in order (1) to promote consistency within the company, (2) to provide for a central repository for documentation and precedential purposes, and (3) to allow the office of ethics to ascertain whether there are any prohibitions on the recipient accepting a significant gift.*

A Company employee may provide Gifts that serve a Company business purpose if: (1) the Fair Market Value of all Gifts provided by the Company to the recipient in a calendar year does not exceed $100, **and** (2) a Company officer approves the Gift. Significant Gifts must have the written approval of a senior vice president and the office of ethics.

<u>Gifts at External Conferences:</u> A Company employee may provide Gifts at external conferences that serve a Company business purpose, if: (1) the Company sponsors the conference or event (e.g., a customer conference); (2) the Fair Market Value of each Gift is not in excess of $100; **and** (3) the Gifts are offered to all of the attendees.

<u>Internal Gifts:</u> The Company has in place a number of internal employee recognition mechanisms through which managers may recognize extraordinary efforts by employees. Other than these recognition programs and as otherwise provided herein, the Company generally prohibits providing and receiving Internal Gifts.

In order to receive an exception to this general prohibition, any employee seeking to provide such Internal Gifts shall request, in writing, the prior, written approval of both the Company's controller and the senior vice president (or higher if the senior vice president seeks to provide the Internal Gift) responsible for the employee's business area. This written request should specify the reasons for the Internal Gift, setting forth any performance or specific efforts by the proposed Internal Gift recipients that is clearly extraordinary or far exceeds the expectations of the employees in the business area that seeks to provide the Internal Gifts. Any such approval shall be granted within the sole discretion of both the controller and the designated senior vice president (or higher if the senior vice president seeks to provide the Internal Gift). In no event may an Internal Gift be provided to a Company contractor.

Internal Gifts at Internal Conferences: A Company employee may provide Internal Gifts at Internal Conferences that serve a Company business purpose, if: (1) the Fair Market Value of each Internal Gift does not exceed $50; (2) only Company employees attend the conference or event (e.g., the annual meeting of the Company's sales group); **and** (3) the Gifts are offered to all attendees. In no event may an Internal Gift at an Internal Conference be provided to a contractor.

C. Providing Gifts and Entertainment to Government Employees
   Company Employees **may** provide Gifts and Entertainment to Government Employees only if: (1) the Gift or Entertainment is approved in writing in advance by the legal department; or (2) in the case of a Gift, the recipient is a U.S. Federal Government Employee and the Gift is a light refreshment (*e.g.,* soft drinks, coffee, chips, donuts, and cookies) provided during a business meeting and is not part of a meal.

NOTE: *The legal department should be involved in the approval of these gifts and entertainment so that it has an opportunity to review all relevant legal and regulatory issues that arise in what can be a very complex framework. The written requirement allows for proper documentation and holds the employee responsible for preparing the documentation and securing the necessary prior approval. Business units that frequently provide gifts or entertainment in this context and have significant training on these matters (e.g., lobbyists) might be granted a reprieve from this requirement in limited circumstances pursuant to written guidelines.*

> *This provision is set out as an example of specific instructions and authorizations for activities for those government officials with which the company deals frequently, to make the policy more practical and informative. A similar provision might be established for certain state or local officials with which the company has an ongoing relationship.*

D. Exceeding Established Monetary Limitations

A higher monetary limit on providing Gifts or Entertainment and providing Gifts at conferences must be approved by: (1) a senior vice president, **or,** (2) if the approval benefits a senior vice president or higher officer, the officer's manager. An officer **should not** approve a higher monetary limit if such higher limit poses an actual or apparent conflict of interest, violates any applicable law or regulation, or violates a policy governing the recipient's conduct.

Except with respect to Gifts and Entertainment for Government Employees, an employee may request approval to provide a Gift or Entertainment after providing the Gift or Entertainment. However, if the request for approval is denied, or the Gift or Entertainment otherwise violates this Policy, the employee shall be obligated to pay personally for the Gift or Entertainment, and may be subject to disciplinary action, including but not limited to termination of employment.

> **NOTE:** *As a practical matter, there are recurring events in the ordinary course of business that an employee knows will be approved (e.g., a reasonably priced business dinner in New York City may be acceptable even though it consistently exceeds preestablished company limits). While the employee is liable for exercising good judgment in recognizing these events, this provision does away with the need for preapprovals that are more form than substance.*

Officer approval levels specifically provided for in this Policy may not be delegated to a lower level Employee (*e.g.,* a senior vice president's approval may not be delegated to a vice president).

E. Accepting Gifts and Entertainment

As a general matter, employees **may not** accept Gifts or Entertainment that violate this Policy, pose an actual or apparent conflict of interest, violate any applicable law or regulation, or violate a policy governing the donor's conduct.

A Company employee **may** accept a Gift or Entertainment from a Third Party if either: (1) the Fair Market Value of all Gifts or Entertainments received by the employee from the Third Party in a calendar year is not greater than $100; **or** (2) in the case of Entertainment with a Fair Market Value greater than $100, the Entertainment is reasonable, customary, and acceptable business practice.

NOTE: *Most companies establish a monetary limitation on gifts that serves as a bright line as to what is appropriate. Other companies utilize written criteria for determining whether the gift or entertainment is appropriate that make the determination more subjective. Both alternatives may be coupled with a requirement to seek approval from a more senior level manager or the ethics office under certain circumstances.*

A Company employee **may not**: (1) accept Gifts of cash or securities; or (2) accept any Significant Gift or Significant Entertainment without the written approval of the Office of Ethics; or (3) solicit any Gift or Entertainment from a Third Party.

If an employee receives or accepts a Gift or Entertainment that violates this Policy, the employee must notify the chief compliance officer, the ethics officer, or the law department about the Gift or Entertainment, and the employee must abide by any final determination of the office of ethics regarding the Gift or Entertainment, including, but not limited to, an instruction to return a Gift or reimburse a Third Party for Entertainment. If an employee receives a Gift that is in violation of this Policy, but under circumstances where it would be difficult or awkward to decline the Gift, the employee may accept the Gift, but must provide the Gift to the office of ethics which will either: (1) return the gift with a polite explanation to the donor as to why it cannot be accepted; or (2) donate the Gift to charity and inform the donor of its disposition and the reason why it could not be accepted.

Failure of an employee to meet the requirements of this Policy may lead to disciplinary action, including, but not limited to, termination of employment.

<u>Waivers</u>

NOTE: *No matter how carefully a policy is crafted there inevitably will be appropriate reasons for granting a waiver. While care must be taken to ensure that waivers are infrequent and do not undermine the purpose of the policy and its consistent application, allowing for them simply constitutes reasonable planning. Ethics offices are well advised, however, to create objective standards for granting waivers ahead of time and apply them consistently to avoid abuse or the appearance of abuse.*

Waivers of this Policy may be granted by the chief compliance officer after consultation with the senior vice president in the chain of command for the employee(s) affected. If the employee affected is a senior vice president (or higher), then consultation shall be with the supervising officer for the senior vice president (or higher). All such waivers, and the basis therefore, shall be fully documented by the office of ethics.

NOTE: *Care must be taken in granting waivers to assess their full implications. Waivers that also would constitute a waiver of the company's code of conduct for an employee designated as an "officer" under Rule 16a-1(f) of the Securities and Exchange Commission's rules may require public disclosure.*

Administrative Provisions

<u>Version Control:</u> This Policy replaces the Gifts and Entertainment Policy dated January 20, 2005.

<u>Policy Review:</u> This Policy will be reviewed on an annual basis.

Repository: This Policy will be stored on the Company intranet website.

Additional References

Gifts and Entertainment FAQs

[Related Policies]

NOTE: *For a wide variety of reasons, including taking disciplinary action for past activities, companies should create and track the versions of a policy.*

Companies should establish a procedure for regularly reviewing policies and modifying them as necessary. Policies that have become stale or are observed in the breach because of changing circumstances can create a liability for the company.

Employees must have ready access to corporate policies, and companies should establish central repositories to facilitate access to those policies.

FAQs that include hypothetical fact situations are an effective way for communicating the practical application of a policy.

To make this policy more effective, consider whether to highlight other policies that may relate to this one (for example, conflict of interest, expense report, political contributions policies, etc.).

H. INSIDER TRADING POLICY

1. Introduction

The insider trading policy that follows applies to all transactions in securities of the company. For purposes of the policy, the term "securities" includes common stock, options for common stock, and other securities that may be issued from time to time, such as convertible debentures or preferred stock, as well as derivative securities relating to a company's stock, such as exchange-traded options. The policy applies to all insiders of the company, and this term applies to all officers, directors, team members, consultants, representatives, and contractors.

According to the Securities and Exchange Commission, "insider trading" refers to "buying or selling a Security, in breach of a fiduciary duty or other relationship of trust or confidence while in possession of material, nonpublic information about the security." SEC Form 2226 (6-89). It also may include the act of disclosing such information, using such information to trade securities, or trading on misappropriated information. Publicly traded companies adopt insider trading policies to serve a number of compliance goals:

- To prevent insider trading by company insiders;
- To establish a compliance roadmap so that the company can assert various affirmative defenses in the event of noncompliance; and
- To facilitate timely Section 16 reporting and short-swing profit recovery.

While these goals should be familiar to in-house counsel, the process of implementing a compliance program can be difficult even with the most well-drafted compliance policies.

While there are some judicial decisions in enforcement cases that draw the line on what is, and is not, a company's securities, most insider trading policies will address a company's common and preferred stock and virtually all conceivable derivative securities, including puts, calls, and options. The courts have accepted the need to protect the investing public against individuals who trade with an unfair informational advantage gained by their positions within companies or through their access to material nonpublic information. Courts and regulators have focused on a "parity of information" concern. The concept of an "insider" covers not only those individuals who have high-level positions within a company and who must, under the securities laws, report transactions involving their trades of company shares (ordinarily called "Section 16 insiders"), but it also covers so-called "situational" insiders or "temporary" insiders because such individuals can use the temporary knowledge to benefit themselves. Generally, courts hold that insiders must either disclose or abstain from trading to avoid insider trading liability, meaning that such individuals need to make public the information that the general public lacks before trading in the securities of the company in order to avoid liability under the court-created insider trading doctrine.

2. Form: Insider Trading Policy

[Company] Policy Against Insider Trading

I. PROVISIONS APPLICABLE TO ALL INSIDERS

A. Statement of Policy

1. [Company name] ("Company") policy prohibits the unauthorized disclosure of any nonpublic information acquired in the workplace and the use of "Material Nonpublic Information" (defined below) in securities trading. It is the policy of this Company that any insider who has Material Nonpublic Information may neither buy nor sell securities of the Company nor engage in any other action to take advantage of that information or pass it on to others.

2. Material Nonpublic Information includes information that has not been released, is not otherwise available to the general public, and that a reasonable investor would likely consider to be important in making an investment decision to buy or sell the Company's securities. Positive or negative information may be material.

NOTE: *The generally accepted test for determining materiality is quite low. Basically it asks whether a reasonable investor would have wanted to have known such information before making the trading decision to buy or sell the security. It is somewhat difficult for compliance purposes to always know what information that publicly traded companies need to disclose, and when it must be disclosed to avoid making some inadvertent violation of an SEC rule or regulation. Whether a fact is material "depends on the significance the reasonable investor would place on the withheld or misrepresented information." Basic Inc. v. Levinson, 485 U.S. 224, 240 (1988). A misrepresentation or omission is material if the information "would have been viewed by the reasonable investor as having significantly altered the 'total mix' of information made available." TSC Industries, Inc. v. Northway, Inc., 426 U.S. 438, 449 (1976).*

Examples of Material Nonpublic Information include without limitation:

- financial results;
- projections of future earnings or losses;
- changes in manufacturing productivity;
- news of a proposed merger or acquisition;
- impending bankruptcy;
- gain or loss of a substantial customer;
- significant new product announcements;
- parts shortages;
- changes in dividend policy;
- stock splits;
- significant litigation exposure;
- stock or debt offerings; and,
- significant changes in senior management.

NOTE: *Some of the most difficult tasks in managing an insider trading policy are the judgment calls that in-house counsel must make when determining whether an individual subject to the policy has material nonpublic information. The standard definition of the term, used in many compliance policies is the information that would be considered to be material by a reasonable investor and is known to company insiders, but not known outside the company. That boilerplate definition is difficult to apply because it requires the attorney to divine what things a "reasonable investor" would consider to be "material," which is necessarily subjective and especially vulnerable to second-guessing. For example, company insiders might be aware of an unannounced contract that has a certain public relations value, but is otherwise devoid of solid financial commitments that a reasonable investor would consider material to the company's bottom line. Nevertheless, the public relations aspect of the contract could be sufficient to move the company's stock. Should in-house counsel consider that contract to be "material" because of the possibility that its announcement might move the stock price irrationally?*

Questions of materiality in evaluating requests by insiders to trade have always been difficult, but are now even more so in light of the

SEC's 2005 modifications to Form 8-K. Those modifications, adopted as part of the SEC's implementation of the Sarbanes-Oxley Act of 2002, provide for an expedited filing obligation (generally between two and four business days) upon the occurrence of specified material events. One such event that triggers a reporting obligation within four business days is the entry into a "material definitive agreement."

See also, Staff Accounting Bulletin No. 99, 64 Fed. Reg. 45,150 (August 19, 1999), in which the SEC instructed companies and their auditors not to make exclusive use of quantitative measures for determining the materiality of information under their disclosure obligations. The commission has made it clear that determining materiality is not solely a quantitative exercise, but instead requires a qualitative assessment as well regarding the importance of the information.

3. No insider or member of such person's immediate family or household who possesses Material Nonpublic Information shall engage in any transaction involving a purchase or sale of the Company's securities during any period commencing with the date that s/he possesses the Material Nonpublic Information and ending at the close of business on the *second trading day following the public disclosure of such information,* or at such time as the information is no longer material.

4. Insiders must not disclose Material Nonpublic Information except to individuals in the Company whose jobs require them to have the information. Insiders must not disclose sensitive or nonpublic information to anyone outside the Company. The Company has standard procedures for the release of material information, and no disclosure should be made without following them. For more information on the Company's procedures for the release of material information, please contact [insert contact information].

B. Potential Liability and Disciplinary Action

1. Individuals who trade on Material Nonpublic Information (or disclose such information to others) may be subject

to severe penalties under federal and state securities laws,
including:

- criminal fines up to $1 million and imprisonment for up
  to 10 years;
- a civil penalty of up to three times the profit gained or the
  losses avoided on the transaction; and
- disgorgement of profits gained or losses avoided on the
  transaction.

NOTE: *The federal securities laws involve two major statutes: The
Securities Act of 1933, Pub. L. No. 73-22, 48 Stat. 74, codified as
amended at 15 U.S.C. §§ 77a-77aa, and the Securities Exchange Act
of 1934, Pub. L. No. 73-291, 48 Stat. 881, codified as amended at 15
U.S.C. § 78a-78ll.*

Insiders who violate this policy also may be sued by persons
who bought or sold the securities at the same time. Persons
who disclose Material Nonpublic Information to others who
then trade in securities while possessing that information
may be liable to disgorge the profits or to pay the avoided
losses of those to whom the information was disclosed, as
well as being made subject to civil penalties.

2. In addition, any insider who violates this policy is subject
   to disciplinary action, including dismissal or termination
   for cause. The Company also may be entitled to pursue
   legal action against anyone who violates this policy. Where
   appropriate, the Company also may report violations to
   appropriate government agencies, including the Securities
   and Exchange Commission and the U.S. Department of
   Justice.

3. For purposes of this policy, the Company has determined
   that the compliance officer shall be the Company's general
   counsel or any attorney in the Company's legal department
   serving as the general counsel's designee.

C. Certain Exemptions

For purposes of this policy, (i) purchases of shares under the Company's employee stock purchase plan, and (ii) the exercise of options in which the option exercise price is paid by the employee and the resulting shares are held by the employee and not sold are exempt from this policy. In addition, bona fide gifts and interspousal transfers are similarly exempt from this policy. However, all sales of shares purchased under the employee stock purchase plan and all sales of shares issued as the result of an option exercise are subject to this policy.

II. PROVISIONS APPLICABLE TO TRADE-RESTRICTED INSIDERS

A. "Trade-Restricted" Insiders

The term "Trade-Restricted Insiders" means all officers and members of the Company's board of directors and certain other insiders designated as trade-restricted by the officer to whom they report or by the compliance officer. (Insiders designated as "trade-restricted" have been or will be notified of such designation.)

B. Trading Calendar

To protect the Company and any officers and directors from committing an inadvertent violation of the insider trading prohibitions, a blackout period is implemented as part of the Company's policies and procedures, during which period no Trade-Restricted Insider shall be allowed to engage in any transaction involving the purchase or sale of the Company's securities. Specifically, the blackout period during which Trade-Restricted Insiders are prohibited from engaging in any transactions involving the Company's securities covers the last three weeks of any fiscal quarter through the close of business on the second trading day following public disclosure of the Company's quarterly or annual financial results. Note also that the Company may designate additional periods during which transactions by Trade-Restricted Insiders are prohibited. To assist those individuals who fall within the scope of these rules, the Company will publish a trading calendar annually and make the calendar available to all Trade-Restricted Insiders.

C. Restrictions on Speculative Transactions Regarding Trade-Restricted Insiders

Trade-Restricted Insiders shall not engage in speculative transactions involving the Company's securities, including short sales of the Company's common stock, or puts, calls, covered calls, or other options on the Company's common stock.

III. PROVISIONS APPLICABLE TO SECTION 16 REPORTING PERSONS

A. Preclearance of Trades

1. A "Section 16 Reporting Person" means any of the following, all of whom are subject to the reporting requirements of Section 16 of the Securities and Exchange Act of 1934, as amended: All members of the board of directors, officers, beneficial owners of more than 10% of any class of equity securities, and insiders performing significant policy-making functions for the Company. Section 16 Reporting Persons may trade in the Company's stock only when they have approval for any trade from the Company's compliance officer or his designee. In evaluating a request for approval, the compliance officer or his designee will base the determination on whether Material Nonpublic Information exists. The compliance officer or his designee will respond to any request to trade within 24 hours of receiving such request. Approved trades must then be concluded within 24 hours of the approval, but may not be concluded if during that period the affected insider becomes aware of Material Nonpublic Information.

NOTE: *There are safe harbor provisions provided by the SEC, by which insiders can limit the dangers from the insider trading prohibitions. But since these safe harbors require specific steps, such as the development of prearranged trading plans that eliminate the opportunity for insiders to take advantage of any informational advantage that they have obtained by virtue of their positions with the company, Section 16 reporting individuals always should coordinate with compliance officers to ensure that these requirements are properly met.*

B. <u>Additional Requirements Regarding Section 16 Reporting Persons</u>

Section 16 Reporting Persons also must comply with the reporting obligations and limitations on short-swing transactions set forth in Section 16 of the Securities and Exchange Act of 1934, as amended. The practical effect of these provisions is that Section 16 Reporting Persons who buy and sell the Company's securities within a six-month period must disgorge all profits to the Company whether or not they knew of any Material Nonpublic Information.

Under these provisions, and so long as certain other criteria are met, neither the receipt of an option under the Company's option plan, nor the exercise of that option, nor the receipt of stock under the Company's employee stock purchase plan is deemed to be a purchase under Section 16; however, the sale of any such shares constitutes a sale for purposes of Section 16. The Company has provided or will provide separate memoranda and other appropriate materials to its Section 16 Reporting Persons regarding compliance with Section 16 and its rules.

IV. INQUIRIES

If you have any doubts about whether you possess Material Nonpublic Information, or whether any trading would violate this policy, or if you have any other questions regarding this policy in general, please contact the general counsel or compliance officer.

3. Form: Code of Conduct

[COMPANY] CODE OF CONDUCT

1. Title. This code of conduct ("Code") is intended by [company name] (the "Company") to comply with:
   a. Section 406 of the Sarbanes-Oxley Act of 2002 and the rules and regulations issued by the Securities and Exchange Commission (including Item 406 of Regulation S-K) promulgated thereunder (collectively, the "Act"), and

> **NOTE:** *The actual title of Sarbanes-Oxley is "The Public Company Accounting Reform Act of 2002," 107 Pub. L. No. 107-204, 116 Stat. 745 (July 30, 2002). The general impact of the act's measures can be summarized as increased and more real-time disclosures being required of publicly traded companies and their key personnel.*

   b. the listing requirements set forth in the NASDAQ Stock Market's Marketplace Rule 4350(n).
2. Applicability. This Code applies to the Company's directors, officers (including the Company's chief executive officer, chief financial officer, and principal accounting officer or controller), and other employees.
3. Provisions. Each person who is subject to this Code should:
   a. Conduct himself or herself honestly and ethically, including the ethical handling of actual or apparent conflicts of interest between personal and professional relationships.
   b. Provide full, fair, accurate, timely, and understandable disclosure in reports and documents that the Company files with, or submits to, the Securities and Exchange Commission and in other public communications made by the Company.
   c. Comply with applicable governmental laws, rules, and regulations.
   In addition, no person subject to this Code may directly or indirectly take action to fraudulently influence, coerce, manipulate, or mislead the Company's independent public auditors for the

purpose of rendering the financial statements of the Company or its subsidiaries misleading.

4. Waivers. Waivers of the provisions in this Code may be approved only by the audit committee of the board of directors ("Committee") or by its chairman; provided that, in the latter case, notice shall be given to the entire Committee as soon as practicable, and any member of the Committee may call a meeting of the full Committee to ratify or terminate such waiver. Waivers must be reported to Company's general counsel on the same day that they are granted. The Company must publicly report waivers for directors and the chief executive officer, chief financial officer, and the principal accounting officer in accordance with, and to the extent required by, the Act and applicable listing requirements.

5. Amendments. This Code may be amended only by the Committee or by the board of directors. Any such amendment must be reported to the Company's general counsel on the same day that the amendment is approved. Amendments will be publicly reported in accordance with the Act and applicable listing requirements.

6. Enforcement. Any breach of this Code is a serious violation and may trigger disciplinary action.

7. Reporting Violations. Any person who believes that a person may have violated this Code promptly must report such matter in the manner described in the Company's "nonretaliation and compliance management procedure," available at [insert URL for document]. The Company will not retaliate against any employee who reports what he or she in good faith believes to be a violation of this Code.

4. Form: Nonretaliation and Complaint Management Policy

[COMPANY] NONRETALIATION & COMPLAINT MANAGEMENT POLICY

This nonretaliation and complaint management policy (this "Policy") is intended by [company name] (the "Company") to comply with (a) Section 301 of the Sarbanes-Oxley Act of 2002 and the rules and regulations (including Item 406 of Regulation S-K of the Securities and Exchange Commission) promulgated thereunder (collectively, the "Act"), and (b) the listing requirements set forth in the NASDAQ Stock Market's Marketplace Rule 4350(d)(3).

1. Applicability: This Code applies to all Company employees, officers, and directors.
2. Policy: The Company will not subject any employee, officer, or director to any disciplinary or retaliatory action as a result of such person having:
   a. disclosed to a federal law enforcement or government agency information that the person has reasonable cause to believe evidences a violation or possible violation of federal, state, or other applicable laws or regulations; or
   b. provided information, caused information to be provided, or otherwise assisted in an investigation for a proceeding regarding any conduct that such person reasonably believes violates:
      i. federal criminal law relating to securities fraud, mail fraud, bank fraud, or wire fraud; or
      ii. any rule or regulation of the Securities and Exchange Commission; or
      iii. any provision of federal law relating to fraud against shareholders;

      where the information or assistance is provided to, or the investigation is being conduct by, a federal regulatory agency, a member of Congress, or a person at the Company with supervisory or similar authority over the employee; or
   c. filed, or caused to be filed, testified, participated in, or otherwise assisted in a proceeding filed or about to be filed (to the knowledge of the Company) that relates to an alleged violation of:

     i. federal criminal law relating to securities fraud, mail fraud, bank fraud, or wire fraud; or

     ii. any rule or regulation of the Securities and Exchange Commission; or

     iii. any provision of federal law relating to fraud against shareholders; or

  d. disclosed violations of the Company's Code to the Company's personnel, federal law enforcement, governmental or regulatory agencies or bodies; or

  e. reported violations of NASDAQ rules applicable to the Company, including any trading in Company stock based on inside information to Company personnel, federal law enforcement, governmental or regulatory agencies or bodies.

3. <u>Compliance Officer:</u> The Company has appointed a compliance officer who is responsible for administering this Policy. The compliance officer is responsible for receiving, collecting, reviewing, and processing complaints and reports by employees and others on the matters described in this Policy. Persons subject to this Policy are encouraged to discuss issues and concerns of the type covered by this Policy with their supervisors who, in turn, are responsible for informing the compliance officer of any concerns raised. If an employee of the Company prefers not to discuss sensitive matters with his or her own supervisor, the employee may instead discuss such matters with the compliance officer or utilize the anonymous complaint procedure described in Section 5 below. The compliance officer will refer complaints arising under this Policy as directed by the audit committee of the board of directors.

    The Company's compliance officer is the [general counsel], who may be reached at [e-mail address] or by mail at [compliance officer name, company name, company mailing address.]

NOTE: *Many companies have appointed a chief compliance officer who is not the company's general counsel. In fact, some government officials discourage the combination of chief compliance officer and chief legal officer or general counsel. The trend seems to be toward a separation of those two corporate functions, though even when separate, the two functions cooperate closely.*

---

4. Complaint Procedure: Any officer, director, or employee of the Company may submit a complaint (a) regarding the Company's accounting, internal accounting controls, or auditing matters (including questionable accounting or auditing matters) (collectively, "Accounting Issues") or (b) regarding the Company's compliance with any applicable U.S. federal or state law or regulation (collectively, "Legal Issues"), with the compliance officer by making a report through the [third-party vendor] service available at [third-party vendor website]. The identity of any Company employee submitting a complaint under this Policy will be kept anonymous to the extent legally possible if the person making such complaint so requests in the first submission made by such person. In addition, individuals who are not affiliated with the Company may communicate complaints about Accounting Issues by submitting such complaints through [third-party vendor website]. In the case of such individuals, the complainant must give his/her identity in the complaint.

5. Contents of Complaints: Persons submitting complaints under this Policy are encouraged to provide as much detail as possible so that the compliance officer and audit committee may determine the veracity of the report. Each such report should include:
   1. When the subject activity occurred;
   2. Who was involved;
   3. The nature of the activity, Accounting Issue, or Legal Issue (as applicable);
   4. Why the activity is of concern;
   5. What documentation exists regarding the activity, providing copies if possible;
   6. Who else is aware of the activity; and
   7. A list of actions already taken to bring this matter to the attention of the Company or any third party and their response.

6. Record Keeping: The compliance officer will maintain a secure file with all reports received under this Policy. The compliance officer will maintain reports, and evaluations of those reports, for at least five years after the date when made, after which time such documents will be destroyed.

7. Reporting: The compliance officer will evaluate each report under this Policy and report to the audit committee on a periodic basis with respect to each such report and evaluation.

8. <u>Limitations on Protected Disclosures:</u> Employees, officers, or directors who file reports or provide evidence that they know to be false or, in the case of Sections 3(a), 3(b), 3(d) and 3(e) of this Policy, who do not reasonably believe in the truth and accuracy of such information, are not protected by this Policy and may be subject to disciplinary action, including termination of employment.

9. <u>Reporting Violations of This Policy:</u> If an employee of the Company believes he or she has been subjected to any action that violates this Policy, he or she may file a complaint with the compliance officer or the most senior officer in the Company's human resources department. If it is determined that an employee has experienced any improper employment action in violation of this Policy, such employee will be entitled to appropriate corrective action.

I. INTERNATIONAL TRADE PRACTICES

1. Introduction

When operating in other countries, a company must be mindful of the laws of those countries, as well as the laws of the United States that impact global operations. Sometimes, the applicability of U.S. laws hinges on the activity itself, and sometimes on the identities of the parties to the transaction. The policy below provides guidance on some of the primary areas of focus for such statutes, like the Foreign Corrupt Practices Act, as to which a company might wish to educate its employees and agents so as to minimize the possibility of violations. This policy does not, however, pretend to serve as a comprehensive view of the various subject areas in which U.S. laws might apply to international business or in which foreign laws might impact a U.S. company doing business overseas.

2. Form: International Business Practices Policy

International Business Practices
[Name of company]
Corporate Policy and Procedures

Subject: International Business (other than Export Control): Legal Compliance: Foreign Corrupt Practices Act, Economic Sanctions, and Anti-Terrorism Laws

1. Purpose: To enhance understanding and establish a framework of permitted and prohibited practices for those in the Company that are engaged in the conduct of our business internationally, including with international customers, agents, consultants, and foreign governments, and support corporate efforts to engage in business with international business partners only with proper care and diligence, and in full compliance with applicable U.S. and non-U.S. law and regulations.

2. Scope: "Company" means the parent company, subsidiaries, controlled affiliated entities, and noncontrolled affiliates of which the Company appoints officers or directors, and all business units.

3. General Policy Statement: The Company's international business continues to grow at a time when coping with the global economic and political environment has never been more challenging. It is

the policy of the Company to conduct its international business responsibly and in compliance with all applicable United States and foreign laws and regulations, including the U.S. Foreign Corrupt Practices Act of 1977 (FCPA), 15 U.S.C. §§ 78dd-1, *et seq.*, economic sanctions, and anti-terrorism laws (prohibited lists). Our policy requires our employees, agents, and consultants to exercise appropriate care and diligence in order to ensure such compliance and to notify the Company's compliance officer of any violations.

NOTE: *For the full text of the FCPA, its legislative history, opinion and review procedure releases, and additional resources and links, see the FCPA section of the website of the U.S. Department of Justice (www. usdoj.gov/criminal/fraud/fcpa/).*

---

4. Policy Statement: U.S. Foreign Corrupt Practices Act (FCPA)
   a. Prohibitions: The FCPA prohibits giving or promising to give, directly or indirectly through a third party, money or anything of value intended to improperly influence business decisions of a "foreign official," any foreign political party or party official, or any candidate for foreign political office to obtain or retain business or secure any improper advantage in obtaining business. Any such payments are strictly prohibited, even if they are considered "accepted practice" in the conduct of business in some countries.
   b. Foreign official: A "foreign official" means any officer or employee of a foreign government, or any department, agency, or instrumentality thereof, or of a public international organization, or any person acting in an official capacity for or on behalf of any such government or department, agency, or instrumentality, or for or on behalf of any such public international organization. It should be noted that a foreign government agency or instrumentality may include government-owned or controlled corporations or business ventures.
   c. Covered persons: The FCPA applies to all officers, directors, employees, agents, consultants, or any other person acting for

the Company and its controlled affiliates in the United States and outside the United States.

NOTE: *The anti-bribery provisions of the FCPA apply to U.S. citizens, permanent residents, "issuers," "domestic concerns," and "any person" who violates the FCPA while in the United States. "Any person" includes foreign persons and corporations. Foreign persons are subject to the FCPA when they perform an act in furtherance of an unlawful act while in the United States or its territories. U.S. corporations may be held liable for the acts of foreign subsidiaries where they themselves authorized, directed, or controlled (or even had knowledge of) the activity in question, as may U.S. citizens or residents ("domestic concerns") who were employed by or acting on behalf of such foreign-incorporated subsidiaries. See www.usdoj.gov/criminal/fraud/fcpa/.*

The Company is liable for violation of the FCPA through any corrupt payments made by its intermediaries, while knowing (or being aware of a high probability) that all or part of the payment will go to a foreign official. To qualify as "knowing," it is sufficient if the Company practiced a conscious disregard or deliberate ignorance with respect to the facts. In order to ensure full compliance with the requirements of the FCPA by its intermediaries, the Company has established a policy for the appointment and retention of international consultants and sales representatives, which is set forth hereunder in Section 5.

NOTE: *Intermediaries include third parties (both corporate and individual) with which the company has a business relationship, such as agents, sales representatives, and joint venture partners.*

---

d. <u>Penalties:</u> The FCPA provides for severe civil and criminal penalties, including imprisonment, for violations. By law, fines imposed on individuals cannot be reimbursed by the Company. The consequences of violations for the Company may affect the Company's ability to conduct its business, and may include suspension of the Company's right to do business with the U.S.

government and ineligibility to receive export licenses. The Company will take all necessary disciplinary action, including dismissal, against any employee violating the FCPA and the Company's policies.

e. Record keeping: The FCPA requires the Company and its subsidiaries and jointly owned ventures to maintain internal accounting controls and to keep books and records that accurately reflect all transactions and accurately account for the disposition of their assets. The Company may be directly liable for any violation of this provision by its subsidiaries and other (partially) owned or controlled ventures.

NOTE: *The recordkeeping and internal controls provisions of the FCPA apply to issuers and reporting companies. These obligations extend to include subsidiaries and jointly owned ventures if the parent company has at least 50% of the voting power. It should be noted, however, that the company has an obligation to make good faith efforts in this regard if it has less than 50% of the voting power.*

---

f. Permissible: Payments of ordinary, legitimate business expenses incurred by or on behalf of a foreign official, a foreign political party or party official, or any candidate for foreign political office for demonstrating products or services or performing a contractual obligation are permissible under the FCPA. As it may be difficult to determine whether a particular payment should be considered as permissible under the FCPA, the law department should be consulted in advance when considering making a payment to any such parties. It should be noted that a payment that otherwise would be impermissible under the FCPA may be permissible if such payment is legal under the written laws of a country.

g. Exceptions: The FCPA permits, under very limited circumstances, making a payment to a foreign official to facilitate or expedite performance of "routine governmental actions," commonly referred to as "facilitating payments." The FCPA lists as examples obtaining permits, licenses, or other official documents; processing visas and work orders; providing police protection or mail pickup and delivery, or scheduling inspections associated with contract performance or transit of goods across country; and providing phone service, power and water supply, loading and unloading cargo, or protecting perishable products. However, even if made for one of these purposes, a payment is not necessarily legal under the FCPA. Therefore, the Company requires the approval of the law department prior to making such a payment. If there is any question whether any payment is covered under this procedure, the law department should be consulted in advance.

NOTE: *It is an affirmative defense if a payment was lawful pursuant to the written laws of a foreign country. This exception is of limited practical use, as not only will it be rare for a corrupt payment to be lawful, but the burden of proving that the payment met the requirements of the statute falls on the defense.*

---

   h. <u>Training:</u> The Company has established an FCPA training program. The program is web-based and all people identified as covered persons in Paragraph (c) above are required to complete the program upon becoming affiliated with the Company, and thereafter on an annual basis. In addition to the web-based training, the Company may require that any covered persons receive additional training as it may see fit.

   i. <u>Certification:</u> In conjunction with the annual training, all covered persons are required to certify that they have not committed and are not aware of any violations of the FCPA.

   j. <u>Violations:</u> If any person becomes aware of a violation of the FCPA, he/she will immediately notify the compliance officer.

5. <u>FCPA Compliance Procedures:</u>
   a. <u>Vetting International Business Partners.</u> In order to comply with the FCPA, Company employees must find out basic information about the other parties, whether individuals or entities, involved in its international business transactions. Two of the most significant FCPA compliance risks are: (1) the Company uses an intermediary (e.g., sales representative, consultant, distributor, etc.) in a sale to a foreign government, and the intermediary "bribes" a

government official to win or keep the business; or (2) the Company inadvertently gives "something of value" to a government official in violation of the FCPA, because the Company was not aware that the recipient of the payment, such as a joint venture partner or an employee of a government-owned entity (such as a utility or hospital), is a "foreign official" under the FCPA. Adequate due diligence should be performed as appropriate to avoid these and other significant compliance risks.

(i) Responsible parties to foreign transactions will conduct due diligence (1) to determine the degree to which the corruption of foreign officials in the country in which the proposed business activities will take place is a risk factor that may impede the Company's ability to comply with the FCPA; and (2) sufficient to verify that each proposed business partner (entities, owners, managers, and key employees), is a bona fide business operation of acceptable financial standing, capable of performing under the proposed contract, and that its owners, managers, and key employees are not foreign officials. Business references should be contacted to attest to the reputation of, and if possible, to opine as to the disposition of the proposed partner to comply with the FCPA.

(ii) A high incidence of corruption, or the participation directly or indirectly of foreign officials in the proposed transaction, or other risk factors identified during due diligence, are "red flags" that may necessitate further due diligence, special documentation (such as certifications), and other steps to manage and contain risk.

b. <u>International Agreements.</u> All international agreements will be in writing. Commissions, fees, or other compensation paid pursuant to any international agreement will be reasonable with respect to the services performed, and will be paid by wire transfer or check to the bank account of the proposed partner in the country where services are performed. Responsible parties should consult the law department in drafting representations and warranties, termination, and legal compliance provisions, and other terms and conditions appropriate to agreements documenting transactions with inherent FCPA compliance risks.

6. Procedures: Economic Sanctions; Prohibited Lists
   a. Transactions Covered: In an increasingly global economy, the Company participates in a growing number of transactions with foreign nationals and/or foreign entities (each, a "Foreign Person"). Each of these transactions is subject to certain U.S. laws and regulations restricting trade. It is the policy of the Company to comply with all applicable U.S. laws and regulations. The procedures set forth in this section are designed to help the Company in meeting its compliance obligations with respect to international transactions, and will be applicable to all of the Company's agreements with Foreign Persons, including agreements with sales representatives and consultants, distributors, licensors and licensees, joint venture partners, investment partners, customers, and suppliers of raw materials and equipment.
   b. Applicable Regulations: Foreign trade is regulated by a number of U.S. government agencies. Among the most significant of these are the Departments of State, Commerce, and the Treasury. The Department of the Treasury, through its Office of Foreign Assets Control (OFAC), exerts the broadest controls by prohibiting or limiting trade with certain countries and Foreign Persons. Lists of prohibited parties and trade restrictions, issued by the Department of the Treasury and other government agencies are commonly referred to as the "Prohibited Lists." In some cases, OFAC even imposes its own special licensing requirements. Many of these regulations are general trade restrictions, unrelated to a particular product, while others may target specific types of products, assets, or finances.

> **NOTE:** *This book contains a separate policy with respect to the Office of Foreign Assets Control, to which you can refer if your company has operations that might be impacted by the regulations of OFAC.*

   c. Due Diligence: Responsible parties should review current due diligence practices and make any changes necessary to ensure corporate compliance with U.S. trade restrictions. Because the

Prohibited Lists are updated regularly, due diligence must be an ongoing process, performed on a transaction-by-transaction basis.

NOTE: *Given the number of prohibited lists, and the fact that they change from time to time, legal counsel should consider using an online service to perform routine compliance checks. Access to the Bureau of Export Administration's searchable database is available by subscription. Some private companies also provide online search services. After the user enters the names of the foreign persons who would be involved in a proposed transaction, the service will scan the prohibited lists for matching names.*

Before committing the Company to participate in any foreign business transaction, the responsible employees will conduct adequate due diligence to ensure that:

  (i) the proposed transaction or business arrangement will not violate any economic sanctions effected by the U.S. government;

 (ii) the Company will meet all applicable licensing requirements;

(iii) the names of the Foreign Persons involved in a proposed transaction or arrangement do not appear on lists of countries subject to embargo or other economic sanctions, are not those of terrorists or criminals identified on military or law enforcement "wanted" lists, and/or are not Foreign Persons who have been debarred from doing business with the U.S. Government (*see, e.g.,* www.ustreas.gov/offices/enforcement/lists/). If a proposed business partner's name matches a name appearing on a Prohibited List, you must conduct further inquiry to confirm that the proposed business partner is not, in fact, the prohibited party.

(iv) the proposed activities will comply with other applicable U.S. laws or regulations. Any abnormal facts or suspicious circumstances uncovered during due diligence that might raise legal compliance issues should be investigated and discussed with legal counsel before proceeding with a transaction.

J. OFFICE OF FOREIGN ASSET CONTROL

1. Introduction

The Office of Foreign Asset Control (OFAC) of the U.S. Department of the Treasury administers and enforces economic and trade sanctions based on U.S. foreign policy and national security goals against targeted foreign countries, terrorists, international narcotics traffickers, and those engaged in activities related to the proliferation of weapons of mass destruction. OFAC acts under presidential wartime and national emergency powers, as well as authority granted by specific legislation, to impose controls on transactions and freeze foreign assets under U.S. jurisdiction. Many of the sanctions are based on United Nations and other international mandates, are multilateral in scope, and involve close cooperation with allied governments.

The laws and regulations administered by OFAC prohibit or restrict U.S. persons from engaging in transactions involving certain countries, groups, and individuals. Specifically, OFAC currently administers full economic embargoes against Cuba, Iran, and Sudan, and partial embargoes against the countries in the Western Balkans, Burma, Iraq, Liberia, North Korea, Syria, and Zimbabwe. OFAC also administers targeted sanctions against certain specified narcotics traffickers, terrorists, and weapons proliferators, and prohibits U.S. persons from engaging in transactions with any individual or entity listed on OFAC's List of Specifically Designated Nationals and Blocked Persons (the "SDN List").

Information on the economic sanctions and trade restrictions administered by OFAC are available at: www.treas.gov/offices/enforcement/ofac/.

2. Form: Office of Foreign Asset Control Policy

Statement of Commitment

The Company is committed to establishing and implementing the appropriate policies and procedures to comply with the laws and regulations administered by the Office of Foreign Asset Control (OFAC), a unit within the United States Department of the Treasury (the "OFAC Laws").

All [services provided by and all transactions conducted by (revise as appropriate to reflect company's business)] [insert name of company] ("the Company") must comply with the OFAC laws and regulations. All investments and transactions in the United States or involving U.S. persons anywhere in the world must comply with OFAC's regulations.

> **NOTE:** *In order to highlight for employees the significance that the company attaches to this policy, discuss roles of senior management and the board of directors in this process. For example: "Senior management has developed, and the board of directors has approved, this policy."*

Major Policy Elements

It is the Company's policy to provide for a system of internal controls reasonably designed to ensure compliance with the OFAC Laws. The system of internal controls will include:

- Development of written policies and procedures relating to OFAC compliance;
- Designation of a qualified OFAC compliance officer responsible for coordinating and monitoring the OFAC compliance program;
- [Periodic], independent testing of the program; and
- The provision of ongoing OFAC training for appropriate personnel.

> **NOTE:** *The frequency of audits of compliance with the OFAC laws, and the frequency and extent of training on this subject, should be determined on the basis of a risk assessment in which the company's operations are reviewed by competent personnel and the risk of OFAC law violations is gauged.*

The goals and objectives of this OFAC policy are to:

- Enable the Company to comply with the laws, regulations, and guidelines enforced by OFAC;
- Cooperate with law enforcement authorities to the fullest extent permitted by OFAC laws and regulations;
- Promote employee awareness of the Company's commitment and obligations to adhere to OFAC laws and regulations; and

- To manage and mitigate compliance risk, operational risk, reputational risk, and strategic risk related to OFAC laws and regulations.

Consequences of Noncompliance

Failure to comply with OFAC laws and regulations may result in civil and criminal penalties. Individual violations also can result in up to 10 years' imprisonment. In addition, a violation of these laws and regulations could result in reputational damage to the Company. Noncompliance with any aspect of the OFAC compliance program may impact the employee's performance evaluation and could result in disciplinary action, including termination.

OFAC Compliance Officer

The [board of directors/senior management] has appointed an OFAC compliance officer (the "OFAC Officer"). The OFAC Officer is responsible for coordinating and monitoring the Company's OFAC compliance program and for managing all aspects of the Company's adherence to the OFAC laws and regulations, including:

- Providing guidance to management and employees on OFAC compliance matters;
- Monitoring legal and regulatory developments and best practices in the OFAC area;
- Keeping the board of directors and senior management informed of ongoing compliance with OFAC requirements, and recommending changes or updates to the program that would ensure continued compliance;
- Carrying out the direction of the board with respect to OFAC matters;
- Coordinating OFAC training for appropriate employees; and
- Filing any required reports with OFAC and ensuring that the appropriate records are maintained.

Training

To promote employee awareness of the requirements imposed by the OFAC laws and regulations, and to help employees understand their roles and responsibilities in the OFAC compliance program, the Company will provide OFAC training to designated employees on a [specify the interval, *e.g.*, annual] basis. The OFAC Officer will be responsible for the content of the OFAC training.

Independent Review

The [insert appropriate title or department of the Company, *e.g.*, internal audit] is responsible for conducting independent reviews of the program on a [specify time period, *e.g.* annual] basis. The [insert appropriate title or department of the Company, *e.g.*, internal audit] will report the results of such independent reviews to senior management and [insert names of any other individuals or groups that should be informed, *e.g., the audit committee of the board*].

Records Retention

The Company will comply with the record retention requirements for all records compiled and maintained in accordance with the relevant OFAC regulations. All documents required to be retained under the OFAC regulations must be maintained for a minimum of five years and may be required to be retained for a longer duration, depending upon the type of record.

NOTE: *The records retention provisions of this OFAC policy must dovetail with the company's general records retention policy. For additional guidance, see the records retention policy later in the pages that follow.*

K. POLITICAL ACTIVITIES

1. Introduction

Political activities by or on behalf of corporations and other entities face considerable restrictions and regulation, particularly in the federal arena. Nonetheless, mechanisms exist that legally permit a corporation's participation in the political process—namely, by and through the creation of a political action committee (PAC). A corporation may administer its PAC, and its PAC may engage in certain political activities, subject to strict limitations. Accordingly, care must be taken to ensure that the corporation is not facilitating contributions to political campaigns, or otherwise perceived as endorsing candidates or underwriting the personal political activities of its employees. While employees are encouraged to participate in the political process, such participation must be separate from the corporation's, and must be conducted on employees' personal time. This policy does not address what types of political activities an employee may conduct on her personal time.

Similarly, corporations may seek to affect public policies by lobbying public officials. While creating and maintaining channels of communication with public officials is important to the well-being of a corporation, the corporation's in-house and external lobbyists must take care not to engage in questionable conduct that potentially could damage a corporation's reputation or, worse yet, trigger a criminal investigation. If in doubt about whether any proposed action would damage the corporation's reputation, and possibly trigger a criminal investigation, lobbyists should always consult a corporation's legal counsel.

NOTE: *Changes in the U.S. House of Representatives and U.S. Senate ethics rules, and possible statutory changes to the Lobbying Disclosure Act and federal post-employment laws, will affect certain parts of this sample political activities policy. On January 5, 2007, the U.S. House of Representatives passed H.Res. 6, which revised certain House ethics rules for the 110th Congress. Similarly, on January 18, 2007, the U.S. Senate passed S. 1, a bill to provide greater transparency in the legislative process, that also revised certain Senate ethics rules for the 110th Congress. In addition, the Senate bill also proposed statutory changes to the current federal post-employment regime* *and to the Lobbying Disclosure Act—these statutory changes must be resolved and approved by members of the Senate and the House conference teams before they become law. As of February 6, 2007, it was not clear when the Senate and House conference teams would meet to reconcile these differences. Furthermore, both the House and Senate Ethics Committees are still examining and interpreting the revised ethics rules. If you have any questions about tailoring the above policy to conform to these changes and any finalized statutory changes (should there be any), please contact the chapter leaders listed at the beginning of this publication, and they can direct you to the specific lawyers who worked on this policy.*

2. Form: Political Activities Policy

Effective Date:

Supersedes:

Policy Owner (*Business Unit*):   Compliance

Overview

[Company]'s (the "Company") policy on political and lobbying activities provides guidance to its employees. This policy sets appropriate and reasonable limitations on activities related to lobbying government officials and conducting political activities with those inside and outside the Company. United States federal government policies and programs represent a continually growing influence on corporate business operations and market strategy. Government regulations may be major drivers of corporate profitability. It has become increasingly important for corporations to play a part in educating lawmakers on the effect of government policy and legislation on their businesses.

Scope

This policy governing lobbying and political activities is directed to all officers, directors, and employees of the Company, who shall be referred to collectively as "Employees." It is Company policy to comply with the letter and spirit of all statutory and regulatory requirements relating to lobbying and political activities. All Company Employees are responsible for ensuring that this policy is understood and implemented consistently with these requirements.

Policy Details: Lobbying

1. Lobbying covers many kinds of activities, requires disclosure, and is subject to specific rules. You may be engaged in lobbying if your work involves:
   - Contacts with legislators, regulators, executive branch officials, or their staffs;
   - Government contract sales; or
   - Efforts to influence legislative or administrative action.

2. For example, depending on the nature of the contact, compensation paid, and the number of contacts, your interaction with a legislative branch official, such as a member of Congress or such member's staff, may trigger, and require that the Company comply with, the registration and reporting requirements under the federal Lobbying Disclosure Act. 2 U.S.C. § 1601 *et seq.* One who otherwise meets the definition of a lobbyist must register with the Secretary of the Senate and the Clerk of the House within 45 days of first making a lobbying contact on behalf of a client or being retained to make such contact (whichever is earlier). 2 U.S.C. § 1603(a)(1).

3. The Company would be exempt from registration if the total expenses by its Employees for lobbying activities do not exceed and are not expected to exceed $24,500 during a semiannual period.

4. Each person employed by the lobbying entity who will make more than one lobbying contact and whose total lobbying activity for that client constitutes 20% or more of its work for that client over a six-month period must be separately listed as a lobbyist in the registration. 2 U.S.C. § 1603(a)(2).

5. Registered lobbyists also must file two semiannual reports that state a good-faith estimate of the total expenses incurred in connection with lobbying activities during the semiannual period. 2 U.S.C. § 1604.

6. A lobbying contact is any oral or written communication (including e-mail) to a covered executive or legislative branch official made on behalf of a client with regard to:
   • Formulation, modification, or adoption of federal legislation, federal rule, regulation, executive order, or any other program, policy, or position of the federal government;
   • Administration or execution of a federal program or policy; or
   • Nomination or confirmation of a person for a position subject to Senate confirmation.

7. A covered official is any policymaking official in the federal government, such as the President; the Vice President, any executive branch political appointee; civilian senior executive schedule employee; military personnel (0–7 and higher); and members of Congress and their staffs.

8. Contacts that do not qualify as lobbying contacts include:
   • Request for a meeting or for status of an action or any similar administrative request;

- Information provided in writing in response to an oral/written request by a covered official for specific information;
- Information required by subpoena, civil investigative demand, or otherwise compelled to be disclosed by statute, regulation, or other action of Congress or an agency; and
- Communications made in response to a notice in the *Federal Register*, *Commerce Business Daily*, or other similar publication.

9. Executive branch personnel are subject to strict restrictions on the gifts that they may accept from sources outside the U.S. government. Generally, they may not accept gifts that are given because of their official position or that come from certain "prohibited sources." These sources include persons (or an organization made up of such persons) who:

    (a) are seeking official action by the executive branch person's agency;

    (b) are doing or seeking to do business with the executive branch person's agency;

    (c) are regulated by the executive branch person's agency; or

    (d) have interests that substantially may be affected by performance or nonperformance of the executive branch person's official duties.

10. There are exceptions to the ban on gifts, which allow the acceptance by executive branch employees of gifts in the following circumstances:

    (a) where the aggregate retail value of the gift is $20 or less, so long as the aggregate value of all gifts from one source is less than $50 in a calendar year;

    (b) where the gift is based solely on a family relationship or personal friendship;

    (c) where the gift is based on a proper outside business or employment relationship; or

    (d) where the gift is in connection with certain proper political activities.

11. Similarly, there are exceptions to the legislative branch gift ban that allow the acceptance of gifts in the following circumstances:

    (a) where the retail value of the gift is $50 or less, and the aggregate value of all gifts worth more than $10 received from one source is less than $100 in a calendar year;

    (b) where the gift is based solely on a family relationship or personal friendship; or

    (c) where the gift is based on a proper outside business or employment relationship.

12. Additionally, both executive and legislative branch personnel may accept gifts of free attendance at certain widely attended gatherings, provided that certain conditions are met, such as the event must be sponsored by the Company and attendance must be open to individuals from throughout a given industry or profession. (*See* Company Gift Policy.)

13. Before any Company Employee gives a gift to executive branch or legislative branch personnel, the Employee must obtain approval from the responsible corporate official or the legal department to give the gift.

14. You must discuss these activities with the compliance officer or the law department to determine whether your activities and contacts with legislators and their staffs under relevant federal and/or state laws would cause registration, disclosure, and other rules to apply.

15. Only the legal department is authorized to approve lobbying agreements with third-party lobbyists or the use of Company Employees for the purpose of lobbying on behalf of the Company.

16. All Company Employees first shall obtain the written approval of the legal department before engaging in any lobbying activities. Such Employees will ensure all lobbying efforts are properly recorded on their time cards and expense reports and in a contact log.

17. The Company controller shall monitor and record all expenditures incurred for lobbying contracts, such as direct payments, third-party fees, and Employee salaries and expenses. Company accounting records shall identify lobbying expenditures by specific government recipient, organization, and project. The Company controller shall ensure compliance with the disclosure and reporting requirements of the Lobbying Act, including filing the Company's Lobbying Act registrations and semiannual reports, if appropriate.

18. Any Company Employee who knows of any violation of this policy, or suspects that a violation has taken place or could take place, must immediately advise the legal department.

> **NOTE:** *If the company is also a federal government contractor, the following section (bracketed paragraphs A through L) should be included in the policy.*

[A. The Byrd Amendment, 31 U.S.C. § 1352, requires qualifying recipients of appropriated funds to file declarations of lobbying contracts with government agencies providing those funds. It prohibits the use of government appropriations from being expended on lobbying activities.

B. The Byrd Amendment, implemented by FAR Subpart 3.8, requires government contractors who request or receive a government contract, grant, loan, cooperative agreement, or loan guarantee to file with the associated government agency a written declaration of lobbying contacts in accordance with 31 U.S.C. § 1352(b).

C. When a contract value exceeds $100,000, government contractors must file a disclosure (a) with each submission for "award" (as well as extension, continuation, renewal, amendment, or modification) of a contract, grant, loan, cooperative agreement, or loan guarantee with an agency, (b) on award of a contract, grant, loan, cooperative agreement, or loan guarantee, if there has been no prior filing, or (c) quarterly, if there has been a "material change" in the accuracy of information previously disclosed.

D. Certification and disclosure requirements of the Byrd Amendment are included in solicitations and contracts expected to exceed $100,000 under FAR 52.203-11, "Certification and Disclosure Regarding Payments to Influence Certain Federal Transactions," and FAR 52.203-12, "Limitation on Payments to Influence Certain Federal Transactions."

E. FAR 52.203-12 also applies to government subcontractors at all tiers who request or receive a subcontract in an amount exceeding $100,000. Subcontractors at each tier must submit a disclosure form and certification. The disclosure form and certificate shall be forwarded from tier to tier until received by the prime contractor. The prime contractor shall submit all disclosure forms to the contracting officer of the government contract on a quarterly basis. The prime contractor shall maintain a file with all lower-tier subcontractors' certificates of compliance.

F. The Byrd Amendment requires the disclosure of third-party lobbying efforts on behalf of specifically identifiable individuals, even when the lobbying is carried out using nonappropriated funds. This does not prohibit such third-party lobbying, but only requires its disclosure.

G. In addition to requiring those who request or receive government contracts to disclose the names and activities of lobbyists, the Byrd Amendment prohibits the use of "appropriated funds" to attempt to influence the award of any contract over $100,000. It prohibits an awardee of a government "contract, grant, loan, or cooperative agreement" from using "appropriated funds" to attempt to "influence" any officer or employee of any government agency or congress in connection with contract award or modification. The law applies government-wide to prime contractors, nonprofit entities, local governments, and subcontractors at all tiers.

H. "Appropriated funds" are defined as contract-derived funds other than profit.

I. "Appropriated funds" does not apply to (1) reasonable compensation pay to officers or Employees for legislative or agency lobbying activities not directly related to a specific contract award, or (2) payment of either reasonable compensation to officers or Employees, or reasonable payment to nonemployee consultants for professional or technical services rendered directly in preparation, submission, or negotiation of any bid, proposal, or application for meeting requirements imposed by or pursuant to law as a condition for receiving an award.

J. In addition, the controller will sign all Byrd Amendment certificates before submission.

K. The director of contracts shall:
   a) Ensure compliance with the disclosure and certification requirements of the Byrd Amendment;
   b) Provide Byrd Amendment certificates to the controller for signature, and then submit the certificates to the government or higher-tier contractors; and
   c) Submit all Byrd Amendment disclosure forms to the contracting officer for each government contract requiring quarterly disclosure.

L. The manager of purchasing shall collect all lower-tier subcontractor Byrd Amendment disclosure statements and certificates for each applicable government contract. Copies of disclosure statements and certificates shall be maintained in each purchase order or subcontractor file, and also provided to the manager of contracts for submission and for file.]

II. Policy Details: Political Contributions

1. The laws of the United States and certain other countries set strict limits on contributions by corporations to political parties and candidates, and violators are subject to very serious penalties—including imprisonment in the case of individuals.

2. The executive and legislative branch gift rules do not affect otherwise lawful contributions to presidential candidates', representatives', and senators' (collectively, "candidates") designated funds, as follows:

   (a) Company personnel may use personal funds to contribute to a candidate's campaign fund, insofar as such contributions are otherwise lawful.

   (b) Company Employees may contribute to a candidate's legal expense fund insofar as such contributions are otherwise lawful. However, Company Employees who are registered lobbyists or foreign agents may not contribute to such legal expense funds.

   (c) Company Employees may contribute to a charity designated by the candidate in lieu of paying the candidate an honorarium (*i.e.*, a speaking fee), even if the charity was established or is controlled by the candidate. Company Employees who are registered lobbyists or foreign agents, however, may not contribute to charities established or controlled by the candidate.

   (d) Company Employees, except those who are registered lobbyists or foreign agents, may contribute to a charity established or controlled by a candidate insofar as such contributions are otherwise lawful.

3. The Company may not make any direct or indirect contributions to, or expenditures on behalf of, any (1) candidate for elective office, (2) political party, or (3) political committee for any purpose.

4. Further, Company Employees may not use Company property, facilities, or Employee time to support a political cause or candidate.

5. The Federal Election Campaign Act of 1971 (FECA), as amended, regulates contributions to and expenditures on behalf of candidates for federal elective office. The Company is prohibited from making contributions to or expenditures on behalf of candidates for federal office, their campaign committees, or other federal political committees.

6. Under the federal campaign finance regulations, a "contribution" is (i) any gift, subscription, loan, advance, or deposit of money or anything of value made by any person for the purpose of influencing any election for federal office; or (ii) the payment of compensation for the unpaid personal services of another person rendered to a political committee. Examples of contributions include gifts of money; gifts of goods and services (in-kind contributions, such as goods and services offered free of charge or at less than the usual and normal charge); and loans and guarantees or endorsements.

7. An "expenditure" is (i) any purchase, payment, distribution, loan, advance, deposit, or gift of money or anything of value, made by any person for the purpose of influencing any election for federal office; and (ii) a written contract, promise, or agreement to make an expenditure. Examples of expenditures include: (1) use of corporate facilities and personnel for campaign purposes; (2) reimbursement of corporate personnel for political contributions; and (3) compensation of corporate personnel for campaign activities, including continuing to pay benefits during an unpaid leave.

8. Further, Company Employees are prohibited from volunteering their services to a candidate or political committee during normal work hours, unless the Employee is on leave without pay, makes up the lost time, or is on vacation.

9. In addition, Company Employees may not use Company property or facilities, such as telephones or copiers, to support a political cause or candidate.

10. Under FECA, a corporation may establish and administer a political action committee (PAC), but corporate funds may

not be contributed to any such PAC. Accordingly, no Company funds shall be contributed to a PAC.

11. PAC funds must not be commingled with personal or corporate funds. Funds used to pay for the cost of PAC's establishment, administration, and solicitation of political contributions must be kept separate from PAC contributions collected under federal election laws.

12. Avoid coercion or the appearance of coercion. As part of solicitation, notify the Employee of the PAC's political purpose; also, inform the Employee of the right to refuse to contribute without reprisal; and make sure that the voluntary nature of contribution guidelines (if any) is clear.

13. Do not solicit contributions (1) from corporations, from national banks, or from government contractors; (2) from non-U.S. citizens who have not been admitted for permanent residence; and (3) from individuals in a federal building.

14. Additionally, never seek to have someone else (including your corporate expense account) reimburse you for a political contribution, or reimburse anyone else.

15. State laws regulate contributions to or expenditures on behalf of candidates for state office. Some states permit a corporation to make limited contributions to or expenditures on behalf of candidates for state office. Other states follow the federal model and prohibit such corporate contributions.

16. To minimize confusion and ensure compliance, it is the Company's policy to follow the federal model and prohibit political contributions at the state level as well, unless an exception is approved by the compliance officer or legal department.

17. The Company and its operating companies encourage political activity by Employees in support of candidates or parties of their choice. But you should engage in the political process on your own time, with your own resources.

18. The Company encourages Employees to vote and be active in the political process, but Employees must engage in such activities on their own time, using personal, not Company, resources.

19. **Do not** use company time, property, or equipment for personal political activities without authorization from your company's compliance officer or law department.
20. The law department shall approve the establishment of any Company PAC.
21. The compliance officer shall monitor expense account submissions and Company expenditures to ensure that personnel are not reimbursed with Company funds for political contributions and to ensure that the Company does not make any restricted political contributions.

Employee Responsibilities

Any Company Employee who knows of any violation of this policy, or suspects that a violation has taken place or could take place, must immediately advise his/her supervisor, the compliance officer, or the law department.

Laws, regulations, and contractual requirements are subject to change, which could require revision to this policy. All personnel shall keep themselves current with any such changes and shall comply with such changes, regardless of whether or not the change has been incorporated into this policy. Any questions regarding conflicts with this policy shall be addressed to the compliance officer or the law department. Recommendations for revisions to this policy shall be made to the compliance officer.

Any issue not specifically mentioned above should be addressed with the law department.

L. PRIVACY AND DATA PROTECTION

1. Introduction

Privacy, data protection, and personal data security laws, rules, and regulations in more than 60 countries around the world—and in all regions of the world—impact the manner in which companies collect, use, store, consolidate, transfer, share, outsource, and otherwise process personal information about their employees, customers, suppliers, and other stakeholders. Examples include the EU Data Protection Directive 95/46/EC, the U.S. Health Insurance Portability and Accountability Act (HIPAA) Privacy and Security Rules, Russia's About Personal Data Act, Hong Kong's Personal Data (Privacy) Ordinance, Argentina's Personal Data Protection Act, and Canada's Personal Information Protection and Electronic Documents Act (PIPEDA).

While the administrative requirements of these laws, rules, and regulations differ across jurisdictions, the privacy principles upon which most of these laws are based are similar throughout the world. Accordingly, these privacy principles provide a framework for establishing a corporate privacy policy for privacy and data protection that will assist companies in achieving compliance across their operations globally.

2. Form: Privacy and Data Protection Policy

[COMPANY] GLOBAL PRIVACY AND DATA PROTECTION POLICY

[Company name] (the "Company") respects the privacy of its customers, employees, business partners, and others, and strives to process personal information in accordance with the laws of the countries in which it conducts business. This global privacy and data protection policy (the "Policy") sets forth the privacy principles that the Company follows with respect to personal information it collects, uses, and discloses globally, except to the extent the Company is required to collect, use, or disclose personal information to respond to a legal or an ethical obligation, or is expressly permitted or authorized by an applicable law, rule, or regulation to collect, use, or disclose personal information for certain purposes consistent with that law, rule, or regulation.

Scope

This Policy applies to all personal information collected, used, and disclosed by or on behalf of the Company, in any format including electronic, paper, or verbal.

Definitions

For purposes of this Policy, the following definitions shall apply:

"Agent" means any third party that collects or uses personal information under the instructions of, and solely for, the Company or to which the Company discloses personal information for use on the Company's behalf.

"Company" means [define, including its subsidiaries, affiliates, predecessors, successors, divisions, and groups globally], but excluding joint ventures to which the Company is a party.

"Personal Information" means any information or set of information that identifies or is used by or on behalf of the Company to identify an individual. Personal Information does not include information that is encoded or anonymized, or publicly available information that has not been combined with nonpublic personal information.

> **NOTE:** *While the scope of potential data elements that may fall within the scope of personal information is very broad, a useful reference to data elements that are likely to fall within this scope can be found in recent Federal Trade Commission enforcement decisions under Section 5 of the Federal Trade Commission Act, which include within the scope of personal information, "first and last name; a home or other physical address, including street name and city or town; an e-mail address or other online contact information, such as an instant messaging user identifier or a screen name that reveals an individual's e-mail address; a telephone number; a Social Security number; credit or debit card information, including credit and/or debit card number, expiration date, and data stored on the magnetic strip of a credit or debit card; checking account information, including ABA routing number, account number and check number; a driver's license number; or any other information about an individual that is combined with the above." Other useful examples include initials or other combinations of information derived*

from an individual's name; dates of birth; and digital or other electronic signatures. For more information, visit the privacy section of the FTC website at www.ftc.gov/privacy/index.html.

"Sensitive Personal Information" means Personal Information that reveals race, ethnic origin, political opinions, religious or philosophical beliefs, trade union membership, information about an individual's health or sex life, Social Security Number, drivers' license number, or other government-issued identification number, credit or debit card number, or financial account information. In addition, the Company will treat as Sensitive Personal Information any information received from a third party where that third party treats and identifies the information as sensitive.

NOTE: *This definition of "sensitive personal information" combines categories of data identified in the EU Data Protection Directive 95/46/ EC, other privacy laws outside the United States, U.S. federal and state medical and health privacy laws, and U.S. state security breach laws effective as of May 2006. For more information, see the European Union Data Protection website at http://ec.europa.eu/justice_home/fsj/ privacy/index_en.htm and the U.S. Department of Health and Human Services HIPAA website at www.hhs.gov/ocr/hipaa/.*

Privacy principles

<u>Necessity</u>: The Company collects, uses, and discloses the Personal Information necessary for identified business purposes, and retains the information in identifiable form only as long as necessary.

NOTE: *The "necessity" principle derives from the "proportionality principle" found in Article 6(1)(c) of EU Directive 95/46/EC and the "minimum necessary" principle found in the HIPAA Privacy Rule at 45 CFR § 164.514(d). The necessity principle serves as a guide for permitted uses and disclosures, and for defining access controls for personal information.*

<u>Notice:</u> The Company will inform individuals about the purposes for which it collects and uses Personal Information about them, the people or types of people who will have access to it, including the types of nonagent third parties to which the Company discloses that information, and the choices and means, if any, the Company offers individuals for limiting the use and disclosure of Personal Information about them. Notice will be provided in clear and conspicuous language when individuals are first asked to provide Personal Information to the Company, or as soon as practicable thereafter, and in any event before the Company uses or discloses the information for a purpose other than that for which it was originally collected.

NOTE: *Notice is a fundamental principle of fair information practices. The notice principle embodies the concept of transparency in processing personal information. Notice is required by Article 10 of Directive 95/46/EC, by the Safe Harbor Framework for transfers of personal data from the European Economic Area (EEA) to the United States, by the Gramm-Leach-Bliley Act, and by many other privacy laws around the world. The HIPAA Privacy Rule requires covered entities to provide specific forms of notice, including a standard "notice of privacy practices" as well as a specialized notice of any permitted occupational health-related disclosures. Any notice provided must accurately and appropriately represent the company's actual practices, as misrepresentations likely will be considered deceptive trade practices in violation of Section 5 of the Federal Trade Commission Act and applicable state unfair and deceptive trade practices statutes. It is important to note that notice may not be appropriate where providing notice may impede compliance with a legal or ethical obligation. Additionally, in some cases, the company may determine that the individual already has the information that would be provided in the notice. In such a situation, notice need not be given unless required by law.*

<u>Choice:</u> The Company will offer individuals the opportunity to choose whether Personal Information about them is (a) to be disclosed to a nonagent third party, or (b) to be used for a purpose other than the purpose for which it was originally collected or subsequently authorized by the individual, or (c) to continue to be used for certain types

of ongoing processing, such as ongoing commercial e-mail, facsimile, telemarketing, or direct mail communications.

For Sensitive Personal Information, the Company will give individuals the opportunity to affirmatively and explicitly consent (opt-in) to the disclosure of the information to a nonagent third party or to the use of the information for a purpose other than the purpose for which it was originally collected or subsequently authorized by the individual, except where such disclosure or secondary use is required or expressly permitted by law.

The Company will provide individuals with reasonable mechanisms to exercise their choices.

NOTE: *The principle of "choice" encompasses the concepts of (1) an informed decision to permit personal information processing or to participate in an activity that involves known collection, use, and disclosure of personal information, (2) the concept of affirmative, express, or opt-in consent or other permission (e.g., authorization), which may be provided verbally or in writing (including print and electronic), and (3) the concept of opting out or choosing not to participate in collection, use, disclosure, or other processing of personal information that the individual already participates in, either by choice or default. Under EU Directive 95/46/ EC, consent is required to process personal information and explicit consent is required to process sensitive personal information unless otherwise expressly permitted under these articles of the directive. Similarly, under the HIPAA Privacy Rule, a written authorization is required for use and disclosure of protected health information unless otherwise expressly permitted by the HIPAA Privacy Rule. It is important to note that choice may not be appropriate where providing choice may impede compliance with a legal or ethical obligation, or where providing choice may prevent performance of a contract or the conduct of necessary business activities that depend on the processing of personal information already collected.*

Data integrity: The Company will use Personal Information only in ways that are compatible with the purposes for which it was collected or subsequently authorized by the individual. The Company will take reasonable steps to ensure that Personal Information is accurate, complete, current, and relevant to its intended use.

<u>Onward transfer:</u> The Company will obtain written assurances from its agents that they will collect, use, and disclose Personal Information only as instructed by the Company, and that they will safeguard Personal Information with at least the same level of protection as is provided by this Policy as well as applicable laws, rules, regulations, and orders, and that they will require the same of any subcontractor. Where the Company has knowledge that an agent is using or disclosing Personal Information in a manner contrary to this Policy, the Company will take reasonable steps to prevent or stop the use or disclosure.

NOTE: *The principle of "onward transfer" appears in Article 17 of EU Directive 95/46/EC, the Safe Harbor, HIPAA's definition of a "business associate," the FTC Safeguards Rule, and privacy and security laws of certain states, such as California Civil Code section 1798.81.5(c), which requires businesses that disclose personal information pursuant to a contract with a nonaffiliated third party to require by contract that the third party implement and maintain reasonable security procedures and practices appropriate to the nature of the information, and to protect the personal information from unauthorized access, destruction, use, modification, or disclosure.*

<u>Access and correction:</u> Upon request, the Company will grant individuals reasonable access to factual Personal Information that it holds about them. In addition, the Company will take reasonable steps to permit individuals to correct, amend, or delete information that is demonstrated to be factually inaccurate or incomplete.

NOTE: *The rights of access and correction provided for by law generally are not absolute. For example, an individual's right of access does not extend to personal information about another person. The Guidelines adopted by the Commission nationale de l' informatique et des libertés of France (known as CNIL) for the implementation of whistleblowing schemes under the French Data Protection Act, for example, state that an incriminated person's right of access to information about him or her generated during the whistleblowing process does not entitle that person to request disclosure of information about third parties. Additionally, the HIPAA*

Privacy Rule provides for, among other things, a reviewable ground for denial of the right of access where the requested access, in the judgment of a licensed health care professional, is likely to endanger the life or physical safety of the individual or another person. Other limitations on the right of access that should be considered are access that would impede compliance with a legal or ethical obligation, or that would result in breach of a contract or disclosure of proprietary business information. In the employment context, in most cases access to undisclosed compensation or succession planning information will be inappropriate, while an employee's access to his or her business contact information, benefits elections, training records, performance reviews, and related personnel file typically are appropriate. Additionally, OSHA also allows employees to access exposure and medical records (see 29 CFR 1910.1020).

Security: The Company will implement reasonable administrative, physical, and technical safeguards to protect Personal Information in its possession from loss, misuse, and unauthorized access, disclosure, alteration, and destruction, and will contractually require the same of its agents.

The Company will evaluate any security incident reasonably expected to involve Sensitive Personal Information or where otherwise required by law, and will report any unauthorized disclosure of Sensitive Personal Information to governmental authorities and impacted individuals as required by and in accordance with applicable laws.

NOTE: *Traditionally, most privacy laws generally required that personal data be safeguarded appropriately, consistent with the general language of this principle. Many jurisdictions have been adopting more prescriptive security requirements for personal information. For example, in Europe, Belgium, Italy, Poland, Spain, and Sweden have issued specific standards for securing personal information. On the federal level, U.S. financial institutions must comply with the FTC Safeguards Rule and entities covered by HIPAA must comply with the HIPAA Security Rule. The U.S. states of Arkansas, California, Nevada, Rhode Island, and Texas have passed laws requiring businesses to implement reasonable practices and procedures to safeguard personal information.*

> *Additionally, under its authority given by section 5 of the FTC Act, the Federal Trade Commission has been increasingly enforcing the requirement that businesses implement appropriate security measures for personal information. Finally, a majority of U.S. states have enacted, within the past few years, laws requiring companies to notify impacted individuals (and in some cases government authorities) of a security breach involving unauthorized access to or acquisition of sensitive personal information. The first such U.S. state law was enacted in California in 2002.*

Enforcement: The Company will conduct compliance audits, reviews, and assessments of its relevant privacy practices to verify adherence to this Policy. Any employee that the Company determines is in violation of this policy will be subject to disciplinary action up to and including termination of employment.

Dispute resolution: Any questions or concerns regarding the use or disclosure of Personal Information should be directed to the responsible corporate official. The Company will investigate and attempt to resolve complaints and disputes regarding use and disclosure of Personal Information in accordance with the principles contained in this Policy.

Contact information

Questions or comments regarding this Policy should be submitted to: [Insert contact information].

Changes to this policy

This Policy may be amended from time to time, consistent with the requirements of applicable privacy laws, rules, regulations, and orders. The Company will take the following steps to provide notice of any changes to this Policy, such as posting a notice on its corporate website or sending communications regarding planned changes to its customers when such changes materially impact the way in which Personal Information about existing customers is used, and providing choices to existing customers regarding how Personal Information about them will be used and disclosed after the changes are implemented whenever this Policy is changed in a material way.

Effective date: [Month, Day, Year]

M. RECORDS MANAGEMENT

1. Introduction

The purposes and benefits of a properly written and consistently applied records management policy include:

(1) Compliance with records retention laws (such as the Internal Revenue Code, environmental statutes, labor and employment laws, and SEC regulations);

(2) Routine destruction of records no longer serving any business or legal purpose;

(3) Efficient, cost-effective, and systematic storage and retrieval of records (particularly electronic records, whose storage and retrieval costs are rising exponentially);

(4) Preservation of records relevant to pending or reasonably anticipated litigation and government investigations, where the improper destruction of records may result in adverse inferences against the offending party to a lawsuit, and to possible sanctions and/or civil and criminal penalties;

(5) Protection against allegations of selective document destruction; and

(6) Facilitation of the prosecution and defense of legal claims (by maintaining records consistent with relevant statutes of limitations).

A records management program should include a records retention schedule (detailing how long, under normal circumstances, to preserve specific records) and records hold guidelines (providing guidance on when and how to suspend normal records destruction practices in order to meet obligations arising pursuant to litigation or a government investigation). Importantly, it is insufficient merely to design and create a records management policy (and a records retention schedule and records hold guidelines); you must actively implement the policy and also inform and train employees regarding the policy to ensure compliance.

What follows below are some of the key components of a records management policy. Whether you use this or some other template as a basis for creating your company's policy, it is imperative that you tailor the policy to your company's particular circumstances. No single policy can fit all companies.

2. Form: Records Management Policy

I. PURPOSE

[Name of company] and its subsidiaries (collectively, the "Company") have adopted this records management policy (the "Policy") to achieve a consistent, organized, and effective approach to managing Company records, from creation through active use, storage, and disposal. This Policy applies to all Company operations [in the United States] and applies to all records, in both hard copy and electronic forms, as defined below.

NOTE: *Consider whether the company should have a single, global records management policy or different policies in different jurisdictions, given the different litigation environment and records retention laws inside and outside of the United States. Also consider cross referencing related policies such as those concerning e-mail and Internet usage, confidentiality, trade secrets, and privacy.*

The purposes of this Policy are (1) to ensure efficient and effective operation of the business, (2) to comply with regulatory recordkeeping requirements, (3) to preserve the confidentiality of Company information, (4) to maintain a manageable volume of well-organized records, (5) to mitigate the risk of the mistaken use of outdated records, and (6) to minimize storage and other costs associated with the retention of unnecessary records.

Consistent with these objectives, it is the Company's policy that records be retained for as long as (but only so long as) necessary to satisfy legal requirements, financial and audit requirements, and legitimate business purposes.

All employees of the Company are charged with the personal responsibility of complying with this Policy.

NOTE: *Consider whether and to what extent this policy should apply to consultants or other service providers that maintain and/or create company records, such as firms to whom the company outsources certain functions.*

II. DEFINITIONS AND TERMS

A. The term "Record" includes, without limitation, documents and electronically stored information (including writings, drawings, graphs, charts, photographs, sound recordings, images, and other data or data compilations stored in any medium) created for one or more purposes related to the Company's business. For example, and without limitation, "records" may also include books, ledgers, files, memoranda, letters, reports, worksheets, slides, other presentation materials, calendars, appointment books, telephone logs, and T&E reports, whether in hard copy or electronic format, and computerized data and programs, computer hardcopy printouts, computer-related magnetic materials (*e.g.*, word processing and personal computer diskettes, and magnetic tapes and cassettes), microfilm and microfiche, telecommunicated material such as facsimiles, and other electronically stored information such as e-mail.

> **NOTE:** *You should know that nonidentical duplicate copies of a particular record may, for litigation or other purposes, constitute separate and distinct records, all of which must be preserved. For example, a copy of a memo may contain handwritten notes not found on other copies of the same memo, and multiple copies of the same e-mail may contain different "metadata."*

B. A "Records Retention Period" is the length of time for which a record must be retained pursuant to applicable law or in accordance with the Records Retention Schedule.
C. The "Records Retention Schedule" is the schedule that sets forth the length of time that categories of records must be maintained. The Records Retention Schedule lists record types regularly kept by the Company and describes their applicable Retention Periods. Revisions to the Records Retention Schedule will occur as necessary to reflect changes in regulations or business requirements.
D. A "Records Hold" is any period of time during which pertinent records may not be disposed of even if they are no longer needed for legitimate business purposes or if the applicable Records Retention

Period has expired. The circumstances giving rise to a Records Hold are set forth in Section III.C, below.

III. POLICY

A. Maintaining and Disposing of Records
 1. Unless subject to a "Records Hold" (*see* Section III.C below), you should maintain records in accordance with the Company's Records Retention Schedule and, if not listed in the Records Retention Schedule, only as long as needed for a legitimate business purpose (in general, for a maximum of one year).

NOTE: *As discussed above, the company should develop a schedule detailing how long, under normal circumstances, records should be preserved. The retention period for a particular record type is a function of the retention period (if any) dictated by local, state, and federal statutes and regulations, the applicable statutes of limitations, and best business practices. Consider advising employees not to "selectively" destroy records. They should destroy particular classes of records in accordance with the policy and the schedule, but should not destroy specific records on a selective basis.*

---

 2. Records created or received during the course of Company business are Company property and, regardless of their location, do not belong to the individual employee who created, received, or maintains them. Company departments retain custodial responsibility and administrative authority over records.
 3. All Company business records should be maintained on Company property or in a Company-approved offsite storage facility.
 4. Records that do not need to be retained under the Records Retention Schedule or for legitimate business purposes may still need to be retained for litigation, government investigation, or similar purposes. The Company will implement a Records Hold for any such records (*see* Section III.C below).

5. Unless subject to a Records Hold, a record should be disposed of at the end of its retention period.

B. E-Mail

1. E-mail should not be used for official recordkeeping purposes. Unless subject to a Records Hold, e-mail messages will automatically be deleted from a user's mailbox after [___] days.

NOTE: *Company IT policies often call for the automatic deletion of e-mails after a set period of time. The above section reflects such an approach. See further discussion after subsection 2, below.*

---

2. E-mail records that need to be preserved for periods longer than [___] days for regulatory, legal, fiscal, or business purposes should be saved in electronic storage media approved by the IT department, or printed out and preserved as paper records. If you are required to retain e-mails pursuant to a Records Hold, the legal department and the IT department will advise you as to the appropriate storage media and process.

NOTE: *Consider how best to regulate the creation and preservation of e-mail. On the one hand, there are good legal and compliance-related reasons for the company to limit the time period that e-mail may be preserved (note, however, that some companies, such as those in the financial services industry, may be required by law to preserve e-mail for longer periods of time). On the other hand, employees can and do find ways to preserve e-mail for a variety of business (and nonbusiness) purposes and it is not wise to adopt a policy with which your employees will not, as a practical matter, comply.*

C. Suspension of Records Retention Periods—"Records Hold"

1. Events occasionally will require a suspension of applicable Records Retention Periods. In any of the following circumstances, a Records Hold will be in effect and you may not dispose of applicable records until further notice.

2. The circumstances calling for a Records Hold include the following:
   a. You have been advised by the Company that records have been sought, or will imminently be sought, in a pending litigation or government proceeding.
   b. You have been advised by the Company that the Company expects records will be sought in a pending or anticipated litigation or government proceeding.
   c. You are personally aware that records have been or likely will be sought in a pending or anticipated litigation or government proceeding.
3. As to the circumstances described in subparagraphs 2(a) and 2(b) above, you may receive a directive from the legal department or other Company official that certain records are subject to a Records Hold. The directive will describe the types of records subject to the Records Hold. You must follow this type of directive carefully.
4. As to the circumstances described in subparagraph 2(c) above, you may personally become aware of circumstances giving rise to a pending or anticipated litigation or government proceeding even before others in the Company have informed you of a Records Hold. In those circumstances, a Records Hold is in effect and you should suspend disposal of pertinent records. You must also promptly inform the law department and your supervisor of the basis for the Records Hold and seek guidance as to further action with respect to such records.

NOTE: *Discussion of when the duty to preserve potentially relevant evidence attaches may be found in the important, recent series of cases beginning with Zubulake v. UBS Warburg LLC, 220 F.R.D. 212, 216-17 (S.D.N.Y. 2003). See also the Litigation volume of this publication for additional information on "Litigation holds."*

---

5. **In no event should you ever alter, destroy, or conceal any records with the intent to impede, obstruct, or influence any litigation or government proceeding, or in relation to or contemplation of any such litigation or government proceeding.**

6. Unauthorized destruction or disposal of Company records may subject an employee to disciplinary action, including termination.

NOTE: *As discussed in the overview, above, a records management program should, in addition to the records management policy itself, include records hold guidelines that provide guidance on when and how to suspend normal records destruction practices in order to meet obligations arising pursuant to litigation or a government investigation. You should also refer to the records hold letter contained in the Litigation volume of the* Toolkit.

IV. Administration

A. As needed to facilitate effective compliance, the Company will assign responsibility for administering this Policy to a records manager, who will supervise the implementation of the Policy, maintain the Records Retention Schedule, manage active records, and transfer nonactive records to offsite storage locations.

B. You should address questions regarding this Policy and your obligations under the Policy to your supervisor, your records manager, or the legal department.

NOTE: *Consider to whom the records manager should report—for example, to the chief compliance officer? To underscore the importance of the records management program, consider establishing a records management committee (consisting of the compliance, technology, and legal departments) to oversee and approve amendments to the policy, and to review and audit compliance with the records management program. Small companies may not wish to appoint a single records manager with company-wide responsibilities, and may prefer instead to assign this responsibility to someone in each of its various departments.*

V. MANAGEMENT OF OFFSITE RECORDS

A. Records that are no longer in use on a regular basis, but that must still be maintained for the remainder of their respective Records Retention Periods, may be sent offsite. The records manager will arrange for records to be archived at an offsite storage facility on a regular basis.

B. The records manager is responsible for sending records to and from offsite storage, indexing all records maintained in offsite facilities, and overseeing the disposal of offsite records for which the Records Retention Period has expired.

VI. TRAINING AND REVIEW

A. Employees will receive guidance on the records management Policy as necessary, including instruction and advice on the creation, retention, and disposal of records.

B. This Policy and the Records Retention Schedule will be reviewed periodically and amended as necessary to reflect any changes in laws, regulations, or business requirements.

N. SUPPLIER AND VENDOR RELATIONS POLICY

1. Introduction

Some companies urge their suppliers and vendors to adopt compliance policies that mirror those that they themselves have adopted. Indeed, the Sentencing Guidelines for Organizational Defendants include admonitions for large business organizations to address this subject with their vendors and suppliers.

2. Form: Supplier/vendor Relations Policy

[COMPANY] SUPPLIER/VENDOR RELATIONS POLICY

This supplier/vendor relations policy (this "Policy") describes the standards for [Company name]'s (the "Company") employees and agents in conducting business on behalf of the Company. Company employees and agents are required to assist in the effort to maintain these standards. Violations of some of the standards set forth here can result in severe penalties for the Company, including criminal fines, substantial monetary damages, and a serious loss of reputation. In addition, violations can result in harsh penalties for individual employees and agents, including dismissal, monetary penalties, and even imprisonment. Because of these potential penalties, the Company requires strict adherence to these policies.

_____

Vice President, Human Resources

NOTE: *An ethics policy must be supported and followed by top management. If top management implements a program, and fails to adhere to that program, that will not go unnoticed by employees. This could create a potentially worse situation than having no ethics policy at all.*

CONFLICTS OF INTEREST

As discussed previously, when dealing with suppliers, vendors, and others with whom we do business, employees of Company and its subsidiaries and affiliates shall avoid situations where their personal interest could conflict with, or appear to conflict with, the interests of the Company.

Conflicts of interest arise where an individual's position or responsibilities with the Company present an opportunity for personal gain apart from the normal rewards of employment. They also arise where an employee's private interests are inconsistent with those of the Company and create conflicting loyalties. Such conflicting loyalties can cause an employee to give preference to private interests in situations where corporate responsibilities should come first.

While it is not possible to detail every situation where conflicts of interest may arise, the following corporate policies cover the areas that have great potential for conflict.

NOTE: *Review your company's values and build a policy accordingly. Some of the provisions below may not be as important to your organization.*

Personal Financial Interest

Employees should avoid any outside financial interest that might influence their corporate decisions or actions. Such outside commercial interest could include, among other things:

A personal or family financial interest in an enterprise that has business relations with the Company, if such financial interests represent a material part of the employee's net worth or income, or if these business relations with the Company represent a major part of the business of the outside enterprise.

An investment in another business that competes with any of the Company's interests, if the investment represents a material part of income or the net worth of the individual, or of the net worth and income of the outside business, or if the area of competition represents a major part of the activity of the outside business.

An employee or his (her) immediate family member may, however, acquire and hold a nominal amount (*i.e.*, less than 1%) of stock and bonds in a publicly traded company engaged in any business which the Company is engaged. The term "publicly traded company" includes a company whose stock is listed on a national stock exchange or traded in a recognized over-the-counter market.

Dealing with Suppliers and Vendors

The Company is a valuable customer for many suppliers of goods and services and facilities. People who want to do business or to continue to do business with the Company must understand that all purchases by the Company or any of its affiliates will be made exclusively on the basis of price, quality, service, and suitability to the Company's needs.

NOTE: *Consider having an ombudsman or ethics hotline so that vendors can report perceived inappropriate activities on the part of your employees.*

Reciprocity

Suppliers of goods and services will not be asked to buy goods and services from the Company or any of its affiliates in order to become or continue as a supplier. Violation of this principle—sometimes called "reciprocity"—may be a violation of antitrust laws.

The Company considers such reciprocal dealings a harmful practice and a hindrance to ensuring purchase of the best available materials or services at the lowest possible prices.

The Company will not attempt to influence its suppliers to purchase from the customers of the Company or any of its affiliates. When the Company makes purchases, it will not favor firms that are customers of the Company or any of its affiliates.

"Kickbacks" and Rebates

Company purchases or sales of goods and services must not lead to Company employees or their families receiving personal kickbacks or rebates. Employees or their families must not accept any form of under-the-table payment.

Receipt of Gifts and Entertainment

Even when gifts and entertainment are exchanged out of the purest motives of personal friendship, they can be misunderstood. They can appear to be attempts to bribe our employees into directing Company business to a particular supplier. To avoid both the reality and the appearance of improper relations with suppliers or potential suppliers, the following standards will apply to the receipt of gifts and entertainment by Company employees:

Gifts

Employees are prohibited from soliciting gifts, gratuities, or any other personal benefit or favor of any kind from suppliers or potential suppliers. Gifts include not only merchandise and products, but also personal services, theater tickets, and tickets to sports events. Employees are discouraged from accepting unsolicited gifts. They are prohibited from accepting gifts of money and gifts in a form that would induce or obligate them to give special consideration to the person or company making the gift.

Employees may accept unsolicited, nonmonetary gifts provided:

(a) they are items of nominal intrinsic value ($50.00 or less); or
(b) they are advertising and promotional materials, clearly marked with company or brand names.

Any gift of more than nominal intrinsic value ($50.00) must be reported to the vice president of human resources. Some gifts may be personalized or perishable so as to make their return impractical. When possible, any nonreturnable gift should be donated in the name of the Company to a charity, and the giver of the gift should be so informed. Employee acceptance of such nonreturnable gifts can be permitted if the gifts cannot be donated, but the employee should tactfully inform givers that such gifts are discouraged. Employees should ordinarily return to the giver any returnable gifts of more than nominal value ($50.00), with a tactful letter explaining Company policy is to return such gifts, and discouraging future gifts. In rare instances, an employee may be allowed to keep such a returnable gift, but employees wishing to keep such gifts must pay the donors the reasonable value of the goods and services involved. Special company approval by the vice president of human resources is required before an employee may keep such a returnable gift. In these cases, employees are also required to tactfully discourage future gifts.

Entertainment

Employees shall not encourage or solicit entertainment from any individual or company with whom our Company does business. Entertainment includes, but is not limited to, activities such as dinner parties, theater parties, and sports events.

From time to time, employees may accept unsolicited entertainment, but only under the following conditions:

(a) The entertainment occurs infrequently;

(b) The entertainment arises out of the ordinary course of business;

(c) The entertainment involves reasonable, not lavish, expenditures. The amounts involved should be ones employees are accustomed to spending normally for their own business or personal entertainment. Value of entertainment over $50.00 must be reported to the vice president of human resources;

(d) The entertainment takes place in settings that are reasonable, appropriate, and fitting to our employees, their hosts, and their business at hand; and

(e) The employee is not tempted to give, and does not feel obligated to give, to the individual or company providing the entertainment any special consideration.

NOTE: *Values and amounts are judgment calls. What is considered nominal in one organization may not be so in another. Additionally, entertainment allowances entail other potentially damaging pitfalls with regard to harassment and discrimination issues.*

STANDARDS COMPLIANCE

Initial Verification

Upon receiving their copy of the Policy, employees current and future will:

- become thoroughly familiar with the Policy;
- resolve any doubts or questions about the Policy;

- complete the Disclosure Statement, which will inform the Company of any existing holdings or activities that might be, or appear to be, at variance with the Policy;
- take steps to correct existing situations and bring holdings and activities into full compliance; such steps will be reviewed and will be based on the written disclosures submitted by employees; and
- Sign the verification and turn it in to the vice president of human resources.

Maintaining Compliance

A copy of this policy shall be furnished to every employee who, in the performance of his or her job, carries out duties and responsibilities that involve representations or contacts with outsiders on behalf of the Company, or whose duties bring them within the purview of this Policy.

Employees must inform the vice president of human resources of any changes in their holdings or activities that might be, or appear to be, at variance with the standards by submission of revised disclosure statements.

Employees must take steps to correct any such changes, if necessary, to bring holdings and activities into full compliance. Such steps will be reviewed and will be based on the written disclosures submitted by employees.

> **NOTE:** *An ombudsman or employee hotline may be useful in providing guidance on these issues, and may increase the likelihood of compliance with the standards in the policy.*

Policy Violations

Employees should immediately report any transaction or contemplated transaction that appears to violate any provision of the Policy. Failure to do so can have serious consequences for the employees and the Company.

Reports of violations should be made by employees to their supervisors.

Management has the responsibility of promptly and thoroughly investigating all reports.

After a violation is investigated, appropriate action will be taken. Management has the right to determine what disciplinary action will be taken for a violation, ranging from a verbal reprimand to termination. All proposed disciplinary action is subject to review by senior management.

Employees should be aware that, in addition to any disciplinary action taken by the Company, violations of some standards may require restitution and may lead to civil or criminal action against individual employees and corporations involved.

Management has the responsibility of taking remedial steps to correct any operating procedures that may have contributed to violation of the Policy.

Continuance of Existing Personnel Policies

The Company has codified numerous personnel policies, rules, and standards of employee performance that continue in force and are contained in the employee handbook. This Policy is intended to supplement and amplify those established personnel policies, rules, and standards.

It continues to be the responsibility of all members of management to comply with all such policies, rules, and performance standards.

[Company]

Supplier/Vendor Relations Policy

ACKNOWLEDGMENT

I hereby acknowledge receipt and understanding of Supplier/Vendor Relations Policy as revised on _____, and of my obligation to follow and abide by its conditions.

_____

NAME (Print)

_____

SIGNATURE

_____

DATE

O. DEVELOPING A LEGALLY-COMPLIANT CORPORATE INFORMATION SECURITY PROGRAM

Managing corporate information security is a legal obligation. Requirements to address security are set forth in an ever-expanding patchwork of federal and state laws, regulations, and government enforcement actions, as well as common law fiduciary duties and other implied obligations to provide "reasonable" security.

NOTE: *A list of some key security laws and regulations appears in the Appendix to this policy.*

Today, almost all businesses have two key legal obligations regarding the security of their own information:

- A duty to *provide reasonable security* for all corporate data; and
- A duty to *disclose security breaches* involving sensitive personal information.

Yet the nature of these legal obligations to address security often are poorly understood by those in management charged with the responsibility, by the technical experts who must implement them, and by the lawyers and other corporate officials who must ensure compliance.

These laws and regulations rarely specify what specific security measures a business should implement to satisfy its legal obligations. By their terms, most simply obligate companies to establish and maintain "reasonable" or "appropriate" security procedures, controls, safeguards, or measures, but often without any further direction or guidance. Yet a careful review of the applicable statutes, regulations, and cases reveals an amazingly consistent approach that also defines the parameters of a "legal" standard for security.

The legal standard involves a relatively sophisticated approach to compliance. It does not literally dictate what security measures are required to achieve "reasonable security." Instead, it focuses on a process to identify and implement measures that are reasonable under the circumstances to achieve the desired security objectives. This requires companies to engage in an *ongoing and repetitive process* that is designed to assess risks, identify and implement responsive security measures, verify that they are effectively implemented, and ensure that they are continually updated in response to new developments.

In other words, merely implementing seemingly strong security measures is not sufficient *per se*. Security measures must be responsive to existing threats facing the company, and must constantly evolve in light of changes in threats, technology, the company's business, and other factors. Thus, legal compliance requires following that process rather than merely implementing specified security measures.

NOTE: *See, for example, Guin v. Brazos Higher Education Service, Civ. No. 05-668, 2006 U.S. Dist. LEXIS 4846 (D. Minn. February 7, 2006) (embracing the "process" approach to security, and rejecting an argument that a specific security measure (encryption) was legally mandated. Instead, the court focused on the fact that the defendant had followed the proper "process" by putting in place written security policies, doing current risk assessments, and implementing proper safeguards as required by the Gramm-Leach-Bliley Act).*

The essence of the process-oriented approach to security compliance is implementation of a comprehensive written security program that includes:

- *Inventory of information assets*—identifying the systems and information that need to be protected;
- *Risk assessment*—conducting periodic assessments of the risks to those systems and information that the company faces;
- *Implementing responsive security measures*—developing and implementing security measures designed to manage and control the specific risks identified;
- *Addressing third parties*—overseeing third-party service provider arrangements;
- *Awareness, education, and training*—implementing security awareness training and education;

- *Monitoring and testing*—ensuring that the program is properly implemented and effective; and
- *Reviewing and adjusting*—revising the program in light of ongoing changes.

The legally mandated process, as required by existing laws, regulations, and enforcement actions, may be summarized as follows:

A. Inventory of Information Assets
   (Identification and assessment of the assets that require protection.)
   1. Information and Data ("Subject Data")
      (a) Identify the information that the company has that needs to be protected, including:
         (1) Personal information;
         (2) Financial data;
         (3) Tax-related data;
         (4) Trade secret information;
         (5) Transaction information; and
         (6) Other sensitive or confidential information.
      (b) Identify persons or entities that own or control the information that needs to be protected, including:
         (1) Company data;
         (2) Client data; and
         (3) Third-party data.
      (c) Identify the location of the information that needs to be protected, including:
         (1) Information in possession of the company
            (A) Physical location (country, city, office, etc.)
            (B) Responsible person, office, division, etc.
         (2) Information in possession of third parties
            (A) Outsourced service providers (name, country, city, office, etc.)
            (B) Consultants, clients, suppliers, etc. (name, country, city, office, etc.)
   2. Information Systems ("Systems")
      (a) Identify the systems that outsourced service providers maintain in the United States or elsewhere that collect, use, communicate, access, or store the company's Subject Data.

(b) Identify the information systems that are used to collect, use, communicate, access, or store Subject Data, including:
  (1) Information systems in the company's control;
  (2) Information systems under the control of a third-party service provider; and
  (3) Information systems under the control of other third parties.
(c) Identify the persons or entities that own or control the information systems that need to be protected.
(d) Identify the location of the information systems that collect, use, access, or store Subject Data, including:
  (1) Information systems in possession of the company
    (A) Physical location (country, city, office, etc.)
    (B) Responsible person, office, division, etc.
  (2) Information systems in possession of third parties
    (A) Outsourced service providers (name, country, city, office, etc.)
    (B) Consultants, clients, suppliers, etc. (name, country, city, office, etc.)

B. Risk Assessment
  (Identification and assessment of reasonably foreseeable internal and external threats to the Subject Data and the Systems on which it resides, to determine: (1) what can go wrong, (2) how likely it is to occur, and (3) the possible consequences.)

NOTE: *For an excellent discussion of the risk assessment process, see the IT Examination Handbook issued by the Federal Financial Institutions Examination Council in (July 2006), available at www.ffiec.gov/ffiecinfobase/booklets/information_security/information_security.pdf.*

Conduct a comprehensive risk assessment that identifies all the reasonably foreseeable internal and external threats to the security, confidentiality, and integrity of the Subject Data that could result in loss, misuse, unauthorized access, disclosure, alteration, or destruction of the Subject Data and/or the company's Systems on which such Subject Data resides. As part of that process—

(a) Identify the company's major vulnerabilities that, if exploited, could result in loss, misuse, unauthorized access, disclosure, alteration, or destruction of the Subject Data and/or the Systems on which such Subject Data resides;

(b) Assess the likelihood that each identified threat will materialize;

(c) Evaluate the potential damage that would result if such threat materialized; and

(d) Assess the sufficiency of the policies, procedures, information systems, and safeguards in place to control these risks.

NOTE: *With appropriate assistance of in-house and outside experts, members of management are best positioned to gauge the necessary scope of the risk assessment and to measure the effectiveness of techniques that might successfully reduce the risks identified during the assessment process.*

This process will be the baseline against which security measures can be selected, implemented, measured, and validated. The goal is to understand the risks the business faces, determine what level of risk is acceptable, and identify appropriate and cost-effective safeguards to combat any unacceptable risks.

NOTE: *See, for example, Interagency Guidelines Establishing Information Security Standards: Small-Entity Compliance Guide (2005), www.federalreserve.gov/boarddocs/press/bcreg/2005/20051214/ attachment.pdf; Guin v. Brazos Higher Education Service, Civ. No. 05-668, 2006 U.S. Dist. LEXIS 4846 (D. Minn. February 7, 2006).*

C. Develop and Implement a Written Security Program

(The Company should develop, implement, and maintain a comprehensive information security program to manage and control the risks it identified, i.e., to reduce those risks and vulnerabilities to a reasonable and appropriate level)

> **NOTE:** *According to the federal court decision in Guin v. Brazos Higher Education Service, where a proper risk assessment has been done and responsive security measures implemented, the inability to foresee and deter a specific security breach does not constitute a failure to satisfy the duty to provide reasonable security. Guin v. Brazos Higher Education Service, Civ. No. 05-668, 2006 U.S. Dist. LEXIS 4846 (D. Minn. February 7, 2006) at p. 12.*

1. Objectives. The information security program should be designed to accomplish the following objectives:
   (a) To ensure the *availability* of the Systems and Subject Data;
   (b) To protect against *unauthorized access* to the Systems and Subject Data;
   (c) To ensure the *confidentiality* of the Subject Data;
   (d) To ensure the *integrity* of the Subject Data;
   (e) To ensure the *authenticity* of the Subject Data;
   (f) To protect against any reasonably anticipated uses or disclosures of the Subject Data that are not permitted; and
   (g) To ensure compliance by employees and agents.
2. Responsibility.
   (a) One or more employees should be charged with overall responsibility for coordination of the information security program.
   (b) The board of directors should be actively involved by:
      (1) approving the information security program; and
      (2) requiring regular reports (at least annually) regarding:
         (A) The overall status of the security program;
         (B) The company's compliance with regulations and material matters relating to the security program, addressing issues such as:
            (i) Risk assessment;
            (ii) Risk management and control decisions;
            (iii) Service provider arrangements;
            (iv) Results of testing;
         (v) Security breaches or violations and management's responses; and
         (vi) Recommendations for changes in the information security program.

3. Select Security Measures/Controls that will adequately address the legal requirements and adequately respond to the risk assessment

4. Types of Security Measures. The Company's information security program should adequately address the following types of security, in a manner appropriate to the company's size and complexity, the nature and scope of its activities, and the sensitivity of the Subject Data involved:

   (a) Physical security measures, which are designed to protect the tangible items that comprise the physical computer system and network that store the data, including servers, terminals that have access to the system, and storage devices.

   (b) Administrative security measures (sometimes referred to as procedural security measures), which consist of management procedures and constraints, operational procedures, accountability procedures, and supplemental administrative controls to prevent unauthorized access and to provide an acceptable level of protection for computing resources and data. Administrative security procedures frequently include personnel management, training, discipline, etc.

   (c) Technical security measures, which involve the use of safeguards incorporated into computer hardware, software, and related devices. They are designed to ensure system availability, provide access control, authenticate persons seeking access, protect the integrity of information communicated via and stored on the system, and ensure confidentiality where appropriate.

5. Components of the Security Program. When designing the security program, keep in mind that the subject of the security program (*i.e.*, information) exists throughout the company. Both best practices and developing law generally require that all departments in the company that collect, create, store, or access data have an opportunity to provide input into this process, and that all relevant departments in the company address certain *categories* of security controls. Although by no means an exclusive list, the legal standard for security generally requires that companies consider the need for, and adopt as necessary, appropriate security measures in the following categories:

   (a) Physical Facility Protection—measures to protect against destruction, loss, or damage of equipment or information due to potential environmental hazards, such as fire and water damage or technological failures, procedures that govern the receipt and removal of hardware and electronic media into and out of a facility, and procedures that govern the use and security of physical workstations;

(b) Physical Access Controls—access restrictions at buildings, computer facilities, and records storage facilities that permit access only by authorized individuals;

(c) Technical Access Controls—policies and procedures to ensure that authorized persons who need access to the system have appropriate access, and that those who should not have access are prevented from obtaining access, including procedures to determine access authorization, procedures for granting and controlling access, authentication procedures to verify that a person or entity seeking access is the one claimed, and procedures for terminating access;

(d) Intrusion Detection Procedures—procedures to monitor log-in attempts and report discrepancies; procedures to detect actual and attempted attacks on, or intrusions into, company information systems; and procedures for preventing, detecting, and reporting malicious software (*e.g.*, virus software, Trojan horses, etc.);

(e) Employee Procedures—procedures to ensure employee honesty and proper job performance, and controls to prevent employees from compromising system security;

(f) System Modification Procedures—procedures designed to ensure that system modifications are consistent with the company's security program;

(g) Data Integrity, Confidentiality, and Storage—procedures to protect information from unauthorized access, alteration, disclosure, or destruction during storage or transmission;

(h) Data Destruction; Hardware and Media Disposal—procedures regarding final disposition of information and/or hardware on which it resides, and procedures for removal from media before re-use of the media;

(i) Audit Controls—maintenance of records to document repairs and modifications to the physical components to the facility related to security (*e.g.*, walls, doors, locks, etc); and hardware, software, and/or procedural audit control mechanisms that record and examine activity in the systems;

(j) <u>Contingency Plan</u>—procedures designed to ensure the ability to continue operations in the event of an emergency, such as a data backup plan, disaster recovery plan, and emergency mode operation plan; and

(k) <u>Incident Response Plan</u>—a plan for taking responsive actions in the event the company suspects or detects that a security breach has occurred, including ensuring that appropriate persons within the organization are quickly notified, and that prompt action is taken both in terms of responding to the breach (*e.g.*, to stop further information compromise and to work with law enforcement), and in terms of notifying appropriate persons who may be potentially injured by the breach.

When addressing these categories of issues, it is important to note that the law does not typically require implementation of any particular security control. The key is to implement security controls responsive to the identified threats, taking into account the factors noted above (*e.g.*, nature of business, cost, etc.).

D. <u>Addressing Third Parties</u>

(Companies are responsible for the security of all of their corporate data, including data accessible to, or under the control of, third parties. Thus, the security program needs to address security in the context of such third-party relationships.)

If third-party service providers or others will have control of, or access to, the Subject Data, the company must properly oversee such third parties by:

(a) Exercising due diligence in selecting and retaining third-party service providers (and in granting access to other third parties) to ensure that they are capable of maintaining adequate security;

(b) Contractually requiring services providers (and others granted access) to implement and maintain appropriate security; and

(c) Monitoring the performance of such service providers (and others granted access) to ensure compliance.

E. Awareness, Education, and Training

(*Training and education for employees is a critical component of any security program. Even the very best physical, technical, and administrative security measures are of little value if employees do not understand their roles and responsibilities with respect to security.*)

The information security program should include:

(a) Security awareness training for all personnel, including:

    (1) Communication to employees of applicable security policies, procedures, standards, and guidelines; and

    (2) Developing and maintaining relevant employee training materials.

(b) Periodic security reminders to appropriate personnel.

(c) User education concerning virus protection, password management, and how to report discrepancies.

(d) Appropriate sanctions against employees who fail to comply with security policies and procedures.

F. Monitoring and Testing the Security Program

(*Merely implementing security measures is not sufficient. Companies must also ensure that the security measures have been put in place properly and are effective.*)

In accordance with its information security program, the Company should:

(a) Maintain procedures for monitoring compliance with the security program;

(b) Conduct a periodic internal review to verify compliance with the security program;

(c) Conduct an assessment of the sufficiency of any safeguards in place to control identified risks;

(d) Conduct regular testing or monitoring of the effectiveness of the safeguards; and

(e) Conduct a regular review of records of system activity, such as audit logs, access reports, and security incident tracking reports.

G. Reviewing and Adjusting the Security Program

(*Security is a moving target. Businesses must conduct periodic reviews to evaluate and adjust their information security programs in light of ever-changing threats, risks, vulnerabilities, and security measures available to respond to them.*)

In accordance with its information security program, the Company should:

(a) Conduct a periodic internal review to evaluate and adjust the information security program in light of:

    (1) The results of the monitoring and testing;

    (2) Any material changes to the company's business or client arrangements;

    (3) Any changes in technology;

    (4) Any changes in internal or external threats facing the company;

    (5) Any environmental or operational changes; and/or

    (6) Any other circumstances that might have a material impact on the company's Systems or the Subject Data.

(b) Conduct a periodic internal review and assessment (audit) by qualified professionals using procedures and standards generally accepted in the profession to certify that its security program meets or exceeds applicable requirements, and is operating with sufficient effectiveness to provide reasonable assurances that the security, confidentiality, and integrity of information is protected.

(c) Obtain a periodic independent review and assessment (audit) by qualified independent third-party professionals using procedures and standards generally accepted in the profession to certify that its security program meets or exceeds applicable requirements, and is operating with sufficient effectiveness to provide reasonable assurances that the security, confidentiality, and integrity of information is protected.

(d) Adjust the security program in light of the findings or recommendations that come from such reviews.

Appendix

Key Information Security Law References

A. **Federal Statutes**

1. **COPPA:** Children's Online Privacy Protection Act of 1998, 15 U.S.C. § 6501 *et seq.*
2. **E-SIGN:** Electronic Signatures in Global and National Commerce Act, 15 U.S.C. § 7001(d).
3. **FISMA:** Federal Information Security Management Act of 2002, 44 U.S.C. §§ 3541-3549.
4. **GLB Act:** Gramm-Leach-Bliley Act, Pub. L. No. 106-102, §§ 501, 505(b), 15 U.S.C. §§ 6801, 6805.
5. **HIPAA:** Health Insurance Portability and Accountability Act, 42 U.S.C. §§ 1320d-2, 1320d-4.
6. **Homeland Security Act of 2002:** 44 U.S.C. § 3532(b)(1).
7. **Sarbanes-Oxley Act:** Pub. L. No. 107-204, §§ 302, 404, 15 U.S.C. §§ 7241, 7262.
8. **Federal Rules of Evidence 901(a):** *see* American Express v. Vinhnee, 2005 Bankr. LEXIS 2602 (B.A.P. 9th Cir. 2005).

B. **State Statutes**

1. **UETA:** Uniform Electronic Transactions Act, Section 12 (now enacted in 46 states).
2. **Laws Imposing Obligations to Provide Security for Personal Information:**

Arkansas	ARK. CODE ANN. § 4-110-104(b)
California	CAL. CIV. CODE § 1798.81.5(b)
Nevada	NEV. REV. STAT. § 603A.210
Rhode Island	R.I. GEN. LAWS § 11-49.2-2(2) and (3)
Texas	TEX. BUS. & COM. CODE ANN. § 48.102(a)
Utah	UTAH CODE ANN. § 13-42-201

3. **Data Disposal/Destruction Laws:**

Arkansas	ARK. CODE ANN. § 4-110-104(a)
California	CAL. CIV. CODE § 1798.81.
Kentucky	2005 H.B. 54, to be codified in KY. REV. STAT. ch. 365

Hawaii	2006 S.B. 2292
Indiana	IND. CODE § 24-4-14
Michigan	MICH. COMP. LAWS § 445.63, Section 12a
Nevada	NEV. REV. STAT. § 603A.200
New Jersey	A. 4001, 2005 Leg., 211th Sess. (N.J. 2005)
North Carolina	N.C. GEN. STAT. § 75-65
Texas	TEX. BUS. & COM. CODE ANN. § 48.102(b)
Utah	UTAH CODE ANN. § 13-42-201
Vermont	VT. STAT. ANN. tit. 9, § 2445 *et seq.*

4. Security Breach Notification Laws

Arizona	ARIZ. REV. STAT. § 44-7501
Arkansas	ARK. CODE ANN. § 4-110-101 *et seq.*
California	CAL. CIV. CODE § 1798.82
Colorado	COL. REV. STAT. § 6-1-716
Connecticut	CONN. GEN. STAT. 36A-701(b)
Delaware	DEL. CODE ANN. tit. 6, § 12B-101 *et seq.*
District of Columbia	D.C. CODE § 28-3861 *et seq.*
Florida	FLA. STAT. ANN. § 817.5681
Georgia	GA. CODE ANN. § 10-1-910 *et seq.* (Applies to information brokers only.)
Hawaii	HAWAII REV. STAT. §487N-2
Idaho	IDAHO CODE ANN. §§ 28-51-104 to 28-51-107
Illinois	815 ILL. COMP. STAT. 530/1 *et seq.*
Indiana	IND. CODE § 24-4.9
Kansas	KAN. STAT. ANN. §§ 50-7a01, 50-7a02
Louisiana	LA. REV. STAT. ANN. § 51:3071 *et seq.*
Maine	ME. REV. STAT. ANN. tit. 10, §§ 1347 *et seq.*
Michigan	MICH. COMP. LAWS § 445.63, Sections 12, 12a &12b
Minnesota	MINN. STAT. §§ 325E.61, 609.891
Montana	MONT. CODE ANN. § 30-14-1701 *et seq.*

Nebraska	NEB. REV STAT. § 87-801 *et seq.*
Nevada	NEV. REV. STAT. § 603A.010 *et seq.*
New Hampshire	N.H. REV. STAT. ANN. 359-C:19 *et seq.*
New Jersey	N.J. STAT. ANN. 56:8-163
New York	N.Y. BUS. CORP. LAW § 899-aa
North Carolina	N.C. GEN. STAT. § 75-65
North Dakota	N.D. CENT. CODE § 51-30-01 *et seq.*
Ohio	OHIO REV. CODE ANN. § 1349.19, § 1347 *et seq.*
Oklahoma	OKLA. STAT. *tit.,* § 74-3113.1 (applies to state agencies only)
Pennsylvania	73 PA. CONS. STAT. § 2303
Rhode Island	R.I. GEN. LAWS § 11-49.2-1 *et seq.*
Tennessee	TENN. CODE ANN. § 47-18-2107
Texas	TEX. BUS. & COM. CODE ANN. § 48.001 *et seq.*
Utah	UTAH CODE ANN. § 13-42-101 *et seq.*
Vermont	VT. STAT. ANN. tit. 9, § 2430 *et seq.*
Washington	WASH. REV. CODE § 19.255.010
Wisconsin	WIS. STAT. § 895.507

C. Federal Regulations

1. Regulations Imposing Obligation to Provide Security

(a) **COPPA Regulations:** 16 C.F.R. § 312.8.

(b) **FDA Regulations:** 21 C.F.R. Part 11.

(c) **FFIEC Guidance:** Authentication in an Internet Banking Environment, October 12, 2005, www.ffiec.gov/pdf/authentication—guidance.pdf. *See also, Frequently Asked Questions on FFIEC Guidance on Authentication in an Internet Banking Environment,* August 8, 2006 at p.5, www.ncua.gov/letters/2006/CU/06-CU-13_encl.pdf.

(d) **GLB Security Regulations:** Interagency Guidelines Establishing Standards for Safeguarding Consumer Information (to implement §§ 501 and 505(b) of the Gramm-Leach-Bliley Act), 12 C.F.R. Part 30, Appendix B (OCC), 12 C.F.R. Part 208, Appendix D (Federal Reserve System), 12 C.F.R. Part 364, Appendix B (FDIC), and 12 C.F.R. Part 568 (Office of Thrift Supervision).

(e) **GLB Security Regulations (FTC):** FTC Safeguards Rule (to implement §§ 501 and 505(b) of the Gramm-Leach-Bliley Act), 16 C.F.R. Part 314 (FTC).

(f) **HIPAA Security Regulations:** Final HIPAA Security Regulations, 45 C.F.R. Part 164.

(g) **IRS Regulations:** Rev. Proc. 97-22, 1997-1 C.B. 652, 1997-13 I.R.B. 9, and Rev. Proc. 98-25.

(h) **IRS Regulations:** IRS Announcement 98-27, 1998-15 I.R.B. 30, and Tax Regs. 26 C.F.R. § 1.1441-1(e)(4)(iv).

(i) **SEC Regulations:** 17 C.F.R. 240.17a-4, and 17 C.F.R. 257.1(e)(3).

(j) **SEC Regulations:** 17 C.F.R. § 248.30. Procedures to safeguard customer records and information; disposal of consumer report information (applies to any broker, dealer, and investment company, and every investment adviser registered with the SEC).

2. **Data Disposal/Destruction Regulations**

(a) **GLB Data Disposal Rule:** 12 C.F.R. Parts 334, 364

(b) **SEC Regulations:** 17 C.F.R. § 248.30. Procedures to safeguard customer records and information; disposal of consumer report information (applies to any broker, dealer, and investment company, and every investment adviser registered with the SEC).

3. **Security Breach Notification Regulations**

(a) **GLB Security Breach Notification Rule:** Interagency Guidance on Response Programs for Unauthorized Access to Customer Information and Customer Notice, 12 C.F.R. Part 30 (OCC), 12 C.F.R. Part 208 (Federal Reserve System), 12 C.F.R. Part 364 (FDIC), and 12 C.F.R. Part 568 (Office of Thrift Supervision).

(b) **IRS Regulations:** Rev. Proc. 97-22, 1997-1 C.B. 652, 1997-13 I.R.B. 9, and Rev. Proc. 98-25.

D. State Regulations

1. **Insurance—NAIC Model Regulations:** National Association of Insurance Commissioners, Standards for Safeguarding Consumer Information, Model Regulation

2. **Attorneys**—New Jersey Advisory Committee on Professional Ethics, Opinion 701 (2006), http://www.judiciary.state.nj.us/notices/ethics/ACPE_Opinion 701_ElectronicStorage_12022005.pdf

E. **Court Decisions**
1. Bell v. Michigan Council 25, No. 246684, 2005 Mich. App. LEXIS 353 (Mich. App. Feb. 15, 2005) (unpublished opinion)
2. American Express v. Vinhnee, 336 B.R. 437; 2005 Bankr. LEXIS 2602 (9th Cir. Dec. 16, 2005)
3. Guin v. Brazos Higher Education Service, 2006 U.S. Dist. LEXIS 4846 (D. Minn. Feb. 7, 2006)

F. **FTC Decisions and Consent Decrees**
1. In the Matter of Guidance Software (Agreement containing Consent Order, FTC File No. 062 3057, November 16, 2006), www.ftc.gov/op/2006/11/ guidance/.htm
2. In the Matter of CardSystems Solutions, Inc. (Agreement containing Consent Order, FTC File No. 052 3148, February 23, 2006), www.ftc.gov/opa/2006/02/cardsystems_r.htm
3. United States v. ChoicePoint, Inc. (Stipulated Final Judgment, FTC File No. 052 3069, N.D. Ga. Jan. 26, 2006), www.ftc.gov/os/caselist/choicepoint/choicepoint.htm.
4. In the Matter of DSW Inc. (Agreement containing Consent Order, FTC File No. 052 3096, Dec. 1, 2005), www.ftc.gov/opa/2005/12/dsw.htm.
5. In the Matter of BJ's Wholesale Club, Inc. (Agreement containing Consent Order, FTC File No. 042 3160, June 16, 2005), www.ftc.gov/opa/2005/06/bjswholesale.htm.
6. In the Matter of Sunbelt Lending Services, Inc. (Agreement containing Consent Order, FTC File No. 042 3153, Nov. 16, 2004), www.ftc.gov/os/caselist/0423153/04231513.htm.
7. In the Matter of Petco Animal Supplies, Inc. (Agreement containing Consent Order, FTC File No. 042 3153, Nov. 7, 2004), www.ftc.gov/os/caselist/0323221/0323221.htm.
8. In the Matter of MTS, Inc., d/b/a Tower Records/Books/Video (Agreement containing Consent Order, FTC File No. 032-3209, Apr. 21, 2004), www.ftc.gov/os/caselist/0323209/040421agree0323209.pdf.

9. In the Matter of Guess?, Inc. (Agreement containing Consent Order, FTC File No. 022 3260, June 18, 2003), www.ftc.gov/os/2003/06/guessagree.htm.

10. FTC V. Microsoft (Consent Decree, Aug. 7, 2002), www.ftc.gov/os/2002/08/microsoftagree.pdf.

11. In the Matter of Eli Lilly and Company (Decision and Order, FTC Docket No. C-4047, May 8, 2002), www.ftc.gov/os/2002/05/elilillydo.htm.

G. State Attorneys General Consent Decrees

1. In the Matter of Providence Health System—Oregon (Attorney General of Oregon, Assurance of Discontinuance, Sept. 26, 2006), www.doj.state.or.us/media/pdf/finfraud_providence_avc.pdf.

2. In the Matter of Barnes & Noble.com, LLC (Attorney General of New York, Assurance of Discontinuance, Apr. 20, 2004), www.bakerinfo.com/ecommerce/barnes-noble.pdf.

3. In the Matter of Ziff Davis Media Inc. (Attorneys General of California, New York, and Vermont, Assurance of Discontinuance, Aug. 28, 2002), www.oag.state.ny.us/press/2002/aug/aug28a_02_attach.pdf.

H. European Union

1. **EU Data Protection Directive:** European Union Directive 95/46/EC of February 20, 1995, on the protection of individuals with regard to the processing of personal data and on the free movement of such data (Data Protection Directive), Article 17, http://europa.eu.int/comm/internal_market/privacy/docs/95-46-ce/dir1995-46_part1_en.pdf.

2. **EU Data Protection Directive:** European Union Directive 2006/24/EC of March 15, 2006, on the retention of data generated or processed in connection with the provision of publicly available electronic communications services or of public communications networks and amending Directive 2002/58/EC, http://eurocrim.jura.uni-tuebingen.de/cms/en/doc/745.pdf.

EXHIBIT A

SENTENCING GUIDELINES FOR ORGANIZATIONAL DEFENDANTS (INCLUDING 2004 CHANGES)

1. INTRODUCTION

The Sentencing Guidelines for Organizational Defendants, first enacted in 1991 and significantly modified in 2004, set out standards by which corporate compliance and ethics programs should be evaluated by federal judges. Even though the guidelines are, by the terms of a 2005 opinion of the U.S. Supreme Court, advisory and not mandatory for use by judges, they continue to serve as benchmarks for such programs.

The guidelines provide the basic structure for a corporate compliance and ethics program. Accordingly, they serve as the touchstone for companies designing such programs. Prosecutors, courts, and other government officials measure corporate compliance and ethics programs against the guidelines in a number of contexts.

2. EFFECTIVE COMPLIANCE AND ETHICS PROGRAM

Historical Note: Effective November 1, 2004 [The Sentencing Guidelines for Organizational Defendants appear as Chapter 8 of the Guidelines Manual promulgated by the United States Sentencing Commission (from which this material was extracted) and can be found at http://www.ussc.gov/2006guid/CHAP8.html.]

§ 8B2.1. Effective Compliance and Ethics Program

(a) To have an effective compliance and ethics program, for purposes of subsection (f) of § 8C2.5 (Culpability Score) and subsection (c)(1) of § 8D1.4 (Recommended Conditions of Probation—Organizations), an organization shall—
  (1) exercise due diligence to prevent and detect criminal conduct; and
  (2) otherwise promote an organizational culture that encourages ethical conduct and a commitment to compliance with the law.
Such compliance and ethics program shall be reasonably designed, implemented, and enforced so that the program is generally effective in preventing and detecting criminal conduct. The failure to

prevent or detect the instant offense does not necessarily mean that the program is not generally effective in preventing and detecting criminal conduct.

(b) Due diligence and the promotion of an organizational culture that encourages ethical conduct and a commitment to compliance with the law within the meaning of subsection (a) minimally require the following:

  (1) The organization shall establish standards and procedures to prevent and detect criminal conduct.

  (2) (A) The organization's governing authority shall be knowledgeable about the content and operation of the compliance and ethics program and shall exercise reasonable oversight with respect to the implementation and effectiveness of the compliance and ethics program.

  (B) High-level personnel of the organization shall ensure that the organization has an effective compliance and ethics program, as described in this guideline. Specific individual(s) within high-level personnel shall be assigned overall responsibility for the compliance and ethics program.

NOTE: *Subsections B and C separate the responsibility to ensure effectiveness of the compliance and ethics program from the responsibility for day-to-day operational responsibility.*

  (C) Specific individual(s) within the organization shall be delegated day-to-day operational responsibility for the compliance and ethics program. Individual(s) with operational responsibility shall report periodically to high-level personnel and, as appropriate, to the governing authority, or an appropriate subgroup of the governing authority, on the effectiveness of the compliance and ethics program. To carry out such operational responsibility, such individual(s) shall be given adequate resources, appropriate authority, and direct access to the governing authority or an appropriate subgroup of the governing authority.

(3) The organization shall use reasonable efforts not to include within the substantial authority personnel of the organization any individual whom the organization knew, or should have known through the exercise of due diligence, has engaged in illegal activities or other conduct inconsistent with an effective compliance and ethics program.

NOTE: *The term "reasonable efforts" is not defined, however, leaving a great deal of uncertainty. At a minimum, some investigation of an individual's propensity for such activities identified in this section, as might be evidenced by past behavior, is appropriate.*

---

(4) (A) The organization shall take reasonable steps to communicate periodically and in a practical manner its standards and procedures, and other aspects of the compliance and ethics program, to the individuals referred to in subdivision (B) by conducting effective training programs and otherwise disseminating information appropriate to such individuals' respective roles and responsibilities.

(B) The individuals referred to in subdivision (A) are the members of the governing authority, high-level personnel, substantial authority personnel, the organization's employees, and, as appropriate, the organization's agents.

(5) The organization shall take reasonable steps—

(A) to ensure that the organization's compliance and ethics program is followed, including monitoring and auditing to detect criminal conduct;

(B) to evaluate periodically the effectiveness of the organization's compliance and ethics program; and

(C) to have and publicize a system, which may include mechanisms that allow for anonymity or confidentiality, whereby the organization's employees and agents may report or seek guidance regarding potential or actual criminal conduct without fear of retaliation.

> **NOTE:** *The guidelines require that employees and agents have a means by which to seek guidance regarding potential criminal conduct. Hotlines, both telephone and online, and mailboxes to which inquiries can be addressed, have been used for this purpose. The law department should play a substantial role in such a mechanism.*

(6) The organization's compliance and ethics program shall be promoted and enforced consistently throughout the organization through (A) appropriate incentives to perform in accordance with the compliance and ethics program; and (B) appropriate disciplinary measures for engaging in criminal conduct and for failing to take reasonable steps to prevent or detect criminal conduct.

(7) After criminal conduct has been detected, the organization shall take reasonable steps to respond appropriately to the criminal conduct and to prevent further similar criminal conduct, including making any necessary modifications to the organization's compliance and ethics program.

   (a) In implementing subsection (b), the organization shall periodically assess the risk of criminal conduct and shall take appropriate steps to design, implement, or modify each requirement set forth in subsection (b) to reduce the risk of criminal conduct identified through this process.

> **NOTE:** *After the initial design and implementation of a corporate ethics and compliance program, a company should periodically review the program's operation. In addition, the company should review the scope of the program to assure itself that the program still addresses the salient legal and business risks that the company faces, because such risks can change over time on account of changes in the law or regulations, changes to the business (mergers, new business opportunities, etc.), and organizational flux.*

Commentary

Application Notes:

1. *Definitions.*—*For purposes of this guideline:*

"Compliance and ethics program" means a program designed to prevent and detect criminal conduct.

"Governing authority" means (A) the Board of Directors; or (B) if the organization does not have a Board of Directors, the highest-level governing body of the organization.

"High-level personnel of the organization" and "substantial authority personnel" have the meaning given those terms in the Commentary to § 8A1.2 (Application Instructions—Organizations).

"Standards and procedures" means standards of conduct and internal controls that are reasonably capable of reducing the likelihood of criminal conduct.

2. *Factors to Consider in Meeting Requirements of this Guideline.* –
   (A) *In General.*—*Each of the requirements set forth in this guideline shall be met by an organization; however, in determining what specific actions are necessary to meet those requirements, factors that shall be considered include: (i) applicable industry practice or the standards called for by any applicable governmental regulation; (ii) the size of the organization; and (iii) similar misconduct.*
   (B) *Applicable Governmental Regulation and Industry Practice.*—*An organization's failure to incorporate and follow applicable industry practice or the standards called for by any applicable governmental regulation weighs against a finding of an effective compliance and ethics program.*
   (C) *The Size of the Organization.*—
       (i) *In General.*—*The formality and scope of actions that an organization shall take to meet the requirements of this guideline, including the necessary features of the organization's standards and procedures, depend on the size of the organization.*
       (ii) *Large Organizations.*—*A large organization generally shall devote more formal operations and greater resources*

in meeting the requirements of this guideline than shall a small organization. As appropriate, a large organization should encourage small organizations (especially those that have, or seek to have, a business relationship with the large organization) to implement effective compliance and ethics programs.

(iii) <u>Small Organizations.</u>—In meeting the requirements of this guideline, small organizations shall demonstrate the same degree of commitment to ethical conduct and compliance with the law as large organizations. However, a small organization may meet the requirements of this guideline with less formality and fewer resources than would be expected of large organizations. In appropriate circumstances, reliance on existing resources and simple systems can demonstrate a degree of commitment that, for a large organization, would only be demonstrated through more formally planned and implemented systems.

Examples of the informality and use of fewer resources with which a small organization may meet the requirements of this guideline include the following: (I) the governing authority's discharge of its responsibility for oversight of the compliance and ethics program by directly managing the organization's compliance and ethics efforts; (II) training employees through informal staff meetings, and monitoring through regular "walk-arounds" or continuous observation while managing the organization; (III) using available personnel, rather than employing separate staff, to carry out the compliance and ethics program; and (IV) modeling its own compliance and ethics program on existing, well-regarded compliance and ethics programs and best practices of other similar organizations.

(D) <u>Recurrence of Similar Misconduct.</u>—Recurrence of similar misconduct creates doubt regarding whether the organization took reasonable steps to meet the requirements of this guideline. For purposes of this subdivision, "similar misconduct" has the meaning given that term in the Commentary to § 8A1.2 (Application Instructions—Organizations).

3. *Application of Subsection (b)(2).*—High-level personnel and substantial authority personnel of the organization shall be knowledgeable about the content and operation of the compliance and ethics program, shall perform their assigned duties consistent with the exercise of due diligence, and shall promote an organizational culture that encourages ethical conduct and a commitment to compliance with the law.

If the specific individual(s) assigned overall responsibility for the compliance and ethics program does not have day-to-day operational responsibility for the program, then the individual(s) with day-to-day operational responsibility for the program typically should, no less than annually, give the governing authority or an appropriate subgroup thereof information on the implementation and effectiveness of the compliance and ethics program.

> **NOTE:** *This requirement supplements the distinction between authority for the program and responsibility for its day-to-day operation.*

4. *Application of Subsection (b)(3).*—
   (A) *Consistency with Other Law.*—Nothing in subsection (b)(3) is intended to require conduct inconsistent with any Federal, State, or local law, including any law governing employment or hiring practices.
   (B) *Implementation.*—In implementing subsection (b)(3), the organization shall hire and promote individuals so as to ensure that all individuals within the high-level personnel and substantial authority personnel of the organization will perform their assigned duties in a manner consistent with the exercise of due diligence and the promotion of an organizational culture that encourages ethical conduct and a commitment to compliance with the law under subsection (a). With respect to the hiring or promotion of such individuals, an organization shall consider the relatedness of the individual's illegal activities and other misconduct (i.e., other conduct inconsistent with an effective compliance and ethics program) to the specific responsibilities the individual is anticipated to be assigned and other factors such as: (i) the

recency of the individual's illegal activities and other misconduct; and (ii) whether the individual has engaged in other such illegal activities and other such misconduct.

5. <u>Application of Subsection (b)(6).</u>—Adequate discipline of individuals responsible for an offense is a necessary component of enforcement; however, the form of discipline that will be appropriate will be case specific.

6. <u>Application of Subsection (c).</u>—To meet the requirements of subsection (c), an organization shall:

(A) Assess periodically the risk that criminal conduct will occur, including assessing the following:

    (i) The nature and seriousness of such criminal conduct.

    (ii) The likelihood that certain criminal conduct may occur because of the nature of the organization's business. If, because of the nature of an organization's business, there is a substantial risk that certain types of criminal conduct may occur, the organization shall take reasonable steps to prevent and detect that type of criminal conduct. For example, an organization that, due to the nature of its business, employs sales personnel who have flexibility to set prices shall establish standards and procedures designed to prevent and detect price-fixing. An organization that, due to the nature of its business, employs sales personnel who have flexibility to represent the material characteristics of a product shall establish standards and procedures designed to prevent and detect fraud.

    (iii) The prior history of the organization. The prior history of an organization may indicate types of criminal conduct that it shall take actions to prevent and detect.

(B) Prioritize periodically, as appropriate, the actions taken pursuant to any requirement set forth in subsection (b), in order to focus on preventing and detecting the criminal conduct identified under subdivision (A) of this note as most serious, and most likely, to occur.

(C) Modify, as appropriate, the actions taken pursuant to any requirement set forth in subsection (b) to reduce the risk of criminal conduct identified under subdivision (A) of this note as most serious, and most likely, to occur.

<u>Background:</u> *This section sets forth the requirements for an effective compliance and ethics program. This section responds to section 805(a)(2)(5) of the Sarbanes-Oxley Act of 2002, Public Law 107–204, which directed the Commission to review and amend, as appropriate, the guidelines and related policy statements to ensure that the guidelines that apply to organizations in this publication "are sufficient to deter and punish organizational criminal misconduct."*

The requirements set forth in this guideline are intended to achieve reasonable prevention and detection of criminal conduct for which the organization would be vicariously liable. The prior diligence of an organization in seeking to prevent and detect criminal conduct has a direct bearing on the appropriate penalties and probation terms for the organization if it is convicted and sentenced for a criminal offense.

<u>Historical Note:</u> Effective November 1, 2004 (*citation omitted*).

EXHIBIT B

THE McNULTY MEMO OF DECEMBER 2006

1. Introduction

The guidance provided to United States Attorneys around the nation as to how they should take corporate compliance and ethics programs into account when considering whether and how to charge companies with federal crimes is contained in the McNulty memo, issued in late 2006. That memo updated earlier memos on that subject from 1999 and 2003.

Because prosecutors review many more situations for possible criminal charges than they ever wind up pursuing in court, the standards that they use in making the assessment as to whether to bring such charges—and which charges to bring if they determine to do so—loom large in the compliance field. Accordingly, understanding those standards enables in-house counsel to better counsel their companies when designing and implementing corporate ethics and compliance programs.

2. Text of Memo

U.S. Department of Justice

Office of the Deputy Attorney General

The Deputy Attorney General   Washington, D.C. 20530

MEMORANDUM

TO: Heads of Department Components
            United States Attorneys

FROM: Paul J. McNulty
            Deputy Attorney General

SUBJECT: Principles of Federal Prosecution of Business Organizations

Federal Prosecution of Business Organizations[i]

---

[i] While these guidelines refer to corporations, they apply to the consideration of the prosecution of all types of business organizations, including partnerships, sole proprietorships, government entities, and unincorporated associations.

I. Duties of the Federal Prosecutor; Duties of Corporate Leaders

The prosecution of corporate crime is a high priority for the Department of Justice. By investigating wrongdoing and bringing charges for criminal conduct, the Department plays an important role in protecting investors and ensuring public confidence in business entities and in the investment markets in which those entities participate. In this respect, federal prosecutors and corporate leaders share a common goal. Directors and officers owe a fiduciary duty to the corporation's shareholders, the corporation's true owners, and they owe duties of honest dealing to the investing public in connection with the corporation's regulatory filings and public statements. The faithful execution of these duties by corporate leadership serves the same values in promoting public trust and confidence that our criminal prosecutions are designed to serve.

A prosecutor's duty to enforce the law requires the investigation and prosecution of criminal wrongdoing if it is discovered. In carrying out this mission with the diligence and resolve necessary to vindicate the important public interests discussed above, prosecutors should be mindful of the common cause we share with responsible corporate leaders. Prosecutors should also be mindful that confidence in the Department is affected both by the results we achieve and by the real and perceived ways in which we achieve them. Thus, the manner in which we do our job as prosecutors—the professionalism we demonstrate, our resourcefulness in seeking information, and our willingness to secure the facts in a manner that encourages corporate compliance and self-regulation—impacts public perception of our mission. Federal prosecutors recognize that they must maintain public confidence in the way in which they exercise their charging discretion, and that professionalism and civility have always played an important part in putting these principles into action.

II. Charging a Corporation: General Principles

A. <u>General Principle:</u> Corporations should not be treated leniently because of their artificial nature nor should they be subject to harsher treatment. Vigorous enforcement of the criminal laws against corporate wrongdoers, where appropriate, results in great benefits for law enforcement and the public, particularly in the area of white-collar crime. Indicting corporations for wrongdoing enables the government to address and be a force for positive change of corporate culture, alter corporate behavior, and prevent, discover, and punish white-collar crime.

B. Comment: In all cases involving corporate wrongdoing, prosecutors should consider the factors discussed herein. First and foremost, prosecutors should be aware of the important public benefits that may flow from indicting a corporation in appropriate cases. For instance, corporations are likely to take immediate remedial steps when one is indicted for criminal conduct that is pervasive throughout a particular industry, and thus an indictment often provides a unique opportunity for deterrence on a massive scale. In addition, a corporate indictment may result in specific deterrence by changing the culture of the indicted corporation and the behavior of its employees. Finally, certain crimes that carry with them a substantial risk of great public harm, e.g., environmental crimes or financial frauds, are by their nature most likely to be committed by businesses, and there may, therefore, be a substantial federal interest in indicting the corporation.

Charging a corporation, however, does not mean that individual directors, officers, employees, or shareholders should not also be charged. Prosecution of a corporation is not a substitute for the prosecution of criminally culpable individuals within or without the corporation. Because a corporation can act only through individuals, imposition of individual criminal liability may provide the strongest deterrent against future corporate wrongdoing. Only rarely should provable individual culpability not be pursued, even in the face of an offer of a corporate guilty plea or some other disposition of the charges against the corporation.

Corporations are "legal persons," capable of suing and being sued, and capable of committing crimes. Under the doctrine of *respondeat superior*, a corporation may be held criminally liable for the illegal acts of its directors, officers, employees, and agents. To hold a corporation liable for these actions, the government must establish that the corporate agent's actions (i) were within the scope of his duties and (ii) were intended, at least in part, to benefit the corporation. In all cases involving wrongdoing by corporate agents, prosecutors should consider the corporation, as well as the responsible individuals, as potential criminal targets.

Agents, however, may act for mixed reasons—both for self-aggrandizement (both direct and indirect) and for the benefit of the corporation and a corporation may be held liable as long as one motivation of its agent is to benefit the corporation. *See United States v. Potter,* 463 F.3d 9, 25 (1st Cir. 2006) (stating that the test to determine whether an agent is acting within the scope of employment is whether the agent is performing acts of the kind which he is authorized to perform, and those acts are motivated—at least in part—by an intent to benefit the corporation). In *United States v. Automated Medical Laboratories,* 770 F.2d 399 (4th Cir. 1985), the Fourth Circuit affirmed a corporation's conviction for the actions of a subsidiary's employee despite its claim that the employee was acting for his own benefit, namely his "ambitious nature and his desire to ascend the corporate ladder." The court stated, "*Partucci* was clearly acting in part to benefit AML since his advancement within the corporation depended on AML's well-being and its lack of difficulties with the FDA." Furthermore, in *United States v. Sun-Diamond Growers of California,* 138 F.3d 961, 969-70 (D.C. Cir. 1998), *aff'd on other grounds,* 526 U.S. 398 (1999), the D.C. Circuit rejected a corporation's argument that it should not be held criminally liable for the actions of its vice-president since the vice-president's scheme was designed to—and did in fact—defraud [the corporation], not benefit it." According to the court, the fact that the vice-president deceived the corporation and used its money to contribute illegally to a congressional campaign did not preclude a valid finding that he acted to benefit the corporation. Part of the vice-president's job was to cultivate the corporation's relationship with the congressional candidate's brother, the Secretary of Agriculture. Therefore, the court held, the jury was entitled to conclude that the vice-president had acted with the intent, "however befuddled," to further the interests of his employer. *See also United States v. Cincotta,* 689 F.2d 238, 241-42 (1st Cir. 1982) (upholding a corporation's conviction, notwithstanding the substantial personal benefit reaped by its miscreant agents, because the fraudulent scheme required money to pass through the corporation's treasury and the fraudulently obtained goods were resold to the corporation's customers in the corporation's name).

Moreover, the corporation need not even necessarily profit from its agent's actions for it to be held liable. In *Automated Medical Laboratories*, the Fourth Circuit stated:

> [B]enefit is not a "touchstone of criminal corporate liability; benefit at best is an evidential, not an operative, fact." Thus, whether the agent's actions ultimately redounded to the benefit of the corporation is less significant than whether the agent acted with the intent to benefit the corporation. The basic purpose of requiring that an agent have acted with the intent to benefit the corporation, however, is to insulate the corporation from criminal liability for actions of its agents which <u>may</u> be inimical to the interests of the corporation or which may have been undertaken solely to advance the interests of that agent or of a party other than the corporation.

770 F.2d at 407 (emphasis added; *quoting Old Monastery Co. v. United States*, 147 F.2d 905, 908 (4th Cir.), *cert. denied*, 326 U.S. 734 (1945)).

III. Charging a Corporation: Factors to Be Considered

A. <u>General Principle:</u> Generally, prosecutors should apply the same factors in determining whether to charge a corporation as they do with respect to individuals. *See* USAM § 9-27.220, *et seq.* Thus, the prosecutor should weigh all of the factors normally considered in the sound exercise of prosecutorial judgment: the sufficiency of the evidence; the likelihood of success at trial; the probable deterrent, rehabilitative, and other consequences of conviction; and the adequacy of noncriminal approaches. *See id.* However, due to the nature of the corporate "person," some additional factors are present. In conducting an investigation, determining whether to bring charges, and negotiating plea agreements, prosecutors must consider the following factors in reaching a decision as to the proper treatment of a corporate target:

   1. the nature and seriousness of the offense, including the risk of harm to the public, and applicable policies and priorities, if any, governing the prosecution of corporations for particular categories of crime (see section IV, infra);

2. the pervasiveness of wrongdoing within the corporation, including the complicity in, or condonation of, the wrongdoing by corporate management (see section V, infra);

3. the corporation's history of similar conduct, including prior criminal, civil, and regulatory enforcement actions against it (see section VI, infra);

4. the corporation's timely and voluntary disclosure of wrongdoing and its willingness to cooperate in the investigation of its agents (see section VII, infra);

NOTE: *The McNulty Memorandum differs from its predecessor (the "Thompson Memorandum"), among other ways, in that it deleted the following phrase from the fourth numbered paragraph: "including, if necessary, the waiver of corporate attorney-client and work product protection." This change constituted part of the Department of Justice's effort to reduce the perception that federal prosecutors routinely seek a waiver of a corporation's attorney-client and work product privileges as a price for the credit due a corporation (in the process by which the prosecutors consider whether and how to charge for federal crimes) for cooperation.*

---

5. the existence and adequacy of the corporation's <u>pre-existing</u> compliance program (*see* section VIII, *infra*);

6. the corporation's remedial actions, including any efforts to implement an effective corporate compliance program or to improve an existing one, to replace responsible management, to discipline or terminate wrongdoers, to pay restitution, and to cooperate with the relevant government agencies (*see* section IX, *infra*);

7. collateral consequences, including disproportionate harm to shareholders, pension holders and employees not proven personally culpable and impact on the public arising from the prosecution (*see* section X, *infra*);

8. the adequacy of the prosecution of individuals responsible for the corporation's malfeasance; and

9. the adequacy of remedies such as civil or regulatory enforcement actions (*see* section XI, *infra*).

B. <u>Comment:</u> In determining whether to charge a corporation, the foregoing factors must be considered. The factors listed in this section are intended to be illustrative of those that should be considered and not a complete or exhaustive list. Some or all of these factors may or may not apply to specific cases, and in some cases one factor may override all others. For example, the nature and seriousness of the offense may be such as to warrant prosecution regardless of the other factors. In most cases, however, no single factor will be dispositive. Further, national law enforcement policies in various enforcement areas may require that more or less weight be given to certain of these factors than to others. Of course, prosecutors must exercise their judgment in applying and balancing these factors and this process does not mandate a particular result.

In making a decision to charge a corporation, the prosecutor generally has wide latitude in determining when, whom, how, and even whether to prosecute for violations of federal criminal law. In exercising that discretion, prosecutors should consider the following general statements of principles that summarize appropriate considerations to be weighed and desirable practices to be followed in discharging their prosecutorial responsibilities. In doing so, prosecutors should ensure that the general purposes of the criminal law—assurance of warranted punishment, deterrence of further criminal conduct, protection of the public from dangerous and fraudulent conduct, rehabilitation of offenders, and restitution for victims and affected communities—are adequately met, taking into account the special nature of the corporate "person."

IV. Charging a Corporation: Special Policy Concerns

A. <u>General Principle:</u> The nature and seriousness of the crime, including the risk of harm to the public from the criminal conduct, are obviously primary factors in determining whether to charge a corporation. In addition, corporate conduct, particularly that of national and multi-national corporations, necessarily intersects with federal economic, taxation, and criminal law enforcement policies. In applying these principles, prosecutors must consider the practices and policies of the appropriate Division of the Department, and must comply with those policies to the extent required.

B. <u>Comment:</u> In determining whether to charge a corporation, prosecutors should take into account federal law enforcement priorities as discussed above. *See* USAM § 9-27-230. In addition, however, prosecutors must be aware of the specific policy goals and incentive programs established by the respective Divisions and regulatory agencies. Thus, whereas natural persons may be given incremental degrees of credit (ranging from immunity to lesser charges to sentencing considerations) for turning themselves in, making statements against their penal interest, and cooperating in the government's investigation of their own and others' wrongdoing, the same approach may not be appropriate in all circumstances with respect to corporations. As an example, it is entirely proper in many investigations for a prosecutor to consider the corporation's pre-indictment conduct, *e.g.*, voluntary disclosure, cooperation, remediation, or restitution, in determining whether to seek an indictment. However, this would not necessarily be appropriate in an antitrust investigation, in which antitrust violations, by definition, go to the heart of the corporation's business and for which the Antitrust Division has therefore established a firm policy, understood in the business community, that credit should not be given at the charging stage for a compliance program and that amnesty is available only to the first corporation to make full disclosure to the government. As another example, the Tax Division has a strong preference for prosecuting responsible individuals, rather than entities, for corporate tax offenses. Thus, in determining whether or not to charge a corporation, prosecutors must consult with the Criminal, Antitrust, Tax, and Environmental and Natural Resources Divisions, if appropriate or required.

V. **Charging a Corporation: Pervasiveness of Wrongdoing Within the Corporation**

A. <u>General Principle:</u> A corporation can only act through natural persons, and it is therefore held responsible for the acts of such persons fairly attributable to it. Charging a corporation for even minor misconduct may be appropriate where the wrong-doing was pervasive and was undertaken by a large number of employees or by all the employees in a particular role within the corporation, *e.g.*, salesmen or procurement officers, or was condoned by upper management. On the other hand, in certain limited circumstances, it may not be appropriate to impose liability upon a corporation, particularly one with a compliance program in place, under a strict *respondeat superior* theory for the single isolated act of a rogue employee. There is, of course, a wide spectrum between these two extremes, and a prosecutor should exercise sound discretion in evaluating the pervasiveness of wrongdoing within a corporation.

B. Comment: Of these factors, the most important is the role of management. Although acts of even low-level employees may result in criminal liability, a corporation is directed by its management and management is responsible for a corporate culture in which criminal conduct is either discouraged or tacitly encouraged. As stated in commentary to the Sentencing Guidelines:

> Pervasiveness [is] case specific and [will] depend on the number, and degree of responsibility, of individuals [with] substantial authority . . . who participated in, condoned, or were willfully ignorant of the offense. Fewer individuals need to be involved for a finding of pervasiveness if those individuals exercised a relatively high degree of authority. Pervasiveness can occur either within an organization as a whole or within a unit of an organization. *See* USSG § 8C2.5, comment. (n. 4).

VI. Charging a Corporation: The Corporation's Past History

A. General Principle: Prosecutors may consider a corporation's history of similar conduct, including prior criminal, civil, and regulatory enforcement actions against it, in determining whether to bring criminal charges.

B. Comment: A corporation, like a natural person, is expected to learn from its mistakes. A history of similar conduct may be probative of a corporate culture that encouraged, or at least condoned, such conduct, regardless of any compliance programs. Criminal prosecution of a corporation may be particularly appropriate where the corporation previously had been subject to noncriminal guidance, warnings, or sanctions, or previous criminal charges, and it either had not taken adequate action to prevent future unlawful conduct or had continued to engage in the conduct in spite of the warnings or enforcement actions taken against it. In making this determination, the corporate structure itself, *e.g.*, subsidiaries or operating divisions, should be ignored, and enforcement actions taken against the corporation or any of its divisions, subsidiaries, and affiliates should be considered. *See* USSG § 8C2.5(c) & comment. (n. 6).

VII. Charging a Corporation: The Value of Cooperation

A. <u>General Principle:</u> In determining whether to charge a corporation, that corporation's timely and voluntary disclosure of wrongdoing and its cooperation with the government's investigation may be relevant factors. In gauging the extent of the corporation's cooperation, the prosecutor may consider, among other things, whether the corporation made a voluntary and timely disclosure, and the corporation's willingness to provide relevant evidence and to identify the culprits within the corporation, including senior executives.

B. <u>Comment:</u> In investigating wrongdoing by or within a corporation, a prosecutor is likely to encounter several obstacles resulting from the nature of the corporation itself. It will often be difficult to determine which individual took which action on behalf of the corporation. Lines of authority and responsibility may be shared among operating divisions or departments, and records and personnel may be spread throughout the United States or even among several countries. Where the criminal conduct continued over an extended period of time, the culpable or knowledgeable personnel may have been promoted, transferred, or fired, or they may have quit or retired. Accordingly, a corporation's cooperation may be critical in identifying the culprits and locating relevant evidence. Relevant considerations in determining whether a corporation has cooperated are set forth below.

1. <u>Qualifying for Immunity, Amnesty or Pretrial Diversion.</u>
   In some circumstances, granting a corporation immunity
   or amnesty or pretrial diversion may be considered in the
   course of the government's investigation. In such circumstances, prosecutors should refer to the principles governing non-prosecution agreements generally. *See* USAM
   § 9-27.600-650. These principles permit a non-prosecution
   agreement in exchange for cooperation when a corporation's
   "timely cooperation appears to be necessary to the public
   interest and other means of obtaining the desired cooperation are unavailable or would not be effective." Prosecutors
   should note that in the case of national or multi-national
   corporations, multi-district or global agreements may be
   necessary. Such agreements may only be entered into with
   the approval of each affected district or the appropriate
   Department official. *See* USAM § 9-27.641.

   In addition, the Department, in conjunction with regulatory agencies and other executive branch departments,
   encourages corporations, as part of their compliance programs, to conduct internal investigations and to disclose their
   findings to the appropriate authorities. Some agencies, such
   as the Securities and Exchange Commission and the Environmental Protection Agency, as well as the Department's
   Environmental and Natural Resources Division, have formal
   voluntary disclosure programs in which self-reporting, coupled with remediation and additional criteria, may qualify
   the corporation for amnesty or reduced sanctions. Even in
   the absence of a formal program, prosecutors may consider
   a corporation's timely and voluntary disclosure in evaluating
   the adequacy of the corporation's compliance program and
   its management's commitment to the compliance program.
   However, prosecution and economic policies specific to the
   industry or statute may require prosecution notwithstanding
   a corporation's willingness to cooperate. This creates a strong
   incentive for corporation's participating in anti-competitive
   conduct to be the first to cooperate. In addition, amnesty,
   immunity, or reduced sanctions may not be appropriate
   where the corporation's business is permeated with fraud or
   other crimes.

2. <u>Waiving Attorney-Client and Work-Product Protections</u>[ii].
   The attorney-client and work product protections serve an extremely important function in the U.S. legal system. The attorney-client privilege is one of the oldest and most sacrosanct privileges under U.S. law. *See Upjohn v. United States*, 449 U.S. 383, 389 (1976). As the Supreme Court has stated "its purposes is to encourage full and frank communication between attorneys and their clients and thereby promote broader public interests in the observance of law and administration of justice." *Id.* The work product doctrine also serves similarly important interests.

   Waiver of attorney-client and work product protections is not a prerequisite to a finding that a company has cooperated in the government's investigation. However, a company's disclosure of privileged information may permit the government to expedite its investigation. In addition, the disclosure of privileged information may be critical in enabling the government to evaluate the accuracy and completeness of the company's voluntary disclosure.

   Prosecutors may only request waiver of attorney-client or work product protections when there is a legitimate need for the privileged information to fulfill their law enforcement obligations. A legitimate need for the information is not established by concluding it is merely desirable or convenient to obtain privileged information. The test requires a careful balancing of important policy considerations underlying the attorney-client privilege and work product doctrine and the law enforcement needs of the government's investigation.

   Whether there is a legitimate need depends upon:
   (1) the likelihood and degree to which the privileged information will benefit the government's investigation;

[ii] The Sentencing Guidelines reward voluntary disclosure and cooperation with a reduction in the corporation's offense level. *See* USSG §8C2.5(g). The reference to consideration of a corporation's waiver of attorney-client and work-product protections in reducing a corporation's culpability score in Application Note 12, was deleted effective November 1, 2006. *See* USSG §8C2.5(g), comment. (n. 12).

(2) whether the information sought can be obtained in a timely and complete fashion by using alternative means that do not require waiver;

(3) the completeness of the voluntary disclosure already provided; and

(4) the collateral consequences to a corporation of a waiver.

If a legitimate need exists, prosecutors should seek the least intrusive waiver necessary to conduct a complete and thorough investigation, and should follow a step-by-step approach to requesting information. Prosecutors should first request purely factual information, which may or may not be privileged, relating to the underlying misconduct ("Category I"). Examples of Category I information could include, without limitation, copies of key documents, witness statements, or purely factual interview memoranda regarding the underlying misconduct, organization charts created by company counsel, factual chronologies, factual summaries, or reports (or portions thereof) containing investigative facts documented by counsel.

Before requesting that a corporation waive the attorney-client or work product protections for Category I information, prosecutors must obtain written authorization from the United States Attorney who must provide a copy of the request to, and consult with, the Assistant Attorney General for the Criminal Division before granting or denying the request. A prosecutor's request to the United States Attorney for authorization to seek a waiver must set forth law enforcement's legitimate need for the information and identify the scope of the waiver sought. A copy of each waiver request and authorization for Category I information must be maintained in the files of the United States Attorney. If the request is authorized, the United States Attorney must communicate the request in writing to the corporation.

A corporation's response to the government's request for waiver of privilege for Category I information may be considered in determining whether a corporation has cooperated in the government's investigation.

Only if the purely factual information provides an incomplete basis to conduct a thorough investigation should prosecutors then request that the corporation provide attorney-client communications or nonfactual attorney work product ("Category II"). This information includes legal advice given to the corporation before, during, and after the underlying misconduct occurred.

This category of privileged information might include the production of attorney notes, memoranda or reports (or portions thereof) containing counsel's mental impressions and conclusions, legal determinations reached as a result of an internal investigation, or legal advice given to the corporation.

Prosecutors are cautioned that Category II information should only be sought in rare circumstances.

Before requesting that a corporation waive the attorney-client or work product protections for Category II information, the United States Attorney must obtain written authorization from the Deputy Attorney General. A United States Attorney's request for authorization to seek a waiver must set forth law enforcement's legitimate need for the information and identify the scope of the waiver sought. A copy of each waiver request and authorization for Category II information must be maintained in the files of the Deputy Attorney General. If the request is authorized, the United States Attorney must communicate the request in writing to the corporation.

If a corporation declines to provide a waiver for Category II information after a written request from the United States Attorney, prosecutors must not consider this declination against the corporation in making a charging decision. Prosecutors must always favorably consider a corporation's acquiescence to the government's waiver request in determining whether a corporation has cooperated in the government's investigation.

Requests for Category II information requiring the approval of the Deputy Attorney General do not include:

(1) legal advice contemporaneous to the underlying misconduct when the corporation or one of its employees is relying upon the advice-of-counsel defense; and

(2) legal advice or communications in furtherance of a crime or fraud, coming within the crimes-fraud exception to the attorney-client privilege.

In these two instances, prosecutors should follow the authorization process established for requesting waiver for Category I information.

For federal prosecutors in litigating Divisions within Main Justice, waiver requests for Category I information must be submitted for approval to the Assistant Attorney General of the Division and waiver requests for Category II information must be submitted by the Assistant Attorney General for approval to the Deputy Attorney General. If the request is authorized, the Assistant Attorney General must communicate the request in writing to the corporation.

Federal prosecutors are not required to obtain authorization if the corporation voluntarily offers privileged documents without a request by the government. However, voluntary waivers must be reported to the United States Attorney or the Assistant Attorney General in the Division where the case originated. A record of these reports must be maintained in the files of that office.

3. <u>Shielding Culpable Employees and Agents.</u> Another factor to be weighed by the prosecutors is whether the corporation appears to be protecting its culpable employees and agents. Thus, while cases will differ depending on the circumstances, a corporation's promise of support to culpable employees and agents, *e.g.*, through retaining the employees without sanction for their misconduct or through providing information to the employees about the government's investigation pursuant to a joint defense agreement, may be considered by the prosecutor in weighing the extent and value of a corporation's cooperation.

Prosecutors generally should not take into account whether a corporation is advancing attorneys' fees to employees or agents under investigation or indictment. Many state indemnification statutes grant corporations the power to advance the legal fees of officers under investigation prior to a formal determination of guilt. As a consequence, many corporations enter into contractual obligations to advance attorneys' fees through provisions contained in their corporate charters, bylaws or employment agreements. Therefore, a corporation's compliance with governing state law and its contractual obligations cannot be considered a failure to cooperate.[iii] This prohibition is not meant to prevent a prosecutor from asking questions about an attorney's representation of a corporation or its employees.[iv]

4. <u>Obstructing the Investigation.</u> Another factor to be weighed by the prosecutor is whether the corporation, while purporting to cooperate, has engaged in conduct intended to impede the investigation (whether or not rising to the level of criminal obstruction). Examples of such conduct include: overly broad or frivolous assertions of privilege to withhold the disclosure of relevant, non-privileged documents, inappropriate directions to employees or their counsel, such as directions not to cooperate openly and fully with the investigation including, for example, the direction to decline to be interviewed; making presentations or submissions that contain misleading assertions or omissions; incomplete or delayed production of records; and failure to promptly disclose illegal conduct known to the corporation.

5. <u>Offering Cooperation: No Entitlement to Immunity.</u> Finally, a corporation's offer of cooperation does not automatically entitle it to immunity from prosecution. A corporation

---

[iii] In extremely rare cases, the advancement of attorneys' fees may be taken into account when the totality of the circumstances show that it was intended to impede a criminal investigation. In these cases, fee advancement is considered with many other telling facts to make a determination that the corporation is acting improperly to shield itself and its culpable employees from government scrutiny. *See* discussion in Brief of Appellant-United States, *United States v. Smith and Watson*, No. 06-3999-cr (2d Cir. Nov. 6, 2006). Where these circumstances exist, approval must be obtained from the Deputy Attorney General before prosecutors may consider this factor in their charging decisions. Prosecutors should follow the authorization process for waiver requests of Category II information (*see* section VII-2, *infra*).

[iv] Routine questions regarding the representation status of a corporation and its employees, including how and by whom attorneys' fees are paid, frequently arise in the course of an investigation. They may be necessary to assess other issues, such as conflict-of-interest. Such questions are appropriate and this guidance is not intended to prohibit such inquiry.

should not be able to escape liability merely by offering up its directors, officers, employees, or agents as in lieu of its own prosecution. Thus, a corporation's willingness to cooperate is merely one relevant factor, that needs to be considered in conjunction with the other factors, particularly those relating to the corporation's past history and the role of management in the wrongdoing.

VIII. Charging a Corporation: Corporate Compliance Programs

NOTE: *Section VIII of the memo sets out the views of the Department of Justice regarding corporate compliance programs, and provides clues as to what weight U.S. Attorneys might give to the existence and operation of such a program when contemplating whether and how to charge a company for violations of federal law. The views regarding how independently corporate directors oversee management's proposed actions (see the text following footnote 6) may be of considerable interest to federal prosecutors and, for that reason, to in-house counsel when counseling their corporate clients and senior management. The ultimate goal of the memo is to provide guidance for U.S. Attorneys as to how they can "determine whether a corporation's compliance program is merely a 'paper program' or whether it was designed and implemented in an effective manner." This section should be read in conjunction with the Sentencing Guidelines, to which it refers in several places.*

A. <u>General Principle:</u> Compliance programs are established by corporate management to prevent and to detect misconduct and to ensure that corporate activities are conducted in accordance with all applicable criminal and civil laws, regulations, and rules. The Department encourages such corporate self-policing, including voluntary disclosures to the government of any problems that a corporation discovers on its own. However, the existence of a compliance program is not sufficient, in and of itself, to justify not charging a corporation for criminal conduct undertaken by its officers, directors, employees, or agents.

Indeed, the commission of such crimes in the face of a compliance program may suggest that the corporate management is not adequately enforcing its program. In addition, the nature of some crimes, *e.g.*, antitrust violations, may be such that national law enforcement policies mandate prosecutions of corporations notwithstanding the existence of a compliance program.

B. <u>Comment:</u> A corporate compliance program, even one specifically prohibiting the very conduct in question, does not absolve the corporation from criminal liability under the doctrine of *respondeat superior*. *See United States v. Basic Construction Co.*, 711 F.2d 570 (4th Cir. 1983) ("[A] corporation may be held criminally responsible for antitrust violations committed by its employees if they were acting within the scope of their authority, or apparent authority, and for the benefit of the corporation, even if . . . such acts were against corporate policy or express instructions."). In *United States v. Potter*, 463 F.3d 9, 25-26 (1st Cir. 2006. According to the court, a corporation cannot "avoid liability by adopting abstract rules" that forbid its agents from engaging in illegal acts; "even a specific directive to an agent or employee or honest efforts to police such rules do not automatically free the company for the wrongful acts of agents." Similarly, in *United States v. Hilton Hotels Corp.*, 467 F.2d 1000 (9th Cir. 1972), *cert. denied*, 409 U.S. 1125 (1973), the Ninth Circuit affirmed antitrust liability based upon a purchasing agent for a single hotel threatening a single supplier with a boycott unless it paid dues to a local marketing association, even though the agent's actions were contrary to corporate policy and directly against express instructions from his superiors. The court reasoned that Congress, in enacting the Sherman Antitrust Act, "intended to impose liability upon business entities for the acts of those to whom they choose to delegate the conduct of their affairs, thus stimulating a maximum effort by owners and managers to assure adherence by such agents to the requirements of the Act."[v] It concluded that

---

[v] Although this case and *Basic Construction* are both antitrust cases, their reasoning applies to other criminal violations. In the *Hilton* case, for instance, the Ninth Circuit noted that Sherman Act violations are commercial offenses "usually motivated by a desire to enhance profits," thus, bringing the case within the normal rule that a "purpose to benefit the corporation is necessary to bring the agent's acts within the scope of his employment." 467 F.2d at 1006 & n4. In addition,

"general policy statements" and even direct instructions from the agent's superiors were not sufficient; "Appellant could not gain exculpation by issuing general instructions without undertaking to enforce those instructions by means commensurate with the obvious risks." *See also United States v. Beusch*, 596 F.2d 871, 878 (9th Cir. 1979) ("[A] corporation may be liable for the acts of its employees done contrary to express instructions and policies, but . . . the existence of such instructions and policies may be considered in determining whether the employee in fact acted to benefit the corporation."); *United States v. American Radiator & Standard Sanitary Corp.*, 433 F.2d 174 (3rd Cir. 1970) (affirming conviction of corporation based upon its officer's participation in price-fixing scheme, despite corporation's defense that officer's conduct violated its "rigid anti-fraternization policy" against any socialization (and exchange of price information) with its competitors; "When the act of the agent is within the scope of his employment or his apparent authority, the corporation is held legally responsible for it, although what he did may be contrary to his actual instructions and may be unlawful.").

While the Department recognizes that no compliance program can ever prevent all criminal activity by a corporation's employees, the critical factors in evaluating any program are whether the program is adequately designed for maximum effectiveness in preventing and detecting wrongdoing by employees and whether corporate management is enforcing the program or is tacitly encouraging or pressuring employees to engage in misconduct to achieve business objectives. The Department has no formal guidelines for corporate compliance programs. The fundamental questions any prosecutor should ask are: "Is the corporation's compliance program well designed?" and "Does the corporation's compliance program work?" In answering these questions, the prosecutor should consider the comprehensiveness of the compliance program; the extent and pervasiveness of the criminal conduct; the number and level of the corporate employees involved; the seriousness, duration, and frequency of

---

in *United States v. Automated Medical Laboratories*, 770 F.2d 399, 406 n.5 (4th Cir. 1985), the Fourth Circuit stated "that Basic Construction states a generally applicable rule on corporate criminal liability despite the fact that it addresses violations of the antitrust laws."

the misconduct; and any remedial actions taken by the corporation, including restitution, disciplinary action, and revisions to corporate compliance programs.[vi] Prosecutors should also consider the promptness of any disclosure of wrongdoing to the government and the corporation's cooperation in the government's investigation. In evaluating compliance programs, prosecutors may consider whether the corporation has established corporate governance mechanisms that can effectively detect and prevent misconduct. For example, do the corporation's directors exercise independent review over proposed corporate actions rather than unquestioningly ratifying officers' recommendations; are the directors provided with information sufficient to enable the exercise of independent judgment, are internal audit functions conducted at a level sufficient to ensure their independence and accuracy and have the directors established an information and reporting system in the organization reasonably designed to provide management and the board of directors with timely and accurate information sufficient to allow them to reach an informed decision regarding the organization's compliance with the law. *In re: Caremark*, 698 A.2d 959 (Del. Ct. Chan. 1996).

Prosecutors should therefore attempt to determine whether a corporation's compliance program is merely a "paper program" or whether it was designed and implemented in an effective manner. In addition, prosecutors should determine whether the corporation has provided for a staff sufficient to audit, document, analyze, and utilize the results of the corporation's compliance efforts. In addition, prosecutors should determine whether the corporation's employees are adequately informed about the compliance program and are convinced of the corporation's commitment to it. This will enable the prosecutor to make an informed decision as to whether the corporation has adopted and implemented a truly effective compliance program that, when consistent with other federal law enforcement policies, may result in a decision to charge only the corporation's employees and agents.

[vi] For a detailed review of these and other factors concerning corporate compliance programs, *see* USSG §8B2.1.

Compliance programs should be designed to detect the particular types of misconduct most likely to occur in a particular corporation's line of business. Many corporations operate in complex regulatory environments outside the normal experience of criminal prosecutors. Accordingly, prosecutors should consult with relevant federal and state agencies with the expertise to evaluate the adequacy of a program's design and implementation. For instance, state and federal banking, insurance, and medical boards, the Department of Defense, the Department of Health and Human Services, the Environmental Protection Agency, and the Securities and Exchange Commission have considerable experience with compliance programs and can be very helpful to a prosecutor in evaluating such programs. In addition, the Fraud Section of the Criminal Division, the Commercial Litigation Branch of the Civil Division, and the Environmental Crimes Section of the Environment and Natural Resources Division can assist U.S. Attorneys' Offices in finding the appropriate agency office and in providing copies of compliance programs that were developed in previous cases.

IX. Charging a Corporation: Restitution and Remediation

A. <u>General Principle:</u> Although neither a corporation nor an individual target may avoid prosecution merely by paying a sum of money, a prosecutor may consider the corporation's willingness to make restitution and steps already taken to do so. A prosecutor may also consider other remedial actions, such as implementing an effective corporate compliance program, improving an existing compliance program, and disciplining wrongdoers, in determining whether to charge the corporation.

B. <u>Comment:</u> In determining whether or not a corporation should be prosecuted, a prosecutor may consider whether meaningful remedial measures have been taken, including employee discipline and full restitution. A corporation's response to misconduct says much about its willingness to ensure that such misconduct does not recur. Thus, corporations that fully recognize the seriousness of their misconduct and accept responsibility for it should be taking steps to implement the personnel, operational, and organizational changes necessary to establish an awareness among employees that criminal conduct will not be tolerated. Among the factors prosecutors should consider and weigh are whether the corporation appropriately disciplined the wrongdoers and disclosed information concerning their illegal conduct to the government.

Employee discipline is a difficult task for many corporations because of the human element involved and sometimes because of the seniority of the employees concerned. While corporations need to be fair to their employees, they must also be unequivocally committed, at all levels of the corporation, to the highest standards of legal and ethical behavior. Effective internal discipline can be a powerful deterrent against improper behavior by a corporation's employees. In evaluating a corporation's response to wrongdoing, prosecutors may evaluate the willingness of the corporation to discipline culpable employees of all ranks and the adequacy of the discipline imposed. The prosecutor should be satisfied that the corporation's focus is on the integrity and credibility of its remedial and disciplinary measures rather than on the protection of the wrongdoers.

In addition to employee discipline, two other factors used in evaluating a corporation's remedial efforts are restitution and reform. As with natural persons, the decision whether or not to prosecute should not depend upon the target's ability to pay restitution. A corporation's efforts to pay restitution even in advance of any court order is, however, evidence of its "acceptance of responsibility" and, consistent with the practices and policies of the appropriate Division of the Department entrusted with enforcing specific criminal laws, may be considered in determining whether to bring criminal charges. Similarly, although the inadequacy of a corporate compliance program is a factor to consider when deciding whether to charge a corporation, that corporation's quick recognition of the flaws in the program and its efforts to improve the program are also factors to consider.

X. Charging a Corporation: Collateral Consequences

A. <u>General Principle:</u> Prosecutors may consider the collateral consequences of a corporate criminal conviction in determining whether to charge the corporation with a criminal offense.

B. <u>Comment:</u> One of the factors in determining whether to charge a natural person or a corporation is whether the likely punishment is appropriate given the nature and seriousness of the crime. In the corporate context, prosecutors may take into account the possibly substantial consequences to a corporation's officers, directors, employees, and shareholders, many of whom may, depending on the size and nature (*e.g.*, publicly vs. closely held) of the corporation and their role in its operations, have played no role in the criminal conduct, have been completely unaware of it, or have been wholly unable to prevent it. Prosecutors should also be aware of non-penal sanctions that may accompany a criminal charge, such as potential suspension or debarment from eligibility for government contracts or federal funded programs such as health care. Whether or not such non-penal sanctions are appropriate or required in a particular case is the responsibility of the relevant agency, a decision that will be made based on the applicable statutes, regulations, and policies.

Virtually every conviction of a corporation, like virtually every conviction of an individual, will have an impact on innocent third parties, and the mere existence of such an effect is not sufficient to preclude prosecution of the corporation. Therefore, in evaluating the severity of collateral consequences, various factors already discussed, such as the pervasiveness of the criminal conduct and the adequacy of the corporation's compliance programs, should be considered in determining the weight to be given to this factor. For instance, the balance may tip in favor of prosecuting corporations in situations where the scope of the misconduct in a case is widespread and sustained within a corporate division (or spread throughout pockets of the corporate organization). In such cases, the possible unfairness of visiting punishment for the corporation's crimes upon shareholders may be of much less concern where those shareholders have substantially profited, even unknowingly, from widespread or pervasive criminal activity. Similarly, where the top layers of the corporation's management or the shareholders of a closely- held corporation were engaged in or aware of the wrongdoing and the conduct at issue was accepted as a way of doing business for an extended period, debarment may be deemed not collateral, but a direct and entirely appropriate consequence of the corporation's wrongdoing.

The appropriateness of considering such collateral consequences and the weight to be given them may depend on the special policy concerns discussed in section III, *supra*.

XI. Charging a Corporation: Non-Criminal Alternatives

A. <u>General Principle:</u> Although non-criminal alternatives to prosecution often exist, prosecutors may consider whether such sanctions would adequately deter, punish, and rehabilitate a corporation that has engaged in wrongful conduct. In evaluating the adequacy of non-criminal alternatives to prosecution, *e.g.*, civil or regulatory enforcement actions, the prosecutor may consider all relevant factors, including:
   1. the sanctions available under the alternative means of disposition;
   2. the likelihood that an effective sanction will be imposed; and
   3. the effect of non-criminal disposition on Federal law enforcement interests.

B. <u>Comment:</u> The primary goals of criminal law are deterrence, punishment, and rehabilitation. Non-criminal sanctions may not be an appropriate response to an egregious violation, a pattern of wrongdoing, or a history of non-criminal sanctions without proper remediation. In other cases, however, these goals may be satisfied without the necessity of instituting criminal proceedings. In determining whether federal criminal charges are appropriate, the prosecutor should consider the same factors (modified appropriately for the regulatory context) considered when determining whether to leave prosecution of a natural person to another jurisdiction or to seek non-criminal alternatives to prosecution. These factors include: the strength of the regulatory authority's interest; the regulatory authority's ability and willingness to take effective enforcement action; the probable sanction if the regulatory authority's enforcement action is upheld; and the effect of a non-criminal disposition on federal law enforcement interests. *See* USAM §§ 9-27.240, 9-27.250.

XII. Charging a Corporation: Selecting Charges

A. <u>General Principle:</u> Once a prosecutor has decided to charge a corporation, the prosecutor should charge, or should recommend that the grand jury charge, the most serious offense that is consistent with the nature of the defendant's conduct and that is likely to result in a sustainable conviction.

B. <u>Comment:</u> Once the decision to charge is made, the same rules as govern charging natural persons apply. These rules require "a faithful and honest application of the Sentencing Guidelines" and an "individualized assessment of the extent to which particular charges fit the specific circumstances of the case, are consistent with the purposes of the federal criminal code, and maximize the impact of federal resources on crime." *See* USAM § 9-27.300. In making this determination, "it is appropriate that the attorney for the government consider, *inter alia,* such factors as the sentencing guideline range yielded by the charge, whether the penalty yielded by such sentencing range . . . is proportional to the seriousness of the defendant's conduct, and whether the charge achieves such purposes of the criminal law as punishment, protection of the public, specific and general deterrence, and rehabilitation." *See* Attorney General's Memorandum, dated October 12, 1993.

XIII. Plea Agreements with Corporations

A. <u>General Principle:</u> In negotiating plea agreements with corporations, prosecutors should seek a plea to the most serious, readily provable offense charged. In addition, the terms of the plea agreement should contain appropriate provisions to ensure punishment, deterrence, rehabilitation, and compliance with the plea agreement in the corporate context. Although special circumstances may mandate a different conclusion, prosecutors generally should not agree to accept a corporate guilty plea in exchange for non-prosecution or dismissal of charges against individual officers and employees.

B. <u>Comment:</u> Prosecutors may enter into plea agreements with corporations for the same reasons and under the same constraints as apply to plea agreements with natural persons. *See* USAM §§ 9-27.400-500. This means, *inter alia*, that the corporation should be required to plead guilty to the most serious, readily provable offense charged. As is the case with individuals, the attorney making this determination should do so "on the basis of an individualized assessment of the extent to which particular charges fit the specific circumstances of the case, are consistent with the purposes of the federal criminal code, and maximize the impact of federal resources on crime. In making this determination, the attorney for the government considers, *inter alia*, such factors as the sentencing guideline range yielded by the charge, whether the penalty yielded by such sentencing range . . . is proportional to the seriousness of the defendant's conduct, and whether the charge achieves such purposes of the criminal law as punishment, protection of the public, specific and general deterrence, and rehabilitation." *See* Attorney General's Memorandum, dated October 12, 1993. In addition, any negotiated departures from the Sentencing Guidelines must be justifiable under the Guidelines and must be disclosed to the sentencing court. A corporation should be made to realize that pleading guilty to criminal charges constitutes an admission of guilt and not merely a resolution of an inconvenient distraction from its business. As with natural persons, pleas should be structured so that the corporation may not later "proclaim lack of culpability or even complete innocence." *See* USAM §§ 9-27.420(b)(4), 9-27.440, 9-27.500. Thus, for instance, there should be placed upon the record a sufficient factual basis for the plea to prevent later corporate assertions of innocence.

A corporate plea agreement should also contain provisions that recognize the nature of the corporate "person" and ensure that the principles of punishment, deterrence, and rehabilitation are met. In the corporate context, punishment and deterrence are generally accomplished by substantial fines, mandatory restitution, and institution of appropriate compliance measures, including, if necessary, continued judicial oversight or the use of special masters. *See* USSG

§§ 8B1.1, 8C2.1, *et seq.* In addition, where the corporation is a government contractor, permanent or temporary debarment may be appropriate. Where the corporation was engaged in government contracting fraud, a prosecutor may not negotiate away an agency's right to debar or to list the corporate defendant.

In negotiating a plea agreement, prosecutors should also consider the deterrent value of prosecutions of individuals within the corporation. Therefore, one factor that a prosecutor may consider in determining whether to enter into a plea agreement is whether the corporation is seeking immunity for its employees and officers or whether the corporation is willing to cooperate in the investigation of culpable individuals. Prosecutors should rarely negotiate away individual criminal liability in a corporate plea.

Rehabilitation, of course, requires that the corporation undertake to be law-abiding in the future. It is, therefore, appropriate to require the corporation, as a condition of probation, to implement a compliance program or to reform an existing one. As discussed above, prosecutors may consult with the appropriate state and federal agencies and components of the Justice Department to ensure that a proposed compliance program is adequate and meets industry standards and best practices. *See* section VIII, *supra.*

In plea agreements in which the corporation agrees to cooperate, the prosecutor should ensure that the cooperation is complete and truthful. To do so, the prosecutor may request that the corporation waive attorney-client and work product protection, make employees and agents available for debriefing, disclose the results of its internal investigation, file appropriate certified financial statements, agree to governmental or third-party audits, and take whatever other steps are necessary to ensure that the full scope of the corporate wrongdoing is disclosed and that the responsible culprits are identified and, if appropriate, prosecuted. See generally section VII, *supra.*

This memorandum provides only internal Department of Justice guidance. It is not intended to, does not, and may not be relied upon to create any rights, substantive or procedural, enforceable at law by any party in any matter civil or criminal. Nor are any limitations hereby placed on otherwise lawful litigative prerogatives of the Department of Justice.

Index